Praise for

WINNER-TAKE-ALL POLITICS

"Important.... The collapse of the American middle class and the huge transfer of wealth to the already wealthy is the biggest domestic story of our time.... The good news reported by Hacker and Pierson is that American wealth disparities—almost exactly as wide as in 1928—are not the residue of globalization or technology or anything else beyond our control. There's nothing inevitable about them. They're the result of politics and policies, which tilted toward the rich beginning in the 1970s and can, with enough effort, be tilted back *over time* (emphasis added for impatient liberals)."

—Jonathan Alter, *The New York Times Book Review*

"Hacker and Pierson argue strongly that the concentration of income at the top is not just the work of deep economic forces. It is aided and abetted by politicians who favor the very rich or allow policies that once favored the rest of us to erode. Hacker and Pierson look closely, sharply, and entertainingly at the way that interest-group politics and the political power of money have allowed this travesty of democracy to happen. This book is a wake-up call. Read it and wake up."

—Robert Solow, winner of the Nobel Memorial Prize for Economics in 1987

"The clearest explanation yet of the forces that converged over the past three decades or so to undermine the economic well-being of ordinary Americans is contained in *Winner-Take-All Politics*. Jacob Hacker and Paul Pierson argue persuasively that the economic struggles of the middle and working classes in the U.S. since the late 1970s were not primarily the result of globalization and technological changes but rather a long series of policy changes in government that overwhelmingly favored the very rich.... Nothing better illustrates the enormous power that has accrued to this tiny sliver of the population than its continued ability to thrive and prosper despite the Great Recession that was largely the result of their winner-take-all policies, and that has had such a disastrous effect on so many other Americans."

—Bob Herbert, *The New York Times*

"Engrossing. . . . Hacker and Pierson . . . deliver the goods. . . . Their description of the organizational dynamics that have tilted economic policymaking in favor of the wealthy is convincing."

—Justin Fox, *Harvard Business Review*

"'How can hedge-fund managers who are pulling down billions sometimes pay a lower tax rate than do their secretaries?' ask the political scientists Jacob S. Hacker (of Yale) and Paul Pierson (University of California, Berkeley) in their deservedly lauded new book, *Winner-Take-All Politics*. If you want to cry real tears about the American dream—as opposed to the self-canonizing tears of John Boehner—read this book and weep. The authors' answer to that question and others amounts to a devastating indictment of both parties. . . . The book deflates much of the conventional wisdom."

—Frank Rich, *The New York Times*

"Over the past generation, the middle class has been repeatedly battered, and its once-solid foundations have begun to tremble. Uncovering the hidden political story behind this great economic challenge, Jacob Hacker and Paul Pierson shed light on what has gone wrong—and why. Their book is must-reading for anyone who wants to understand how Washington stopped working for the middle class."

—Elizabeth Warren, Assistant to the President and Special Advisor to the Secretary of the Treasury on the Consumer Financial Protection Bureau

"How the U.S. economic system has also moved 'off center' toward an extreme concentration of wealth, and how progressive efforts to reverse that trend have run aground. . . . A very valuable book."

—Ed Kilgore, *Washington Monthly*

"Hacker and Pierson make a compelling case. If Marie Antoinette were alive, she might aver of today's great economically challenged masses, 'Let them nibble on passbook-savings-account interest'—if they can manage to save anything, that is."

—David Holahan, *The Christian Science Monitor*

"A must-read book. . . . It broke down what was at stake in 2010 and will be at stake in 2012 better than anything I've read. . . . Hacker and Pierson show how politics has become 'organized combat.'"

—Joan Walsh, *Salon*

"Two top political scientists tell us when America turned terribly wrong—and how the rich and powerful organized to do the turning. . . . Fascinating."

—Sam Pizzigagi, "Too Much," an online newsletter of the Institute for Policy Studies

"Must buy this book."

—Beezernotes.com

"This is a transformative book. It's the best book on American politics that I've read since *Before the Storm*. . . . If it has the impact it deserves, it will transform American public arguments about politics and policymaking."

—Henry Farrell, Crookedtimber.org

"*Winner-Take-All Politics* is a marvelous connect-the-dots book. It makes not just one point, but a series of points that fit together like train-cars."

—*The Weekly Sift*

"A swiftly written political history that shows why we're where we are and what crippled our government's ability to deal with it."

—*The American Prospect*

"Hacker and Pierson remind us that there are no such things as 'pure' markets, and that markets everywhere are shaped by laws and regulations, cultures and the institutional arrangements that themselves are shaped by the political process."

—Steven Pearlstein, *The Washington Post*

"I really recommend it."

—Chris Hayes, Washington editor of *The Nation* magazine,
on MSNBC's *Countdown with Keith Olbermann*

"Read *Winner-Take-All Politics*. This excellent work is all about how Washington has made the rich richer—and turned its back on the middle class."

—Liz Smith, WOWOWOW.com

"It's a great review of the state-of-the-art thinking on the scope of the inequality explosion and . . . correctly frames this as a non-inevitable consequence of policy decisions. . . . Recommended."

—Matt Yglesias, thinkprogress.org

"This is an important book for raising some of the key questions of our time. I would recommend that people read it and give it serious thought."

—Tyler Cowen, Marginalrevolution.com

Also by Jacob S. Hacker and Paul Pierson

Off Center: The Republican Revolution
and the Erosion of American Democracy

Also by Jacob S. Hacker

The Great Risk Shift: The New Economic Insecurity
and the Decline of the American Dream

The Divided Welfare State: The Battle over Public and Private
Social Benefits in the United States

The Road to Nowhere: The Genesis of President Clinton's Plan
for Health Security

Also by Paul Pierson

Politics in Time: History, Institutions and Social Analysis

Dismantling the Welfare State?
Reagan, Thatcher, and the Politics of Retrenchment

Winner-Take-All
Politics

How Washington Made the Rich Richer—
And Turned Its Back on the Middle Class

Jacob S. Hacker
and Paul Pierson

SIMON & SCHUSTER PAPERBACKS
New York   London   Toronto   Sydney

To our children—Ava and Owen, Sidra and Seth—
inheritors of a hopefully stronger America

Simon & Schuster Paperbacks
A Division of Simon & Schuster, Inc.
1230 Avenue of the Americas
New York, NY 10020

First Simon & Schuster trade paperback edition March 2011

SIMON & SCHUSTER PAPERBACKS and colophon are registered
trademarks of Simon & Schuster, Inc.

For information about special discounts for bulk purchases,
please contact Simon & Schuster Special Sales at
1-866-506-1949 or business@simonandschuster.com.

The Simon & Schuster Speakers Bureau can bring authors to
your live event. For more information or to book an event,
contact the Simon & Schuster Speakers Bureau at
1-866-248-3049 or visit our website at www.simonspeakers.com.

Designed by Joy O'Meara

Manufactured in the United States of America

20   19   18   17   16   15   14   13   12

The Library of Congress has cataloged the hardcover edition as follows:

Hacker, Jacob S.
    Winner-take-all politics : how Washington made the rich richer-and
turned its back on the middle class / Jacob S. Hacker and Paul Pierson.
        p.   cm.
    Includes bibliographical references and index.
    1. Equality—United States.   2. Capitalism—United States.
3. United States—Economic policy.   4. United States—Politics
and Government—1945–1989.   5. United States—Politics and
government—1989–.   I. Pierson, Paul.   II. Title.
    HN89.S6H33   2010
    306.3'42097309045—dc22   2010014515

ISBN 978-1-4165-8869-6
ISBN 978-1-4165-8870-2 (pbk)
ISBN 978-1-4165-9384-3 (ebook)

Contents

The Thirty-Year War

For those working on Wall Street, 2009 was a very good year. At the thirty-eight biggest companies, investors and executives earned a staggering $140 billion in all—the highest number on record.[1] The venerable investment firm Goldman Sachs paid its employees nearly a half million dollars each, capping off one of the best years since its founding in 1869.[2] The sums, while astounding, were hardly unprecedented. Unfettered pay had become the norm on Wall Street over the prior generation, as it had in American boardrooms more broadly. The CEO of Goldman Sachs, Lloyd C. Blankfein, had taken home $68 million in 2007. That same year, the top twenty-five hedge fund managers raked in $892 million on average, according to *Alpha* magazine's annual ranking of the highest earners—Wall Street's equivalent of *People* magazine's "most beautiful people."[3]

What made the 2009 payouts so shocking wasn't the numbers themselves. It was what they said about the American economy—and American government. The Wall Street of well-heeled bankers was thriving, while the Main Street of ordinary workers struggled amid the worst economic downturn since the Great Depression. And Wall Street was thriving because less than two years before it had received hundreds of billions in federal bailout money, along with less visible but far more massive indirect assistance from the Federal Reserve. In the wake of the financial crisis—a crisis prompted in no small part by banks' reckless practices—

government had shoveled cash in the front doors of the nation's leading financial institutions to avert catastrophe. Now Goldman and other big firms were, in essence, discreetly but steadily shoveling a large share of that cash out the back doors into employees' private accounts.

For the very top earners, the payouts were actually less ostentatious than usual, lest they make more conspicuous the scale of the unexpected riches. Big paychecks looked bad, after all, when the rest of the economy was staggering, and when Wall Street lobbyists were ferociously battling proposed reforms of the financial system to clip the banks' wings and forestall another bailout. Out, for the most part, were seven- and eight-figure bonuses. In were complicated "stock options" and "deferred compensation" that promised equally big returns down the road. As the *New York Times* helpfully explained, "Wall Street is confronting a dilemma of riches: How to wrap its eye-popping paychecks in a mantle of moderation."[4]

This was not exactly the dilemma faced by most Americans. While the money spigot flowed freely on Wall Street, the "real economy" remained trapped under the debris of the financial implosion of 2007. Even as Blankfein insisted that Goldman was doing "God's work"—apparently missing the passage in the Bible about how hard it is for a rich man to enter heaven—tens of millions of homeowners were still reeling from the real estate crash that firms like his had helped create through heedless speculation in securities underwritten by subprime loans.[5] Nationwide, home prices had plummeted, wiping out nearly 40 percent of American families' home equity between December 2006 and December 2008.[6] The unemployment rate hovered around 10 percent. For every job opening, there were six job seekers.[7] State and local governments faced with unprecedented budget deficits were slashing gaping holes in the safety net, raising taxes, and threatening to lay off hundreds of thousands of teachers. Leading economists suggested it would be years before the country returned to full employment. The human toll—in shattered careers, disrupted families, and lost security—was incalculable.

These two starkly divergent tales of 2009 represent just the most recent and painful chapter of a longer story. Over the last generation, more and more of the rewards of growth have gone to the rich and superrich. The rest of America, from the poor through the upper middle class, has fallen further and further behind. Like Wall Street's deep-pocketed denizens in 2009, the very richest of Americans have shot into the economic stratosphere, leaving middle- and working-class Americans to watch their fortunate fellowmen's ascent while remaining firmly planted on economic terra firma. In the phrase that leads this book's title, the American economy has become "winner-take-all."

Consider the astonishing statistics. From 1979 until the eve of the Great Recession, the top one percent received 36 percent of all gains in household income—even after taking into account the value of employer-sponsored health insurance, all federal taxes, and all government benefits.[8] (We will examine this "DNA evidence," which provides irrefutable proof of the hyperconcentration of economic gains at the top, in the next chapter.) Economic growth was even more skewed between 2001 and 2006, during which the share of income gains going to the top one percent was over 53 percent. That's right: More than 50 cents of every dollar in additional income pocketed by Americans over this half decade accrued to the richest 1 in 100 households.

Even more striking, the top 0.1 percent—one out of every thousand households—received over 20 percent of all after-tax income gains between 1979 and 2005, compared with the 13.5 percent enjoyed by the bottom 60 percent of households. If the total income growth of these years were a pie, in other words, the slice enjoyed by the roughly 300,000 people in the top tenth of 1 percent would be half again as large as the slice enjoyed by the roughly *180 million* in the bottom 60 percent. Little wonder that the share of Americans who see the United States as divided between "haves" and "have nots" has risen sharply over the past two decades—although, as we will see, the economic winners are more accurately portrayed as the "have-it-alls," so concentrated have the gains been at the very, very top.[9]

These mind-boggling differences have no precedent in the forty years of shared prosperity that marked the U.S. economy before the late 1970s. Nor do they have any real parallel elsewhere in the advanced industrial world. A generation ago, the United States was a recognizable, if somewhat more unequal, member of the cluster of affluent democracies known as mixed economies, where fast growth was widely shared. No more. Since around 1980, we have drifted away from that mixed-economy cluster, and traveled a considerable distance toward another: the capitalist oligarchies, like Brazil, Mexico, and Russia, with their much greater concentration of economic bounty. Of course, the United States is far richer than these oligarchic nations. But, contrary to the rhetoric of inequality's apologists, it has not grown consistently more quickly than other rich democracies that have seen little or no tilt toward winner-take-all. America's runaway rewards for the affluent have not unleashed an economic miracle whose rewards have generously filtered down to the poor and middle class.

Quite the opposite. Like a raging fever that announces a more serious underlying disease, rising inequality is only the clearest indicator of an economic transformation that has touched virtually every aspect of Americans' standard of living. From the erosion of job security to the declining reach of health insurance, from the rising toll of home foreclosures to the growing numbers of personal bankruptcies, from the stagnation of upward social mobility to the skyrocketing of personal debt, the American economy that has delivered so much to the fortunate has worked much less well for most Americans. And this has been true not just over the past three years or thirteen years, but over the past thirty years. Winner-take-all has become the defining feature of American economic life.

How has this happened? If most commentators are to be believed, the answer lies in inevitable shifts in our economy driven by global, universal pressures. Like a doctor forced to dispense difficult truths to a patient in denial, these economic diagnosticians tell us that the shared prosperity of the postwar generation was rooted in a sheltered, low-tech economy that is not coming back. A technological revolution has rendered the world "flat," sweeping away differences rooted in culture and politics and policy. In today's highly globalized and competitive environment, educational achievements and workplace skills are economic destiny, and deep economic cleavages based on those achievements and skills are all but inevitable.

This diagnosis has its distinctive ideological spins, of course: On the one side, liberal economic doctors call for massive investments in education to give more people a shot at entering the winner's circle. On the other side, conservative economic doctors call for more tax cuts and deregulation to unleash the competitive economy still further, with promises that, at some point soon, the gains will "trickle down." But whatever the prescription, the diagnosis ultimately points to the same constellation of factors. Globalization, skill shifts, technological transformation, economic change—the list is familiar from the seemingly endless autopsies that crunch the numbers and report, to use James Carville's famous catchphrase, It's the economy, stupid.

Winner-Take-All Politics offers a very different diagnosis, one rooted in a very different sort of exploration. Rather than doctors dispensing difficult truths, we see ourselves as investigators uncovering buried clues that point to culprits beyond the usual suspects most analysts have fingered. The truths that we find share little in common with the familiar nostrums about the natural course of the American economy. Yet, in some respects, they offer an even more disturbing assessment. They strip away the aura of economic destiny surrounding runaway inequality. But they replace the certainty of a false economic diagnosis with discomforting conclusions—along with a new set of puzzles—about how, and for whom, American politics works.

The puzzles are all around us. How can hedge-fund managers who are pulling down billions sometimes pay a lower tax rate than do their secretaries? And why, in an era of increased economic uncertainty, is it so hard for their secretaries to form or join a union? How have corporate managers—who, along with Wall Street bigwigs, make up more than half of the top 0.1 percent—ascended from pay levels twenty to thirty times that of a typical worker to levels two to three hundred times as great?[10] And why, over a generation in which most Americans have experienced modest economic gains, have politicians slashed taxes on the rich even as the riches of the rich have exploded?

To answer these questions, we need to adopt a perspective that is both broader and deeper than that commonly on offer—to see the big changes in the landscape of American politics that are too often missed or taken for granted, to look inside the black box of government policies that are too often treated as immaterial or uninteresting (but which turn out to be neither). We need to travel down neglected byways of American political and economic life that lead to the heart of the winner-take-all economy, to find the forgotten stories that help us see the profound changes in American democracy that have unfolded in our time. Along the way, we will meet sometimes-little-known figures who helped engineer hidden but profound organizational changes—in American politics and, through those political shifts, in the American economy.

Winner-Take-All Politics is not another of the many book-length indictments of our nation's present economic wrongs, with their familiar finger-pointing at the greed or incompetence of public or private figures. Our current crisis certainly bears emphasis, in part because it so clearly reveals the sources and costs of the winner-take-all economy. And by the end of our investigation, the roots and realities of contemporary discontents will indeed be apparent. But, as will become clear, our current crisis is merely the latest in a long struggle rooted in the interplay of American democracy and American capitalism. This struggle has not unfolded overnight. Nor is it a simple linear tale of sweeping, inevitable change. The advancing tide of the winner-take-all economy sometimes feels like a force of nature. (Certainly, it is convenient for its beneficiaries to describe it that way.) Yet America's slow, steady slide toward economic oligarchy has been neither beyond human control nor bereft of resistance.

We tell the story of a thirty-year war. Marked by bitter conflict, it has involved more than flash-in-the-pan personalities or fleeting electoral victories. Step by step and debate by debate, America's public officials have rewritten the rules of American politics and the American economy in ways that have benefited the few at the expense of the many. Not all have been as candid about what they were doing as former Democratic Senator John Breaux when he joked that his vote could not be bought but could be "rented" by the highest bidder. Nor have many been as rhapsodic as Republican Senator Phil Gramm, who described Wall Street as a "holy place." But, for reasons we shall explain and with consequences we will unveil, all of America's political class have felt the increasing pull of the winner-take-all economy.

Our story unfolds in three parts. Part 1 delves into the mystery of the winner-take-all economy. We come face-to-face with what has really happened in the American marketplace over the last generation: who's won and who's lost in the thirty-year war, and how government has played an integral role in creating these new economic realities. Here, we crunch the economic numbers—the *right* numbers, the numbers that truly get to the heart of what has happened to our economy over the last generation. But we also take our investigation where the right numbers lead and, in doing so, enter surprisingly uncharted territory. To uncover the path to winner-take-all requires seeing the transformation of American government over the last generation, a transformation that has fundamentally changed what government does, and whom it does it for.

But resolving our first mystery only reveals a deeper one: If government has played a central part, how could this happen? In a country where public officials must regularly face the judgment of citizens at the polls, how could their efforts come to so persistently favor the very few? In our search for clues, we show that this is an age-old question, and that the thirty-year war has parallels in our nation's past—in the great debates over government's place in a dynamic, increasingly unequal economy that took place in the first half of the last century.

Part 2 takes us down to the subterranean roots of the winner-take-all economy, which lie, against common expectations, in the political transformations of the 1970s. The seventies are the forgotten decade of American political history. Received wisdom seeks the wellsprings of our polarized and confrontational politics in the cultural clashes and electoral upheavals of the 1960s. Casting liberal movements against conservative political reactions, this familiar storyline misses the true timing and character of the shifts that have generated our deeper crisis—and overlooks some of the central political movements that reshaped the battlefield of combat.

In part 3, we provide a portrait of the new world of American politics forged in this crucible—the world of "Winner-Take-All Politics." We do so through the prism of the nation's two political parties, showing how Republicans and Democrats have both responded, in different ways, to the political pull of America's superrich. Here we see the full causes and consequences of the political transformations of the era. Here we also see the daunting challenges that President Obama has had to grapple with in the latest and most epic battle in the thirty-year war.

We would have liked to end our book by declaring the end of winner-take-all politics. But the effects of a thirty-year war are not wiped away overnight. The hurdles to renewal, rooted in the story we tell, are formidable. Yet, as high as they are, they do not lead us to counsel despair. For the obstacles are not irresistible forces of nature but man-made forces of politics. And they are obstacles that our nation has faced before. The gap between the ideals of American democracy and the realities of American politics has yawned in the past. Reformers have dramatically narrowed this gap in the past as well. Nothing in this history suggests today's barriers will be easily cleared. But there is much to instill determination that they can and must be.

Part I

The Puzzling Politics of Winner-Take-All

Chapter 1

The Winner-Take-All Economy

Americans like crime dramas, and for good reasons. There is an exciting discovery that immediately creates mystery. The scene has clues to pore over (increasingly, with the latest in forensic technology). Suspects are found and interrogated, their motives questioned, their alibis probed. And if the crime drama is worth its salt, there are surprises along the way—unexpected twists and turns that hopefully lead to a satisfying explanation of the once-mysterious felony.

This book starts with a mystery every bit as puzzling as that of the typical crime drama, and far more important for the lives of Americans: Why, after a generation following World War II in which prosperity was broadly distributed up and down the income ladder, did the gains of economic growth start going mostly to those at the top? Why has the economy become more risky and unreliable for most Americans even as it has created vast riches for the well-positioned and well-off? The mystery is dramatic. The scene is strewn with clues. And yet this mystery has continued to bedevil some of the nation's finest economic detectives.

It's not as if the post-1970s transformation of our economy has gone unnoticed, of course: Even before the economic crisis that shook the nation in 2008, scores of economists and experts in allied fields, like sociology and political science, were creatively crunching the numbers and fiercely debating their meaning. Yet again and again, they have found themselves at dead ends or have missed crucial evidence. After countless arrests and interrogations, the demise of broad-based prosperity remains a frustratingly open case, unresolved even as the list of victims grows longer.

All this, we are convinced, is because a crucial suspect has largely escaped careful scrutiny: American politics. Understandably, investigators seeking to explain a set of economic events have sought out economic suspects. But the economic suspects, for the most part, have strong alibis. They were not around at the right time. Or they were in a lot of countries, doing just the same thing that they did in the United States, but without creating an American-style winner-take-all economy.

This chapter is not the place to pin the case on American politics—or spell out exactly *how* American politics did it. These are tasks for the rest of this book. But we will show what a convincing solution has to look like and introduce the clues that lead us to zero in on American politics as our prime suspect. In the next chapter, we will start laying out what we mean when we say, "American politics did it." For, as will become clear, resolving our first mystery only raises a deeper one: How, in a political system built on the ideal of political equality and in which middle-class voters are thought to have tremendous sway, has democratic politics contributed so mightily to the shift toward winner-take-all?

Investigating the Scene

As in any investigation, we cannot find the suspects unless we know more or less what happened. A body dead for twenty-four hours yields a very different set of hunches than one dead for twenty-four years. Likewise, we need to be able to characterize the winner-take-all economy in clear, simple, and empirically verifiable terms to rule certain explanations out and others in. Unfortunately, much of the discussion of our current economic state of affairs has lacked such clarity.

Indeed, most of the economic investigators have actually been looking in the wrong place. Fixated on the widening gap between skilled and unskilled workers, they have divided the economic world into two large groups: the "haves" with college or advanced degrees; the "have-nots" without them. The clues suggest, however, that the real mystery is the runaway incomes and assets of the "have-it-alls"—those on the very highest rungs of the economic ladder. These fortunate few are, in general, no better educated or obviously more skilled than those on the rungs just below, who have experienced little or none of these meteoric gains.

The mystery, further, is not just why the have-it-alls have more and more. It is also how they have managed to restructure the economy to shift the risks of their new economic playground downward, saddling Americans with greater debt, tearing new holes in the safety net, and imposing broad financial risks on Americans as workers, investors, and taxpayers. The rising rewards at the top, as startling and important as they are, are only a symptom of a broader transformation of the American economy. The deeper mystery is how our economy stopped working to provide security and prosperity for the broad middle class. The deeper mystery, the mystery that has yet to be systematically outlined or unraveled, is the rise of the *winner-take-all economy*.

A big reason for the continuing confusion is that the largest body of evidence on which economic investigators have traditionally relied fails to capture the crucial facts. Most of those who have asked how the poor, middle class, and rich have fared have examined national surveys of income, such as the Census Bureau's widely used Current Population Survey—the basis for those annual summaries of income and poverty trends that appear in the news late each summer. These surveys, however, have a serious problem: They do not reach many rich people and, even when they do, do not usually show their exact incomes. (Instead, they cap the maximum amount disclosed, a practice known as top coding.) As a result, most investigators are examining the winner-take-all economy without looking at the winners at all. It is as if *Lifestyles of the Rich and Famous* took you on an exciting tour of the financial life of a couple making $125,000 a year ("Look: their own washer and dryer!").

Enter two young economists who have turned the investigation upside down: Thomas Piketty and Emmanuel Saez. They are a transcontinental team—Piketty is now based at the Paris School of Economics, while Saez is at the University of California, Berkeley (both are natives of France).

In 2009, at age thirty-six, Saez was awarded the John Bates Clark Medal for the economist younger than forty making the greatest contribution to the discipline. The medal was, in large part, for pathbreaking work that he and Piketty have done using income tax statistics to paint a new and revealing portrait of the distribution of economic rewards in the United States and other rich nations.[1]

Piketty and Saez's approach is simple but revolutionary. Rather than talking to witnesses, the most important of whom (the rich) cannot be easily found, they scour the scene itself. More precisely, Piketty and Saez tap into a source of data that is particularly good at revealing what the have-it-alls actually have: namely, income reported when paying taxes. Information that taxpayers provide about their wages, salaries, capital gains, and other income may contain errors—and sometimes deliberate errors. But tax forms require careful documentation that income surveys don't, and taxpayers have strong legal inducements to get the numbers right. More important, the one group that the tax code generally singles out for special scrutiny is the rich, the very people whom income surveys tend to miss. To be sure, the tax data are not without flaws, and Piketty and Saez assiduously try to correct them (for example, they adjust the results to account for the fact that some people don't file tax returns).* But they are enormously better than survey results in capturing the full distribution of economic rewards.

And what the Piketty and Saez evidence uniquely shows is just how sharply our economy has tilted toward winner-take-all. Most of the gains of economic growth since the 1970s have gone precisely to those that the commonly used surveys miss—not just the top 10 percent, but especially the top 1 percent, and especially the highest reaches of the top 1 percent.

---

* We should emphasize that the Piketty and Saez data only allow us to say how well different income *groups* are doing, not how well individual households fare over time—an issue with traditional surveys of income as well. We can say the rich of today are richer than in the past, not how much change there is from year to year in who is rich and who is not. But, as we shall see, taking into account the upward or downward income mobility of households does not change this basic picture. It may even strengthen it, since long-term income mobility is much more limited than Americans believe, and may have declined since the 1960s. In any case, income groups are not statistical fictions. If the rich grow much richer, while the poor and middle class do not, the structure of society will look very different.

Three Big Clues

Compared with the standard surveys that portray the rich as earning upper-middle-class salaries, Piketty and Saez's data are like DNA evidence in a case previously investigated using only eyewitness accounts. As it turns out, the DNA evidence reveals three essential clues that were previously neglected.

Clue #1: Hyperconcentration of Income

The first clue is that the gains of the winner-take-all economy, befitting its name, have been extraordinarily *concentrated*. Though economic gaps have grown across the board, the big action is at the top, especially the very top.

To grasp this point, consider an alternate reality in which income grows at the same pace for all groups in society. In this scenario, the rich get richer at the same rate as everyone else, so the share of national income earned by the rich stays constant. We might call this imaginary country Broadland—a counterfactual parallel to the real world of runaway gains at the top that the writer Robert Frank has evocatively termed "Richistan."[2]

Broadland would not be some kind of egalitarian fantasy. It would simply be a country where economic growth was making the income distribution neither more equal nor less. It would, in fact, be pretty close to the situation that existed from the end of World War II until the early 1970s, a period in which incomes actually grew at a slightly faster rate at the bottom and middle of the economic distribution than at the top.

But Broadland is not the world of the past generation. Instead, the share of income earned by the top 1 percent has increased from around 8 percent in 1974 to more than 18 percent in 2007 (the last year covered by the data)—a more than twofold increase. If you include capital gains like investment and dividend income, the share of the top 1 percent has gone from just over 9 percent to 23.5 percent. The only time since 1913 (the first year of the data) that this share has been higher was 1928, on the eve of the stock market crash that ushered in the Great Depression, when it tickled 24 percent.

But the top 1 percent, while seemingly an exclusive group, is much too broad a category to pinpoint the most fortunate beneficiaries of the post-1970s income explosion at the top. The Piketty and Saez evidence allows us to climb higher up the economic ladder and peer into the pocketbooks of the richest tenth of a percent and even the richest hundredth of a percent—yes, 0.1 percent and 0.01 percent—of Americans. The latter comprise the highest-earning 15,000 or so families in the United States, a group in which we would expect *Lifestyles of the Rich and Famous* to have little trouble finding private jets and opulent mansions.

Plenty of jets and mansions, it turns out: The top 0.1 percent (the richest one in a thousand households) collectively rake in more than $1 trillion a year including capital gains—which works out to an average annual income of more than $7.1 million. In 1974, by comparison, the top 0.1 percent's average income was just over $1 million. (All these incomes are adjusted for inflation by expressing them in 2007 dollars.) In terms of the share of national income earned, the top 0.1 percent have seen their slice of the pie grow from 2.7 percent to 12.3 percent of income—a more than *fourfold* increase.

We shall say more about *who* is in this rarefied group in the chapters to come, but for now, let us simply note that its denizens are not, for the most part, superstars and celebrities in the arts, entertainment, and sports. Nor are they rentiers, living off their accumulated wealth, as was true in the early part of the last century. A substantial majority are company executives and managers, and a growing share of these are financial company executives and managers. High earners in law, medicine, real estate, and other potentially lucrative fields also make an appearance, but they pale in prominence to the "working rich" of the executive world.[3]

By now it will come as no surprise that the gains within this superrich group are themselves highly concentrated. While things have been good for the top 0.1 percent, the top 0.01 percent (the richest one in ten thousand households) has seen an even more spectacular rise. From less than $4 million in average annual income in 1974, the average member of this select group now earns more than $35 million. From earning less than 1 of every 100 dollars, these supremely fortunate souls now earn more than 1 of every 17—or more than 6 percent of national income accruing to 0.01 percent of families. This is the highest share of income going to this group since the data began to be collected in 1913.

The more closely we look at changes in the distribution of economic rewards, the more it becomes clear that the big gains have been concentrated at the very, very top.[4] According to Piketty and Saez's revealing evidence regarding pre-tax incomes, we have gone from Broadland to Richistan—from a world in which most of the nation's income gains accrue to the bottom 90 percent of households (the pattern of the economic expansion of the 1960s) to one in which more than half go to the richest 1 percent (the pattern of the last economic expansion from 2002 to 2007). For those in the tightly circumscribed winner's circle of the winner-take-all economy, the last generation has truly been a golden age.

Clue #2: Sustained Hyperconcentration

The DNA evidence reveals a second important clue: The shift of income toward the top has been *sustained*, increasing steadily (and, by historical standards, extremely rapidly) since around 1980.

Figure 1 tells the story. The poor may not be getting poorer, but the rich have been steadily pulling away: in good times (the strong economy of the mid- to late 1990s) and in bad times (the very weak economy of the early 1980s); under Republican presidents (Reagan, George H. W. Bush, and George W. Bush, whose presidencies are shaded in gray on the figure) and under Democratic President Clinton. The only brief reversals occur during the dives in the stock market that occurred in the late 1980s and around 2000. But the occasional setback associated with a decline in the stock market has only been a springboard to new heights. For thirty years, the good times have just kept rolling.

The solution to our mystery, in short, needs to account for a simple fact: The rising share of national income captured by the richest Americans is a long-term trend beginning around 1980. It is a trend, moreover, that is not

obviously related to either the business cycle or the shifting partisan oc-
cupancy of the White House.[5] The partisan to-and-fro and economic ebb
and flow surely had some part to play. But something else was at work in
creating the winner-take-all economy—something that fostered a sharp
divide between broadly shared prosperity and winner-take-all.

**Figure 1: The Richest 1 Percent's Share of National Income
(Including Capital Gains), 1960–2007**

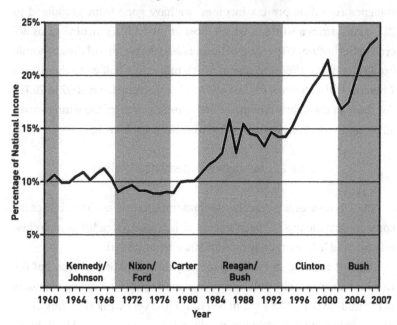

Source: Thomas Piketty and Emmanuel Saez, "Income Inequality in the United States,
1913–1998," *Quarterly Journal of Economics*, vol. 118, no. 1 (2003): 1–39. Data updated through 2007 available at http://elsa.berkeley.edu/~saez/TabFig2007.xls.

Clue #3: Limited Benefits for the Nonrich

We come, finally, to the third clue—and perhaps the most puzzling of all. It is so puzzling, and potentially controversial, that we spend much of the rest of this chapter documenting and delving into it.

The third clue is this: In an era in which those at the top reaped massive gains, the economy stopped working for middle- and working-class Americans. We know that the rich grew fabulously richer over this period. We know that relative to the rich, the rest of Americans lost ground. But what we have not yet investigated is whether they lost ground overall. How well did they fare in an era in which so large a share of economic gains accrued to those above them? Did they become richer and more economically secure? Did they see their chance of rising to the top increase? How much, in other words, did they really benefit from the winner-take-all economy?

The evidence can be summarized in a two-word answer: Not much. When we look at the DNA evidence on U.S. incomes, we find that most Americans experienced extremely modest gains over the era in which the rewards at the top multiplied. This is true, surprisingly and revealingly, even for the mostly highly skilled individuals just below the very top rungs of the income ladder. But the evidence on income gains actually understates the case—by a lot. When we expand our view beyond income to take in the broader canvas of the winner-take-all economy, the argument for thinking that the gains of America's top-heavy economic growth "trickled down" becomes even weaker. This is not just a story of relative income erosion. The fallout of the winner-take-all economy has reached broadly and deeply into the security of the middle class—and, as recent events reveal, the entire American economy.

Trickle-Up Economics

Ronald Reagan famously asked, "Are you better off than you were four years ago?" Our own version of the question is, "Are you better off than you were a generation ago?"—or, more specifically, "How much better off are middle- and lower-income Americans than they were a generation ago?" The answer has substantial implications for how we judge the economic trends of the last thirty years. After all, if everyone experienced very large gains and the rich just happened to experience even larger gains, this might not cause great concern. Indeed, this is the "trickle-down" scenario that advocates of helping the have-it-alls with tax cuts and other goodies constantly trot out: If a rising tide lifts dinghies as well as yachts, who cares if it does a bit more for yachts?

But trickle-down is not the only possibility. Another scenario might be called "trickle-up": The rich are getting fabulously richer while the rest of Americans are basically holding steady or worse. What if the modern economy looks less like an open sea, where rising water lifts all boats, and more like a system of locks, where those who don't get through the gates are left behind? Yachts are rising, but dinghies are largely staying put, locked out (so to speak) from higher waters. Indeed, in this alternative scenario, there is reason to suspect that the dinghies are staying put in part *because* the yachts are rising—that the rich are closing the locks behind them to capture resources that would otherwise have enhanced the living standards of everyone else.

So which of these scenarios is correct—trickle-down or trickle-up? The evidence is not completely consistent, and there is room for debate at the margins. But it's increasingly clear that trickle-down economics is not working as its proponents promise. Trickle-up economics, by contrast, seems to be working all too well.

Bringing In Government Taxes and Benefits

To see trickle-up in action, we need a source of evidence slightly different from that provided by Piketty and Saez. As mentioned, Piketty and Saez look at tax records, so the family incomes they report basically add up the private sources of income that people list on their tax forms: wages, salaries, investment income, gifts, and so on. These income sources do not include government benefits, such as Social Security payments. Nor do they take into account the effect of taxes themselves: They are the incomes on which people pay taxes, not incomes *after* people pay taxes.

These omissions matter for studying inequality, because in all rich nations, including the United States, government taxes and benefits make the distribution of income more equal, taking more from those at the top and providing more to those at the bottom. These omissions also matter because some of the compensation that people receive in the workplace takes the form of noncash benefits like health insurance and retirement pensions. Thus, if we want the most accurate measure of the resources that middle- and lower-income Americans have at their disposal, we need to take into account government's effect on incomes as well as tally up private noncash compensation. The basic tax data include neither.

Fortunately, the Congressional Budget Office—Congress's nonpartisan budget agency, known as CBO—has developed these broader indicators. CBO does this by combining the basic tax data with the results of income surveys that ask people about government and private benefits. In addition, CBO calculates what people with different incomes are required to pay in federal taxes. The result is considered the gold standard for studying family income trends. Although available only back to 1979—unlike the Piketty and Saez data, which go back to 1913—this augmented DNA evidence is as close as we can get to an accurate picture of what happened to the income of American households at the bottom, middle, and top of the distribution over the last generation.[6]

This picture turns out to be stark: The bottom went nowhere, the middle saw a modest gain, and the top ran away with the grand prize.

How Much Did Family Incomes Grow for the Poor, Middle Class, and Rich?

Let us start with the simplest measure of economic gains: the percentage increase in the inflation-adjusted incomes of households on different rungs of the economic ladder. The first point to make is that the overall economy expanded substantially over the twenty-seven years covered by CBO. Between 1979 and 2006—the last year currently available—real average household income, according to the augmented DNA evidence, rose by almost 50 percent, a compounded gain of 1.5 percent per year. A household earning exactly the average income had $47,900 in 1979 and $71,900 in 2006, or half again as much.

This is the happy story. The less happy story, at least for the nonrich, is where the gains of that growth went. Start with those at the bottom: As figure 2 shows, the average income of the poorest 20 percent, or quintile, of American households rose from $14,900 to $16,500, a meager 10 percent gain over twenty-seven years, even after taking into account government taxes and benefits and private employment-based benefits.

What about those in the middle? They did better, but not that much better: The middle quintile of households (that is, the 20 percent of households above the bottom 40 percent and below the top 40 percent) saw their average inflation-adjusted income rise from $42,900 to $52,100—a gain of 21 percent. This may sound good (and because families became smaller over this period, the gains per family member within households are a bit larger). But it works out to a real gain of just 0.7 percent a year, a rate of increase less than half the growth of average income over this period. Not much of a yearly raise.

These numbers look all the more striking when we consider a simple fact: American households are working many more hours today than they were in the late 1970s. This is because women are much more likely to work outside the home than they were a generation ago, augmenting both family income and the amount of time that household members spend in the workforce. Among working-age married couples with children, these extra hours totaled more than ten additional full-time weeks in the workforce (406 hours) in 2000, as compared with 1979. Without those additional hours and income, households in the middle of the distribution would have barely budged upward at all. The incomes of households at the bottom would actually have fallen.[7]

So who received the gains? The simple answer is those at the top, especially the very top. The average after-tax income of the richest 1 percent of households rose from $337,100 a year in 1979 to more than $1.2 *million* in 2006—an increase of nearly 260 percent. Put another way, the average income of the top 1 percent more than tripled in just over a quarter-century. Figure 2 graphically portrays the scale of the disparity. Just getting the 2006 average income of the top 1 percent on the same axis as the average incomes of other groups is a challenge, so stark is the difference.

Figure 2: Average Household After-Tax Income Including Public and Private Benefits, 1979 and 2006

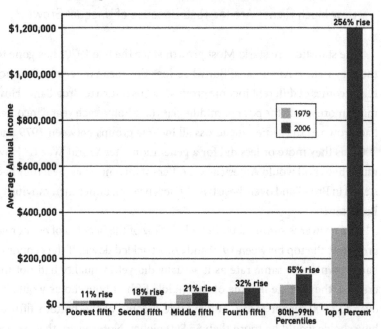

Source: Calculated from Congressional Budget Office (CBO), *Historical Effective Tax Rates, 1979–2006* (Washington, D.C.: CBO, April 2009), www.cbo.gov/publications/collections/tax/2009/average_after-tax_income.xls. Income includes wages, salaries, self-employment income, rents, taxable and nontaxable interest, dividends, realized capital gains, cash transfer payments, and cash retirement benefits, as well as all in-kind benefits, such as Medicare, Medicaid, employer-paid health insurance premiums, food stamps, school lunches and breakfasts, housing assistance, and energy assistance. Federal taxes are subtracted from income and account for not just income and payroll taxes paid directly by individuals and households, but also taxes paid by businesses (corporate income taxes and the employer's share of Social Security, Medicare, and federal unemployment insurance payroll taxes).

And, again, the gains enjoyed by the top 1 percent pale in comparison to those received by the top hundredth of 1 percent—a group CBO separated out in its analysis up through 2005. Between 1979 and 2005, the CBO numbers show, the average after-tax income of households in the top 0.01 percent increased from just over $4 million to nearly $24.3 million—more than quintupling in a little more than a quarter-century.

How Much Richer Are the Rich Because of Unequal Growth?

The statistics are stark: Most growth since the late 1970s has gone to the very richest Americans. But what does this mean in terms of the actual incomes of different income groups? Let us return to Broadland. How much more would the poor or middle class take home each year if incomes had grown at the same rate across all income groups between 1979 and 2006, as they more or less did for a generation after World War II? How much better off would Americans at different income levels be if they had stayed in Broadland over these twenty-seven years, rather than moving to Richistan?

The answer is summed up in table 1: Few of the benefits of economic growth at the top between 1979 and 2007 trickled down. If the economy had grown at the same rate as it actually did yet inequality had not increased, the average income of the middle fifth of households would be over $12,000 higher today. The average income of the bottom fifth of households would be more than $5,800 higher. Note, again, that we are assuming no change in the overall growth of the economy, just a broader distribution of the economy's rewards. Note, too, that we are accounting here for all government taxes and benefits as well as private workplace benefits. And remember: Broadland is not some hyperegalitarian world in which the rich get "soaked"; rather it's a world in which the rich simply experience the same income growth rate as everyone else, just as they basically had before the late 1970s.

Table 1: Richistan vs. Broadland

	Richistan (average actual income in 2006)	Broadland (all groups experience the average rate of household income growth between 1979 and 2006)	How Much Richer or Poorer in Broadland in 2006?
Bottom Fifth	$16,500	$22,366	$5,866 Richer
Second Fifth	$35,400	$45,181	$9,781 Richer
Middle Fifth	$52,100	$64,395	$12,295 Richer
Third Fifth	$73,800	$84,209	$10,409 Richer
80th–90th Percentile	$100,915	$106,696	$5,781 Richer
90th–95th Percentile	$132,258	$128,714	**$3,544 Poorer**
95th–99th Percentile	$211,768	$181,992	**$29,776 Poorer**
Top 1 Percent	$1,200,300	$506,002	**$694,298 Poorer**

So what would have happened to those at the top if they had experienced the same average growth of their income as everyone else? The answer is that they would be pulling down around $500,000 a year on average, rather than the more than $1.2 million the top 1 percent actually earned, on average, in 2006—a nearly $700,000 difference. Unequal growth has been very, very good for the have-it-alls.

When Richistan and Broadland are compared, another arresting conclusion comes into view. Other than the richest 10 percent of Americans, *every income group would have done better if they had experienced the average growth of household income,* that is, if they had lived in Broadland rather than Richistan. (The tipping point where Richistan delivers higher incomes than Broadland is somewhere between the 90th and 95th percentiles, though the gap between Richistan and Broadland is small until the very top of the distribution.) Put another way, the entire bottom 90 percent saw their incomes rise more slowly than average household income between 1979 and 2006. If trickle-up economics has a textbook case, this is it.

A Victimless Crime?

The DNA evidence shows that real household incomes for all groups but the very well-off have risen only modestly, and almost entirely because of increased family work hours. Meanwhile, the overall economy has expanded substantially. The explanation for this disconnect, mathematically speaking, is that most of the gains of growth have gone to Americans at the top of the economic ladder.

But this simple mathematical explanation leaves open an obvious objection: The economy is not zero-sum. Perhaps the gains of the rich, as impressive as they are, did not come at the expense of the rest of Americans. Maybe "Broadland" is not just an imaginary but an unimaginable country. After all, didn't the United States grow much more quickly than other rich nations during this period, allowing the rich to get richer even as the rest of Americans moved ahead as well? In particular, didn't the United States grow a lot faster than Europe, where incomes are generally much more equal and where the massive rise in income inequality seen in the United States did not occur?

The answer is no. The American economic engine ran hotter in some years than the European economic engine. But on average, between 1979 and 2006, economic growth per capita was essentially the same in the fifteen core nations of Europe as it was in the United States.[8] The United States is richer than these nations, but the gap has been surprisingly stable since the late 1970s.

The historical evidence certainly doesn't suggest an American economic miracle alongside European sclerosis. This lends strength to the supposition that the outsized gains of the rich came at the expense of those lower on the economic ladder, who found themselves enjoying less and less of the economic pie. On average, the economic pie grew at essentially the same rate in the United States as it did in nations where the poor and middle class have continued to enjoy a much larger piece.

Indeed, in one important respect, the pie actually grew more quickly in Europe than it did in the United States. Recall that American households are working more hours than they did in the past. The same is true in Europe, but not nearly to the same extent. Women have entered the workforce to roughly the same degree—in fact, the share of the population in the workforce grew more quickly in Europe than in the United States between 1979 and 2006.[9] Yet in Europe average work hours for those in the workforce have declined, so the net effect is only a small increase in overall work hours, compared with a much more substantial rise in the United States.[10] As a result, GDP per hour worked—perhaps the best single measure of a country's economic health—actually rose faster in Europe than in the United States between 1979 and 2006.

To be sure, the story of divergent work hours is complicated: Some of the decline in work hours in Europe is involuntary, due to higher levels of unemployment. But the basic story is that the United States did not grow markedly faster than Europe even as American inequality skyrocketed. Adjusted for the growing work hours of American families—with all the attendant stress and strains that those increased hours have caused—the American economic pie actually grew slightly more slowly.

The Big Zero

If there is a nail in the coffin of the dismissive view about middle-class economic problems, it is the decade that shall not be named: the 2000s. Some call these years the "aughts," others "the aughties," still others "the big zero."[11] The last moniker may be the most appropriate. The decade closed with the nation mired in the worst economic downturn in more than seventy years, with the unemployment rate around 10 percent and with the share of Americans unemployed for more than six months at the highest level ever recorded.[12] Economically speaking, the 2000s was truly a lost decade. At its end, the stock market was partying like it was 1999. Housing prices had crashed. Home ownership was at 2000 levels.[13] Even the most optimistic estimates suggested it would take years to recover from the hemorrhaging of jobs and incomes triggered by the collapse.

Here's the kicker: The aughties were awful even *before* the economy began to crumble in late 2007. They featured six years of consecutive economic growth (from the end of 2001 until the end of 2007) in which the median income of non-elderly households actually fell while the share of Americans living in poverty actually rose. This was the first economic expansion on record in which the typical non-elderly household lost economic ground.[14] Yet it wasn't all bad news. Between 2002 and 2007, the real pretax incomes of those in the top 1 percent rose by 10 percent. Per year.[15]

Beyond Income

Those who are inclined to be dismissive of the evidence just reviewed frequently respond by insisting that the focus on income is short-sighted: We should also look at the chance people will rise up the economic ladder, at their workplace benefits, at their spending and wealth, and so on. True enough. Unfortunately, when we take a broader perspective, the conclusion that our economy has become increasingly winner-take-all only becomes stronger.

Stagnant Social Mobility

Americans have always believed in upward social mobility—both as an ideal and a description of reality. And if social mobility had been rising along with inequality over the last generation, then the growing concentration of income at the top might be less of a concern. One year's poor household might be next year's middle-class or even rich household. Social mobility would soften the sharp edges of a growing class divide.

Alas, the evidence is overwhelming that upward social mobility has *not* increased at the same time that inequality has skyrocketed. Indeed, according to a number of innovative new studies, American mobility may well have declined over the last generation, even as inequality has risen. This is true of both individual mobility ("Am I richer than I was a decade or two ago?") and of intergenerational mobility ("Am I richer than my parents were?").[16] Over a typical decade, for example, just under four in five people stay in the same income quintile or move a single quintile up or down.

We know less about the long-term mobility of the top 1 percent, but all indications are that people in this rarefied group usually don't drop very far down the ladder for any length of time. Looking just at wage and salary income, for example, more than 70 percent of the highest-earning 1 percent of American households in 2004 were among the highest-earning 5 percent of households in 1994. Only around one in ten had risen from the bottom 80 percent—down from around one in seven in the 1970s.[17] And of course, as the gains of economic growth become ever more concentrated, almost by definition fewer individuals will be able to move into the shrinking ranks of the economic winners.

Compared with other rich nations, moreover, U.S. intergenerational mobility is surprisingly low, in part because the gap between income groups is so much bigger. The American Dream portrays the United States as a classless society where anyone can rise to the top, regardless of family background. Yet there is more intergenerational mobility in Australia, Sweden, Norway, Finland, Germany, Spain, France, and Canada. In fact, of affluent countries studied, only Britain and Italy have lower intergenerational mobility than the United States does (and they are basically even with the U.S.).[18]

The differences are often stark. In the United States, more than half of the earnings advantage (or disadvantage) of fathers is passed on to sons. In Canada, only about a fifth or less is. And almost all of the difference is accounted for by the fact that Americans are much more likely to be stuck at the bottom or secure at the top than are Canadians. In short, when mobility is accounted for, the picture of the winner-take-all economy looks no better. If anything, it looks worse.

Broken Benefits

It is often argued that workplace benefits, like health insurance and retirement pensions, alter the story of the winner-take-all economy—and that, in particular, the middle class does better when you take into account the growing share of compensation that comes in the form of such benefits, rather than cold, hard cash. Actually, the CBO numbers we have been looking at already take into account health and pension benefits, so the anemic gains of working- and middle-class Americans cannot be explained away by suggesting that they are getting better and better benefits at their place of work.

But let's take the argument a little further. Are Americans getting better benefits tied to their jobs? Not when it comes to retirement benefits. Employers contribute less to such benefits than they did in the 1970s, and workers are less likely to have an employer-sponsored pension than they were in the late 1970s.[19] And many fewer have a guaranteed defined-benefit pension that pays them a fixed income in retirement. Instead, most Americans who have pensions rely on defined-contribution plans that place all the risk of retirement savings on them. This risk has been driven home by the recent stock market drop, which reduced the median balance in 401(k)s by a third between 2007 and 2008.[20] As notable as the decline is the end point: the typical amount in a 401(k) in 2008 was a paltry $12,655. Given this, it's no shock that the share of Americans who are at risk of retiring without adequate income has risen substantially since the early 1980s.[21]

On the other side of the benefits equation, employers and workers are certainly spending more on health insurance—much, much more. The question is what this spending has bought. Are Americans better insulated against medical costs than they were a generation ago? No. Are they more secure against the medical crises and costs that, studies suggest, are associated with more than half of the rising number of personal bankruptcies?[22] No. Health costs that outstrip the growth of earnings year after year after year—pushing more people out of coverage and more people into hardship—can hardly be seen as an unqualified benefit for the middle class.

That's especially so because these higher costs are not inevitable. The United States spends vastly more than any other rich nation on health care—both as a share of the overall economy and on a per-person basis—even though we are the only affluent democracy that doesn't guarantee insurance to all its citizens. In 2007, the price tag for our exorbitant system came to $7,290 per person. The next most profligate nation, Norway, featured spending of $4,763 per person. Canada's spending per capita is essentially half the U.S. level.[23]

Yet the United States has fewer doctors, hospital beds, and nurses per person than the norm among rich nations, and Americans (while less healthy overall) visit doctors and hospitals less often and have shorter hospital stays. Indeed, by some measures our care looks surprisingly substandard. For example, recent analyses of "amenable mortality"—deaths that could have been prevented with timely care—find that the United States has the highest rate of preventable death before age seventy-five among rich nations, and that it is falling farther and farther behind.[24]

And, of course, the United States has had a higher share of citizens without coverage than any other rich nation, and that share has been growing. In 2006, more than 46 million Americans younger than sixty-five were uninsured—nearly 18 percent of the non-elderly population. Back in 1979, the number of uninsured was 27.5 million, or less than 15 percent of the nonelderly population.[25] Add in workplace benefits and the situation of most Americans looks even more dire than when we focus on income alone.

Consumption to the Rescue?

Can another definition of economic well-being come to the rescue? It has long been known that inequality of spending (or "consumption") is less than inequality of income. The reasons are obvious: The rich save more of their money than the poor; at the same time, two major groups in society—retirees and young adults—often spend more than they earn, thanks to savings and loans. So we should expect less consumption inequality than income inequality. The issue is whether we see the same basic trends in inequality of consumption that we do in inequality of income, namely, a big increase.

Tackling this issue turns out to be extremely difficult, in part because the main source of evidence, the Consumer Expenditure Survey, largely misses the high-income folks who've benefited from the winner-take-all economy. Still, it is increasingly clear there is no "consumption paradox." Consumption inequality is not as great as income inequality, as we'd expect (especially since the evidence fails to capture the big winners at the top). But the two have grown at more or less the same rate over time.[26]

Here again we find smart analysts ignoring the most notable feature of the winner-take-all economy—that it's, well, winner-take-all. Have lower-income Americans been borrowing more to sustain their spending? Definitely. Are the less affluent experiencing lower price inflation than richer Americans thanks to cheap Chinese goods?[27] Perhaps. But none of this is going to alter fundamentally our view of American inequality. The access of the poor to easy credit or Wal-Mart prices has little bearing on the growing gap between the superrich and the merely well-to-do.

Drowning in Debt

Furthermore, the flip side of consumption is savings and investment—and the wealth that comes with savings and investment. After all, it's not as if the rich are giving all the money they don't spend to charities for the poor. In fact, money that high earners do not spend gets turned into wealth, and the share of wealth held by the rich is both high and growing. In 2004, the wealthiest 1 percent of households had an average net worth of nearly $15 million.[28] (At the very top of the ladder, the wealthiest 400 Americans—according to the famous *Forbes* 400 list—had an average net worth of $3.9 billion in 2008, more than six times the 1985 average for the *Forbes* 400.)[29]

The average net worth of the bottom 80 percent of households, in contrast, was around $82,000, and that includes the wealth that households had in their homes. Average net worth for the bottom 40 percent of households was a paltry $2,200 in 2004, less than half the $5,400 that this group enjoyed in 1983. Strikingly, over the entire period between 1983 and 2004, only 10 percent of all wealth gains went to the bottom 80 percent of Americans, an even more skewed pattern of growth than seen in income.[30]

Perhaps more striking, 17 percent of households in 2004 had zero or negative net worth—they owed more than they had. (And this was before the collapse of real estate prices put more homes "underwater"—with home loans exceeding home values—than at any time in U.S. history.) Here we find a major clue to why consumption is not always a good measure of income: For a time, at least, people can spend beyond their income by borrowing, and before the 2007 downturn, Americans were borrowing at record rates. But, as the late economist Herbert Stein is reported to have said, "If something can't go on forever, it won't." The inexorable increase in household debt was not sustainable without comparable income gains— and those gains did not occur. Once again, scouring the scene turns up plenty of additional proof that the winner-take-all economy has produced limited gains for those outside the winner's circle.

The clues are undeniable: Not only did those below the top reaches of the economic ladder find themselves falling ever farther behind the have-it-alls; they reaped surprisingly few of the gains of the massive expansion at the top.

This is an economic puzzle. It is also a political puzzle. Democracy may not be good at a lot of things. But one thing it is supposed to be good at is responding to problems that affect broad majorities. How could events and trends like these evolve with so little response from democratically elected leaders? Indeed, as we shall see, the puzzle is even deeper. For government was no mere bystander in many of these developments. It actually pushed them along. Why?

Before we turn to these questions, however, we have one last piece of unfinished business: We need to explain why the prime suspect that America's economic detectives have fingered is, at most, a modest accomplice to the crime.

The Usual (but Wrong) Suspect

Tune into the cable money stations or read the business press and you are likely to hear an account of rising inequality that goes something like this:

"Education is the key to understanding broad inequality trends."[31]

"To explain increasing inequality we must explain why the economic return to education and to the development of skills more generally has continued to rise."[32]

"We have an economy that increasingly rewards education and skills because of that education."[33]

These quotes were not chosen at random. They are the pronounce-ments, respectively, of the former head of President George W. Bush's Council of Economic Advisers, Gregory Mankiw, a Harvard economist; Fed chairman Ben Bernanke (another economist, formerly of Princeton); and, finally, former President George W. Bush himself.

It might seem that the common element connecting these quotes is that those responsible for them have ties to the Republican Party. After all, rising inequality was an inconvenient reality for a GOP president (and, before 2006, a GOP Congress) intent on cutting taxes for the wealthy. The fact is, however, that these three quotes express what was, until recently at least, the overwhelming consensus view on inequality among econo-mists, a view summarized in the ungainly acronym SBTC.

The SBTC Seduction

SBTC is not a regional telephone company. It stands for "skill-biased technological change," and it is still by far the dominant explanation for American inequality trends.[34] According to the SBTC argument, the last thirty or so years have witnessed a massive shift toward more knowledge-based employment. In the popular version of the argument, this shift has been greatly accelerated by the globalization of the American economy. This transformation has made formal education and advanced skills much more valuable, fueling a growing divide between the highly educated and the rest of American workers.

In some versions of the argument, skill-biased technological change is driven by computers and the Internet. In others, the main culprit is the failure of the educational advancement of most workers to keep pace with the growing skill demands of a global knowledge economy.[35] The account of the crime, however, is the same: SBTC did it.

There are just two problems: SBTC isn't even charged with the right crime. And the suspect has an alibi.

Why Educational Gaps Can't Explain American Top-Heavy Inequality

If there is an Exhibit A in the case that SBTC did it, it is the rising "college wage premium"—the extra amount that college graduates earn relative to their less educated peers. Each year, the College Board publishes a report entitled, "Education Pays," in which it announces that the gap between those who have finished college and those who have not is large and growing. More sophisticated economic analyses usually emphasize the effects of education across the full spectrum of educational achievement, before college and beyond. But they reach the same conclusion: a growing "return to schooling." From here, it's a short leap to the view that the rising bang for one's educational buck is the main cause of growing inequality.

Only it's not. The return to schooling—and especially to a college degree—has risen. But, as we've seen, rising American inequality is not mainly about the gap between the college-educated and the rest, or indeed about educational gaps in general. It is about the pulling away of the very top. Those at the top are often highly educated, yes, but so, too, are those just below them who have been left increasingly behind.

There's more: The college educated did well relative to those below them, but not because they experienced massive economic gains. Rather, they merely managed to avoid the devastatingly slow growth at the bottom.

Assume that the story about a new educational elite is true. The top 20 percent of the income distribution should therefore be composed almost entirely of college graduates. (The share of Americans with a college degree was 29 percent in 2007.) What, then, happened to the household income of someone at the 80th percentile, the starting point for entry into this supposedly favored class? The answer is that it has grown extremely slowly compared with the income of folks at the very top—roughly one-fourth as quickly per year as the average income of the top 1 percent.

That middle-class income growth, moreover, is mostly because of increased household work hours, not increased individual earnings. Hard as it may be to believe, a typical entry-level worker (ages 25–34) with a bachelor's degree or higher earned only $1,000 more for full-time, full-year work in 2006 than did such a worker in 1980 ($45,000 versus $44,000, adjusted for inflation).[36] And college-educated workers are substantially less likely to receive health insurance in their first job than they once were—almost four in ten now start out in the labor market without health benefits.[37] So much for the enormous general rewards of a college degree.

To be sure, some workers with advanced education make enormous sums. But that's exactly the point: A huge amount of inequality occurs among workers who have heeded the advice of "Education Pays" and sought a college degree. Economists call this "within-group inequality" (that is, inequality among people with the same education or skills), and it is one of the strongest pieces of exculpatory evidence on SBTC's side. That is because within-group inequality, by definition, cannot be explained with reference to education, since it occurs among people with the same basic characteristics. And within-group inequality accounts for a major part of the rise in inequality since the 1970s, especially at the very top—where almost everyone has a good education.[38]

Maybe SBTC was at work among these workers in more subtle ways—some argue that college-educated workers with the skills to do routine tasks have lost out to those who do higher-level "abstract tasks"—but the case against SBTC, considered so strong at the outset, becomes harder to make.

But forget about the weak case, because the suspect has a strong alibi.

Why Didn't Other Rich Nations Experience SBTC's Wrath?

SBTC is attractive to economic detectives because it is an all-purpose criminal—one that, its prosecutors argue, can explain both the decline in American inequality in the first half of the twentieth century and its rise in the last thirty years. It is a suspect whose influence should be seen over long spans of time and, more important for the present discussion, across national borders. After all, other rich nations have computers and the Internet too—indeed, quite a few are more networked than we are— and most rich nations are *more* exposed to the global economy than we are. If SBTC did it here, it should have done it elsewhere, where the same technological and global shifts were taking place.

Embarrassingly for the SBTC-did-it consensus, however, SBTC seems to be picky about where to strike. When it comes to rising inequality, the world isn't flat after all. American income inequality is the highest in the advanced industrial world. As one labor economist wryly puts it, "If there were a gold medal for inequality, the United States would win hands down . . . [S]tandard measures show that the United States more closely resembles a developing country than an advanced country on this measure of economic performance."[39]

Yet gaps in skills, as measured by years of schooling, are not larger in the United States than they are in other affluent nations. They are actually smaller. Inequality is dramatically higher in the United States not because of greater skill gaps or greater returns to education, but because within-group inequality is greater than it is in other rich nations. Indeed, there is more inequality among workers with the *same* level of skills (measured by age, education, and literacy) in the United States than there is among *all workers* in some of the more equal rich nations.[40]

The Uniqueness of America's Winner-Take-All Economy

SBTC's alibi appears even stronger when it comes to the meteoric rise of earnings at the very top, because that rise has been substantially more meteoric in the United States than in other rich nations.

Figure 3 shows the share of income, excluding capital gains, going to the top 1 percent of households in twelve nations: Australia, Canada, France, Germany, Ireland, Japan, the Netherlands, New Zealand, Sweden, Switzerland, the United Kingdom, and, of course, the United States.[41] The first bar shows the average share in the mid-1970s (1973–1975); the second shows the average share around the millennium (1998–2000).

One feature of figure 3 that jumps out is that the United States did not look all that exceptional in the early 1970s. Germany, Switzerland, Canada, even France—all had a higher share of national income going to the top 1 percent a generation ago.

Yet that has changed dramatically. The United States is now at the top of the advanced industrial pack, with regard to both the level (16 percent) and the increase (virtually a doubling) of the top 1 percent's share of income. Half of the nations in figure 3—a diverse group that includes France, Germany, Japan, the Netherlands, Sweden, and Switzerland—experienced little or no increase in the share of income going to the top 1 percent. Apparently in these countries SBTC was AWOL.

It's true that the other English-speaking nations in this group—Australia, Canada, Ireland, and the United Kingdom—have followed a path more like the United States'. Still, the United States is well in the lead in the competition for the gold medal for inequality. Whereas the United States experienced a doubling of the income share of the top 1 percent, the other English-speaking nations saw only an average rise of around half that in percentage terms.

The English-speaking world has certainly emulated the American pattern more closely than other nations have. But this is hardly proof that government policy doesn't matter, since these nations have also generally emulated U.S. *public policy* more than other nations have. What's more, the trajectory of the two countries that are most often compared

Figure 3: The Top 1 Percent's Share of National Income
(Excluding Capital Gains), Mid-'70s vs. Circa 2000

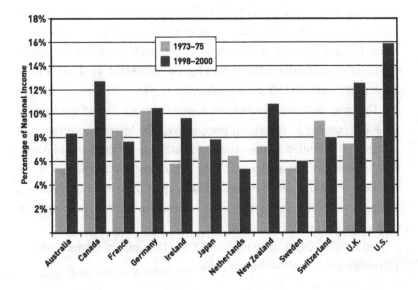

Notes: The first bar for each nation is the top 1 percent's average share of national income (excluding capital gains) in 1973–75 (except for Ireland, for which data are unavailable until 1976; the first bar for Ireland averages the years 1976–79]. The second bar for each nation is the top 1 percent's average share in 1998–2000 (except, for reasons of data availability, France and Germany (1996–98), the Netherlands (1997–99), and Switzerland (1994–96]).

Source: Andrew Leigh, "How Closely Do Top Income Shares Track Other Measures of Inequality?" *The Economic Journal* 117 (November 2007): F589-F603. Data available at http://people.anu.edu.au/andrew.leigh/pdf/TopIncomesPanel.xls. (The figure uses Leigh's data on the top 1 percent excluding capital gains, adjusted for consistency across nations.)

to the United States, the United Kingdom and Canada, cannot be viewed as wholly independent of the rise of America's winner-take-all-economy. As we saw when we started to parse the composition of the top 0.1 percent, the rise in the compensation of the highest earners, especially corporate executives and financial managers, drives much of the outsized gains at the top in the United States. Companies in English-speaking nations compete for these workers, and thus have faced the most pressure to match the massive salaries on offer in the States.[42] This appears to hold particularly true for Canada.* While this contagion effect is hard to pin down, there is little doubt that some of the increase in top incomes in other English-speaking nations reflects competitive pressure to match the more dramatic rise in the United States—a rise that we shall see has a great deal to do with U.S. public policy.

The cross-national window just opened puts the rise of the winner-take-all economy in surprising perspective. The hyperconcentration of income in the United States—the proximate cause of the death of America's broad-based prosperity—is a relatively recent development. It is also a development that sets the United States apart from other rich nations, calling into serious doubt the usual explanation for America's winner-take-all economy, SBTC.

But if SBTC didn't do it, who did? Enter the unusual suspect: American politics.

---

* Perhaps most telling, there is little sign of the same meteoric rise at the top among *French*-speaking portions of Canada. Executives in Quebec do not appear to be competing in the same common labor market that has allowed American pay levels at the top to diffuse to the rest of Canada.

Chapter 2

How the Winner-Take-All Economy Was Made

The winner-take-all economy—the hyperconcentration of rewards at the top that is the defining feature of the post-1970s American economy—poses three big mysteries: Who did it? How? And why? We have seen that the main suspect fingered by most investigators, Skill-Biased Technological Change, is at most a modest accomplice. Now, it is time to turn to the unusual suspect, American government and politics.

No less important, it is time to ask, if American government and politics did it, how? Only after understanding the basic, powerful ways in which government fueled the winner-take-all economy will we be in a position to delve into the "Why" questions: What were the motives behind the public policies that fostered winner-take-all? How, in a representative democracy, could public officials favor such a small slice of Americans for so long? That part of our investigation begins in chapter 3 with a whirlwind tour of American political history that seeks to uncover the reasons why, and the means by which, politicians in our capitalist constitutional democracy do—or do not—seek to redress imbalances of economic resources and power.

We face a high hurdle in our investigation. If there is one thing on which most economic experts seem to agree, it is that government and politics can't be much of an explanation for the hyperconcentration of American incomes at the top. President Bush's treasury secretary, Henry Paulson, may have tipped his Republican hat when he asserted in 2006 that inequality "is simply an economic reality, and it is neither fair nor useful to blame any political party."[1] (No one could doubt which party he thought was being unfairly and uselessly blamed.) Yet Paulson is hardly alone in his exculpatory judgment: Most economists on both sides of the political spectrum argue that government policy is at best a sideshow in the inequality circus. There are exceptions, of course. Nobel Laureate in Economics Paul Krugman has forcefully argued that policy is a crucial reason for rising inequality, and other experts have usefully examined the role of policy in specific areas.[2] But the dominant perspective remains highly skeptical of attributing much influence to government—in part because there has yet to be a systematic accounting of the full range of things that American public officials have done (or, in some cases, deliberately failed to do) to propel the winner-take-all economy.

Think of this chapter as the opening argument of our case. Like any opening argument, it won't address all the questions. In particular, it will leave almost entirely unaddressed the core mystery that motivates the rest of the book: Why have American politicians done so much to build up the winner-take-all economy? But as in any investigation, finding the right suspect—and showing just how powerful the case against that suspect is—represents the first step toward unraveling the larger mysteries that started the search.

Why Politics and Policy Are (Wrongly) Let Off

Much of the widespread doubt about the role of American politics and public policy in fostering rising inequality centers on a simple fact: The great bulk of the growth in inequality has been driven by rising inequalities in what people earn before government taxes and benefits. Simply put, those at the top are raking in a lot more from their jobs than they used to. The winner-take-all economy reflects a winner-take-all labor market.

Enter the doubters: It would be one thing, they argue, if government was taking much less from the rich in taxes or giving much less to the middle class in benefits than it used to. That would be a transparent case of government abetting inequality. But how, the skeptics ask, can government influence what people earn *before they pay taxes or receive government benefits?* On the conservative side, for example, Harvard's Gregory Mankiw insists that while "some pundits are tempted to look inside the Beltway for a cause" of rising inequality, "policymakers do not have the tools to exert such a strong influence over pretax earnings, even if they wanted to do so."[3] On the liberal side, economist and former Clinton Treasury official Brad DeLong of the University of California at Berkeley says, "I can't see the mechanism by which changes in government policies bring about such huge swings in pre-tax income distribution."[4]

This skeptical response, however, makes three elemental mistakes.

The first is to miss the strong evidence that government *is* doing much less to reduce inequality through taxes and benefits at the *very top* of the income ladder. Here again, a fixation on inequality between big chunks of the income distribution misses the extent to which, at the very pinnacle, government policy has grown much more generous toward the fortunate. As we will show, this increasing solicitousness accounts for a surprisingly large part of the economic gains of America's superrich.

Second, the skeptical response feeds off a mistaken presumption that if government and politics really matter, then the only way they can matter is through the passage of a host of new laws actively pursuing the redistribution of income to the top. We'll show that a large number of new laws that greatly exacerbate inequality *have* been created, but we will also show that big legislative initiatives are not the only way to reshape how an economy works and whom it works for. Equally, if not more, important is what we will call "drift"—systematic, prolonged failures of government to respond to the shifting realities of a dynamic economy. We will have a lot to say about drift in this book, because the story of America's winner-take-all economy isn't just about political leaders actively passing laws to abet the rich, but also about political leaders studiously turning the other way (with a lot of encouragement from the rich) when fast-moving economic changes make existing rules and regulations designed to rein in excess at the top obsolete.

The third problem with the skeptical response goes even deeper: The skeptics suggest that the only way government can change the distribution of income is through taxation and government benefits. This is a common view, yet also an extraordinarily blinkered one. Government actually has enormous power to affect the distribution of "market income," that is, earnings before government taxes and benefits take effect. Think about laws governing unions; the minimum wage; regulations of corporate governance; rules for financial markets, including the management of risk for high-stakes economic ventures; and so on. Government rules make the market, and they powerfully shape how, and in whose interests, it operates. This is a fact, not a statement of ideology. And it is a fact that carries very big implications.

Perhaps the biggest implication is that public policy really matters. The rules of the market make a huge difference for people's lives. And what matters is not the broad label applied to what government does ("tax reform," "health care reform") but the underlying details that most commentators blithely ignore. As our investigation proceeds, we will see again and again that the devil truly is in the details of public policy. Policy is not a sideshow; in the modern age of activist government, it is often the main show.

To be sure, it is sometimes difficult to know exactly what the effects of these rules are. But there's no question that these rules, taken together, have a massive cumulative impact. Just stop for a moment to contemplate how different economic affairs would be in our nation without basic property rights or government-regulated financial markets and you begin to appreciate how pervasive the role of government really is. And governments at different times and in different nations can and do make markets in very different ways, and with very different distributional results.

When these mistaken assumptions are corrected—when, that is, we look at what's happened at the very top, take political efforts to block the adaptation of government policy seriously, and look at how markets have been politically reconstructed to aid the privileged—a conclusion that can't be mistaken comes into view: Government has had a huge hand in nurturing America's winner-take-all economy.

To be clear, we are not saying that technological shifts haven't played a role too. Changes in information technology have fostered more concentrated rewards in fields of endeavor, such as sports and entertainment, where the ability to reach large audiences is the main determinant of economic return.[5] Computers, increased global capital flows, and the development of new financial instruments have made it possible for savvy investors to reap (or lose) huge fortunes almost instantly—a point first made by Sherwin Rosen and elaborated by Robert Frank and Philip Cook in their 1995 book, *The Winner-Take-All Society*.[6] But such technologically driven explanations have little to say about why the hyperconcentration of income at the top has been so much more pronounced in the United States than elsewhere. Nor do they come close to explaining just how concentrated economic gains have become.

For example, the "superstar" story of celebrities, artists, and athletes who now reach, and thus make, millions has a good deal of merit. As noted in chapter 1, however, these sorts of professions only account for a tiny share of the richest income group.

Table 1, based on a recent study of tax return data, shows that roughly four in ten taxpayers in the top 0.1 percent in 2004 were executives, managers, or supervisors of firms outside the financial industry (nearly three in ten were executives). By contrast, high-earners in the arts, media, and sports represented just 3 percent of this top-income group.

Table 1: Percentage of Taxpayers in
Top 0.1 Percent (Including Capital Gains), 2004

Executives, managers, supervisors (non-finance)	40.8%
Financial professions, including management	18.4
Not working or deceased	6.3
Lawyers	6.2
Real estate	4.7
Medical	4.4
Entrepreneur not elsewhere classified	3.6
Arts, media, sports	3.1
Computer, math, engineering, technical (nonfinance)	3.0
Business operations (nonfinance)	2.2
Skilled sales (except finance or real estate)	1.9
Professors and scientists	1.1
Farmers & ranchers	1.0
Other	2.6
Unknown	0.7

Source: Jon Bakija and Bradley T. Heim, "Jobs and Income Growth of Top Earners
and the Causes of Changing Income Inequality: Evidence from U.S. Tax Return Data,"
working paper, Williams College, Office of Tax Analysis (March 17, 2009), Table 1.

As for financial professionals, who make up a much larger proportion
of the top 0.1 percent (nearly two in ten taxpayers), it strains credulity to
say they are merely the talented tamers of technological change. After
all, plenty of the so-called financial innovations that their complex com-
puter models helped spawn proved to be just fancier (and riskier) ways of
gambling with other people's money, making quick gains off unsophisti-
cated consumers, or benefiting from short-term market swings. Moreover, most of these "innovations" could occur only because of the failure
to update financial rules to protect against the resulting risks—much to
the chagrin of the rest of Americans who ended up bailing the innovators
out. Former Fed chairman Paul Volcker was no doubt channeling a widespread sentiment when he said in 2009 that the last truly helpful financial
innovation was the ATM.[7]

What is more, government policy not only failed to push back against
the rising tide at the top in finance, corporate pay, and other winner-take-

all domains, but also repeatedly promoted it. Government put its thumb on the scale, hard. What's so striking is that it did so on the side of those who already had more weight. We can see this most clearly in the most transparent case of government abetting inequality: the gutting, over the course of three decades, of progressive taxation at the top of the economic ladder.

A Cut Above

The major rollback of taxation for those at the very top has received surprisingly little notice among today's economic detectives. Most commentators appear to accept—with pleasure or displeasure, depending on their ideological persuasion—that the tax burden of the rich is not an important part of the rise of winner-take-all inequality.

But this is not true. Yes, as the *Wall Street Journal* editorial board never tires of reminding readers, the well-off are paying a larger share of the nation's total income taxes than in the past. But that does not mean that the well-off are paying higher income tax *rates*. The amount of taxes we pay is a function not just of how steep tax rates are but also of how much we earn. And over the last generation, the well-off have earned more and more—so much more that they can pay a larger share of the nation's income taxes and still pay a much lower overall *rate* on their massively larger incomes.

Moreover, income taxes are among the taxes that hit the rich hardest. When you take into account all federal taxes—including payroll taxes, which only hit the rich lightly, and corporate and estate taxes, which once hit the rich much harder than they do today—tax rates on the rich have fallen dramatically.

Perhaps most important, talking about the rich as a monolithic group makes no sense. As we have learned, there are the rich, and there are the *rich*. And what is most striking is that the latter group—the very, very, very rich—have enjoyed by far the greatest drop in their tax rates.

Figure 1, drawn from the research of the economists Thomas Piketty and Emmanuel Saez discussed in the last chapter, shows just how spec-tacular the decline has been for the tiny slivers of the top 1 percent we talked about earlier.[8] This figure tracks the effective average federal rate—what people *actually* pay as a share of their reported income, not the of-ficial rate that enterprising lawyers and accountants make mincemeat of for the rich every day. As can be seen, those in the top 1 percent pay rates that are a full third lower than they used to be despite the fact that they are much richer than those in the top 1 percent were back in 1970. But as the top 1 percent is sliced into smaller and richer groups, the even more startling story becomes clear: The truly advantaged are paying a much smaller share of their reported income than they used to—at the very top (the richest 0.01 percent) less than half as large a share of income. They are not simply richer because their paychecks have grown; they're richer because government taxes them much less heavily than it once did.

Figure 4: Average Federal Tax Rates for Top Income Groups, 1970–2004

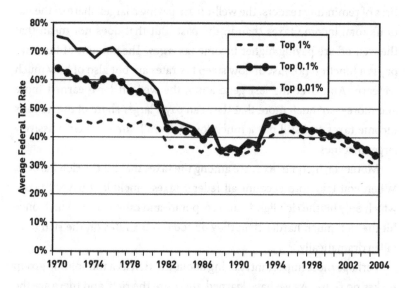

Source: Thomas Piketty and Emmanuel Saez, "How Progressive is the U.S. Federal Tax System? A Historical and International Perspective," *Journal of Economic Per-spectives* 21, no. 1 (Winter 2007); data available at http://elsa.berkeley.edu/~saez/jep=results=standalone.xls.

Tax policy experts have a name for a tax code that taxes higher-income people at a higher rate: "progressive." The federal tax code is still progressive overall. But what used to be a key feature of the code—its steep progressivity at the very top income levels—has simply disappeared. The richest of the rich now pay about the same overall rate as those who are merely rich. Indeed, though figure 1 doesn't show this, the upper middle class—families, say, in the top 10 or 20 percent of the income distribution—are paying an average federal tax rate not much lower than that paid by the superrich. This is a pattern we will see again and again: dramatic benefits for the rich that are so precisely targeted that they are only visible when we put that tiny slice of Americans under our economic microscope. It is as if the government had developed the economic policy equivalent of smart bombs, except these bombs carry payloads of cash for their carefully selected recipients.

How much of the rise in winner-take-all outcomes does this three-decades-long tax-cutting spree account for? Unlike the effect of government on how much people earn, this is relatively easy to calculate (at least to a first approximation), and the numbers are staggering. The top 0.1 percent had about 7.3 percent of total national after-tax income in 2000, up from 1.2 percent in 1970. If the effect of taxes on their income had remained what it was in 1970, they would have had about 4.5 percent of after-tax income.[9] Put more simply, if the effects of taxation on income at the top had been frozen in place in 1970, a very big chunk of the growing distance between the superrich and everyone else would disappear.

This dramatic change in tax policy didn't happen magically. Starting in the 1970s, the people in charge of designing and implementing the tax code increasingly favored those at the very top. The change began before Reagan's election, and continued well after the intellectual case had crumbled for the supply-side theories that had justified his big tax cuts. It resulted from a bidding war in which Democrats as well as Republicans took part, and involved cuts in estate and corporate taxes as well as in income taxes. The one big regularity was an impressive focus on directing benefits not just to the well-to-do but to the superrich. On provisions as diverse as the estate tax and the Alternative Minimum Tax, elected officials repeatedly chose courses of action that advantaged the very wealthy at the expense of the much larger group of the merely affluent.

All this occurred, moreover, even as Americans as a whole remained strongly supportive of making the richest pay more in taxes. In 1939, as the nation still grappled with the Great Depression, 35 percent of Americans agreed with the (very strongly worded) statement that "government should redistribute wealth by heavy taxes on the rich." In 1998, 45 percent agreed; and in 2007, 56 percent did. Public concern about taxes has ebbed and flowed, but large majorities of Americans consistently say higher-income Americans pay too little in taxes and that corporate income taxes—which have fallen to less than 15 percent of all taxes—should be a key source of government revenue.[10] And yet, taxes on the richest of Americans have, for more than thirty years, just kept coming down.

Not all of the tax-cutting has been as prominent as the estate tax cuts of 2001. Given public concerns about tax breaks for the wealthy, politicians have, not surprisingly, opted for more subtle means of achieving similar ends. One is slashing back enforcement of tax law. Call it "do-it-yourself tax cuts." Roughly one out of every six dollars in owed taxes goes unpaid—literally, hundreds of billions a year.[11] Not all of these dollars are owed by the rich, of course. But just as Willie Sutton robbed banks because "that's where the money is," tax evasion by the rich is where the money is. Most Americans, after all, have most of their taxes automatically taken out of their wages. Rich people and corporations, by contrast, are largely responsible for reporting their complex earnings and capital gains, and they have the will and the way to use intricate partnerships, offshore tax havens, and other devices that skirt or cross legal lines. Yet, as the investigative reporter David Cay Johnston has painstakingly documented, audits of high-income taxpayers and businesses have plummeted. About the only area where audits have gone up is among poorer taxpayers who claim the Earned Income Tax Credit.[12]

Another way public officials have cut the taxes of upper-income filers without passing new laws is by leaving in place loopholes through which rich Americans and their accountants shovel lightly taxed cash. Take one of the more egregious examples: the ability of private equity and hedge fund managers to treat much of their extraordinary incomes as capital gains, subject only to a 15 percent tax rate. (In 2006, the top twenty-five hedge fund managers earned nearly $600 million on average, with the richest, James Simons, taking in $1.7 *billion*.)[13] The "carried interest" provision that allows this sweetheart deal is a bug in the tax code that predates the rise of hedge funds. But while this loophole is almost universally viewed as indefensible (and may finally be closed a bit in 2010), it has been protected for years by the fierce lobbying of its deep-pocketed beneficiaries and the strong backing of Wall Street supporters like Senator Chuck Schumer, Democrat of New York.

Given all the energy spent trying to pin rising inequality on relatively dubious suspects, it's striking how little attention is paid to the very easily fingered culprit of declining tax rates on the rich. We've hardly begun laying out the full case for government's role, but there's no doubt that U.S. tax policy has exacerbated American hyperinequality through the demise of progressive taxation at the top of the economic ladder.

Reducing Redistribution

The fixation on inequality between large sections of the income distribution has obscured the extent to which government policy has grown more generous toward those at the very top. The second common oversight mentioned earlier—failing to take seriously how government policy can be undermined by deliberate efforts to block its being updated—has led observers to ignore the extent to which policy has become *less* generous toward the vast majority of Americans who have been on the losing side of rising inequality.

Indeed, a big clue in the cross-national statistics that points toward government policy as the suspect is that the United States stands out in its response to increases in inequality in market earnings since the 1970s. Elsewhere in the advanced industrial world, creeping tendencies toward greater economic disparities—whether due to globalization, technological change, or other broad economic or social forces—have been met with concerted, active resistance. In the United States, this pressure has proceeded with little government interference, aside from policies that have actively pushed it along.

We know this thanks to a major international research effort, the Luxembourg Income Study (LIS). For more than a decade, LIS researchers have been combing through national income data to examine how actively governments redistribute the income that people earn in the market, taking money from people higher on the economic ladder and distributing it to people lower. The LIS data suffer from the now-familiar problem that they are not very good at accounting for the incomes of the very richest. But they nonetheless offer a revealing picture of how countries have responded to rising inequality.

That picture may come as a surprise: We think of the welfare state as embattled, but in the majority of rich nations for which we have evidence, income redistribution over the past few decades has either held steady or actually risen. In many of these countries—and that includes our northern neighbor, Canada—inequality created by the market has been significantly softened by a greater government role.[14]

On American soil, the opposite has been true. Government is doing substantially less to reduce inequality and poverty below the highest rungs of the income ladder than it did a generation ago. We sometimes hear about expanding programs for the poor such as the Earned Income Tax Credit. But against the rising tide of inequality, these programs have represented fragile levees, crumbling under the weight of quickly moving water. Between 1980 and 2003, for example, the percentage by which government taxes and benefits reduced inequality (as measured by the Gini index, a common inequality standard) fell by more than a quarter.[15]

Can the absence of a government response to rising inequality really be treated as a form of policy? Absolutely—when it takes the form of "drift," the deliberate failure to adapt public policies to the shifting realities of a dynamic economy.[16]

The idea of drift is simple, but central to understanding what has transpired in the United States. Major shifts in the economy and society change how public policies work. Think of how rising inflation erodes the value of the federal minimum wage. Workers at the very bottom of the economic ladder have seen their economic standing decline in part because the minimum wage has not been updated to reflect the rising price of consumer goods.[17]

And why has it not been updated? Because intense opponents of the minimum wage have worked tirelessly and effectively to prevent it from being increased to prior levels or pegged to inflation (a proposal that came close to passing in the 1970s). This has been every bit as much a political fight as, say, the Bush tax cuts of 2001 and 2003. But it is a far less visible fight, resulting not in big signing ceremonies, but in *nothing happening*. Our point is that nothing happening to key policies while the economy shifts rapidly can add up to something very big happening to Americans who rely on these policies.

Drift, in other words, is the opposite of our textbook view of how the nation's laws are made. It is the passive-aggressive form of politics, the No Deal rather than the New Deal. Yet it is not the same as simple inaction. Rather, drift has two stages. First, large economic and social transformations outflank or erode existing policies, diminishing their role in American life. Then, political leaders fail to update policies, even when there are viable options, because they face pressure from powerful interests exploiting opportunities for political obstruction.

Drift is not the story of government taught in a civics classroom, but it is a huge and growing part of how policy is actually made in the civics brawl room that is contemporary American politics. Our nation's fragmented political institutions have always made major policy reforms difficult. But, as we will see in the chapters to come, the slog has only grown more strenuous. Perhaps the biggest barrier in the last few decades has been the dramatically expanded use of the Senate filibuster. The insistence on sixty votes to cut off debate has allowed relatively small partisan minorities to block action on issues of concern to large majorities of Americans. Add to these institutional hurdles the increasing polarization of the two major political parties, and you have the perfect recipe for policy drift—and an increasingly threadbare safety net.

Still, a big part of the rise in American inequality has indeed occurred in the market, that is, in what people earn through their work and their assets even before America's (dwindling) government benefits and (less and less progressive) taxes have a chance to do anything. Could government have any role in *this* part of rising inequality? Yes, because government has rewritten the rules of the market in ways that favor those at the top.

Rewriting the Rules

During the 2008 presidential campaign, the Republican candidate John McCain pilloried his opponent, Barack Obama, as the "Redistributor-in-Chief" because Obama called for letting the Bush tax cuts expire for families making more than $250,000 a year. The charge was revealing, not because Obama's tax program was particularly redistributive, but because it reflected a view that is widespread not just among conservative politicians but also among experts and academics who study public policy. If this view has a title, it might be something like "The Rugged Individualist Meets Big Government."

In this familiar story, there are two neatly defined worlds: the market, where the rugged individualist makes his home, and the government, which takes money from the rugged individualist and provides him and others with benefits. The popular version is summed up in tales of independent frontiersmen conquering the West, without the evident help of the U.S. Army or postal service or Lewis and Clark's government-sponsored expedition. In a more contemporary vein, it is captured in the celebration of the can-do spirit of states like Alaska, from which John McCain's running mate, Sarah Palin, prominently hailed. Despite Alaska's status as the state most dependent on federal largesse on a per-person basis, politicians there persist in extolling the state's self-made rise and criticizing the meddling hands of the federal government.[18]

Academics and policy experts are not immune to this view either—though their version generally lacks the ideological tinge. Indeed, in the preceding discussion of the changing role of government, we have largely been following the standard expert convention of parsing inequality into two parts: "market" inequality and "postgovernment" inequality. In this perspective, people earn money in the market thanks to their labor and assets. Governments then take that money through taxes and redistribute it through government transfers. It is a tidy view of the relationship between markets and governments. It is also utterly misleading.

Governments *do* redistribute what people earn. But government policies also shape what people earn in the first place, as well as many other fundamental economic decisions that consumers, businesses, and workers make. Practically every aspect of labor and financial markets is shaped by government policy, for good or ill. As the great political economist Karl Polanyi famously argued in the 1940s, even the ostensibly freest markets require the extensive exercise of the coercive power of the state—to enforce contracts, to govern the formation of unions, to spell out the rights and obligations of corporations, to shape who has standing to bring legal actions, to define what constitutes an unacceptable conflict of interest, and on and on.[19] The libertarian vision of a night-watchman state gently policing an unfettered free market is a philosophical conceit, not a description of reality.

The intertwining of government and markets is nothing new. The frontier was settled because government granted land to the pioneers, killed, drove off, or rounded up Native Americans, created private monopolies to forge a nationwide transportation and industrial network, and linked the land settled with the world's largest postal system. Similarly, the laissez-faire capitalism of the early twentieth century was underpinned by a government that kept unions at bay, created a stable money supply, erected trade barriers that sheltered the new manufacturing giants, protected entrepreneurs from debtors' prison and corporations from liability, and generally made business the business of government.

When the political economy of the Gilded Age collapsed, it was government that reinvented American capitalism. With the arrival of the New Deal, the federal government took on a much more active role in redistributing income through the tax code and public programs. But the activist state that emerged did not just involve a new layer of redistribution. It fundamentally recast the national economy through the construction of a new industrial relations system, detailed and extensive regulation of corporations and financial markets, and a vast network of subsidies to companies producing everything from oil to soybeans. It also made huge direct investments in education and research—the GI Bill, the National Science Foundation, the National Institutes of Health—promoting the development of technological innovations and a skilled workforce that continue to drive American economic productivity.

And so it is with today's winner-take-all economy. Redistribution through taxes and transfers—or rather its absence—is only part of the story, and not even the biggest part. Even the word "redistribution" is symptomatic of the pervasive distortions in contemporary discussion. It suggests the refashioning of a natural order by meddling politicians, a departure from market rewards. But the treatment of the market as some pre-political state of nature is a fiction. Politicians are there at the creation, shaping that "natural" order and what the market rewards. Beginning in the late 1970s, they helped shape it so more and more of the rewards would go to the top.

Beyond the stunning shifts in taxation already described, there were three main areas where government authority gave a huge impetus to the winner-take-all economy: government's treatment of unions, the regulation of executive pay, and the policing of financial markets. These changes are so crucial to understanding how government rewrote the rules that we take them up now as a prelude to our larger story.

The Collapse of American Unions

No one who looks at the American economy of the last generation can fail to be struck by the precipitous decline of organized labor. From a peak of more than one in three workers just after World War II, union membership has declined to around one in nine. All the fall has occurred in the private sector, where unionization plummeted from nearly a quarter of workers in the early 1970s to just over 7 percent today.[20] (By contrast, public-sector unionization increased, partially masking the private-sector collapse.)

This decline has abetted rising inequality in very obvious ways. Wages and benefits are more equal (and higher) where unions operate, and less educationally advantaged workers, in particular, have lost ground as the reach of unions has ebbed.[21] But the near-extinction of private-sector unions has had a much broader and less appreciated effect on the distribution of American economic rewards. It has created a political and economic vacuum that has proven deadly to those seeking to redress winner-take-all inequality and friendly to those seeking to promote and consolidate it.

This is because organized labor's role is not limited to union participation in the determination of wages. Much more fundamental is the potential for unions to offer an organizational counterweight to the power of those at the top. Indeed, while there are many "progressive" groups in the American universe of organized interests, labor is the only major one focused on the broad economic concerns of those with modest incomes. In the United States, and elsewhere, unions are the main political players pushing leaders to address middle-class economic concerns and resisting policy changes that promote inequality. Unions also have the resources and incentives to check corporate practices, such as bloated executive pay packages, that directly produce winner-take-all outcomes. Indeed, even with their current weakness, American unions (through operations like the AFL-CIO Office of Investment) represent one of only two organized groups providing a potential check on the unfettered autonomy of top executives and investors—the other being "investor collectives" like public pension systems and mutual funds. It is surely no coincidence that almost all the advanced industrial democracies that have seen little or no shift toward the top 1 percent have much stronger unions than does the United States.[22]

The conventional view is that American labor's collapse was inevitable and natural, driven by global economic changes that have swept unions aside everywhere. But a quick glance abroad indicates that extreme union decline was not foreordained. While unions have indeed lost members in many Western nations (from a much stronger starting position), their presence has fallen little or not at all in others. In the European Union, union density fell by less than a third between 1970 and 2003. In the United States, despite starting from much lower levels, it fell by nearly half.[23] Yet we do not need to gaze across the Atlantic to see a very different picture of union fortunes. In Canada, where the rate of unionization was nearly identical to the United States' a few decades ago, unions have seen little decline despite similar worker attitudes toward unions in the two nations.

If economic forces did not dictate the implosion of American unions, perhaps American workers have simply lost interest in joining unions. Wrong again. In fact, nonunionized workers have expressed an *increasing* desire to be unionized since the early 1980s. In 2005, more than half of nonunionized private-sector workers said they wanted a union in their workplace, up from around 30 percent in 1984.[24] Compared with other rich democracies, the United States stands out as the country with the greatest unfulfilled demand for union representation.[25]

Looking at surveys like these, it's tempting to pin the blame on labor leaders for having their heads in the sand—and indeed, their initial response was overly complacent.[26] By the late 1970s, however, unions were seeking reforms in labor laws that would have helped them maintain their reach. The most prominent was a major labor law reform bill in 1978. Unions made the bill their top political priority.[27] Employers, energized and organized as they had not been for decades, mobilized in return, targeting Republicans and conservative Southern Democrats. Reform passed the House and commanded majority support in the Senate. But in a sign of the gridlock that would soon seem normal, the bill's opponents were able to sustain a Senate filibuster—despite the presence of large Democratic majorities in the Senate.

The message of the failed reform drive was clear: Business had the upper hand in Washington and the workplace. In the words of economists Frank Levy and Peter Temin, the defeat sent "signals that the third man—government—was leaving the ring."[28] Even before Reagan took office, business adopted a much more aggressive posture in the workplace, newly confident that government would not intervene. When Reagan came to power, he reinforced the message by breaking a high-profile strike by air-traffic controllers, as well as stacking the National Labor Relations Board (NLRB) in favor of management. Within a few years, it was evident to all involved that the established legal framework for recognizing unions—the National Labor Relations Act, or NLRA—placed few real limits on increasingly vigorous antiunion activities. Writing in the *Wall Street Journal* in 1984, a prominent "union avoidance" consultant observed that the "current government and business climate presents a unique opportunity for companies . . . to develop and implement long-term plans for conducting business in a union-free environment." The "critical test," he continued, was whether corporations had the "intellectual discipline and foresight to capitalize on this rare moment in our history."[29]

They did. Reported violations of the NLRA skyrocketed in the late 1970s and early 1980s.[30] Meanwhile, strike rates plummeted, and many of the strikes that did occur were acts of desperation rather than indicators of union muscle.[31] Nor did the assault abate in subsequent years. Between the mid-1980s and late 1990s, the share of NLRA elections featuring five or more union-avoidance tactics more than doubled, to over 80 percent.[32] By 2007, less than a fifth of the declining number of workers organized in the private sector gained recognition through the traditional NLRA process, once the near-exclusive route to unionization.[33]

As the effective sidelining of the NLRA suggests, drift was the most powerful weapon of union opponents. Simply blocking federal actions that countered the economic and state-level shifts that were devastating unions, or that might weaken employers' hand in union struggles, usually proved enough. In part, this reflected a harsh mathematical reality—the smaller the number of unions, the greater the cost per member needed to organize the vast nonunion sector. Once labor decline began to gain momentum, American unions confronted a harsh choice: devoting more of their evaporating resources to organizing, or gambling it on national and state political action to promote new rules.

Drift was especially dangerous to American unions for two other reasons. The first was their very uneven geographic and industrial reach. Well established in certain manufacturing industries in particular states, they were acutely vulnerable to the movement of manufacturing jobs to states where labor rights were more limited, as well as shifts in employment to sectors that had not previously been organized. These features made it easier for employers to pit one group of workers against another, and to move their activities—or threaten to move their activities—to areas where unions were weak or absent, inside or outside the United States.

The second reason is less well understood: American workers are unique in the extent to which they rely on individual firms to protect their health and retirement security.[34] Government's failure to update health-care and retirement policies left unionized companies in sectors from autos to airlines to steel highly vulnerable to the "legacy costs" associated with benefits for aging union workers (that is, the costs of benefits promised in the past, especially those granted to retirees). These costs—which in other rich democracies are either borne by all taxpayers or mandatory across firms—have contributed to slower employment growth in the unionized sector while stiffening corporations' resistance to labor inroads.

A quick glance at Canada's very different postwar experience drives these points home. As figure 5 shows, the gap in unionization between Canada and the United States has dramatically opened over the past four decades. The Canadian economist W. Craig Riddell has found that little of the divergence can be explained by structural features of the two nations' economies, or even by varying worker propensities to join a union.[35] Rather, the difference is due to the much lower (and declining) likelihood in the United States that workers who have an interest in joining a union will actually belong to one. Canadian law, for example, allows for card certification and first-contract arbitration (both features of the Employee Free Choice Act currently promoted by labor unions in the United States). It also bans permanent striker replacements, and imposes strong limits on employer propaganda.[36] Moreover, because Canada has national health insurance and substantially lower medical costs, unionized sectors in Canada also bear far lower legacy costs. All this contrasts starkly with the United States, where national political leaders have done little to ease the burdens of private benefits and where aggressive antiunion activities by employers have met little resistance from public authorities.

Figure 5: Union Share of Wage and Salary Workers
in the U.S. and Canada, 1960–2000

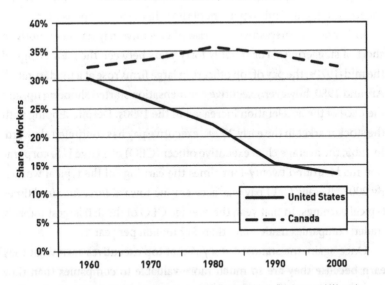

Sources: David Card, Thomas Lemieux, and W. Craig Riddell, "Unions and Wage Inequality," *Journal of Labor Research* 25, no. 4 (2004): 519–59; Sylvia Allegreto, Lawrence Mishel, and Jared Bernstein, *The State of Working America* (Ithaca, NY: Cornell
University Press, 2008).

In short, American unions did not just happen to be in the way of a
fast-moving economic train. They were pushed onto the tracks by American political leaders—in an era in which an organized voice would increasingly be needed to provide an effective counterweight to the rising
influence of those at the top.

Blank Checks in the Boardroom

When the mercurial Home Depot CEO Bob Nardelli reaped a $210 mil-
lion severance package upon his firing in 2007, even as the company's stock
fell, he became a poster child for the pay-without-performance world of
executive compensation.[37] Yet Nardelli was hardly the only corporate ex-

ecutive benefiting handsomely from the winner-take-all economy. As we saw earlier, the highest-paid executives in firms outside the financial sector account for around 40 percent of those in the top 0.1 percent.[38]

In historical perspective, the rise of executive pay has been nothing short of staggering.[39] For roughly forty years between the New Deal and the mid-1970s, the pay of top officers in large firms rose at a modest rate.[40] Around 1980, however, executive compensation started shooting up, and the pace of the acceleration increased in the 1990s. Despite dipping with the stock market in the early 2000s, executive pay has continued skyward. In 1965, the average chief executive officer (CEO) of a large U.S. corporation made around twenty-four times the earnings of the typical worker. By 2007, average CEO pay was accelerating toward *three hundred* times typical earnings. In that year, the average CEO of the 350 largest publicly traded companies made more than $12 million per year.[41]

Once again, the standard story is that top executives earn what they earn because they are so much more valuable to companies than they once were. Government has been a bystander as market forces have benignly played out.

Once again, however, the standard story is wrong. Executive pay is set in a distorted market deeply shaped by public policy. CEOs have been able to take advantage of a corporate governance system that allows them to drive up their own pay, creates ripe conditions for imbalanced bidding wars in which executives hold the cards, and prevents all but the most privileged insiders from understanding what is actually going on.

These arrangements are no accident. Over the last generation— through both changes in public policy and the failure to update government regulations to reflect changing realities—political leaders have promoted a system of executive compensation that grants enormous autonomy to managers, including significant indirect control over their own pay. Bob Nardelli's outsized check could very well have had "Made possible by Washington" written on it.

As with the decline of unions, the experience of other rich nations shows that nothing about modern globalized capitalism makes extraordinary executive salaries inevitable or even likely. American CEOs are paid more than twice the average for other rich nations. In the country with the second-highest CEO pay levels—Switzerland—CEOs are paid on average around three-fifths of what American executives earn.[42] Pay is not only lower in other rich nations; it also takes different forms. American CEOs, for example, receive much of their pay in short-term stock options, which not only lack transparency for stockholders but are also highly lucrative for CEOs who can create quick stock market gains through job cuts, restructuring, or creative accounting. Stock options are used in other nations, too, but they are much more often linked to long-term rather than short-term performance, as well as to firm performance relative to industry norms.[43] Thus, for instance, options can be designed so that when the rising price of oil drives up the share price of energy companies, CEOs receive extra compensation only if their firm's performance exceeds industry averages.

Defenders of American arrangements argue that they are in the best interests of shareholders.[44] By negotiating with executives on behalf of the diffuse interests of those owning stock, this argument goes, boards of directors act as faithful defenders of shareholder value. Many of those who study how this process actually works are more doubtful. Looking at corporate governance in a number of rich democracies, the political economists Peter Gourevitch and James Shinn argue that a better description is "managerism," a system in which managerial elites are in a strong position to extract resources.[45] The financier John Bogle has contended that instead of an "ownership society" in which managers serve owners, the United States is moving toward an "agency society" in which managers serve themselves.[46] Two of the nation's leading experts on corporate compensation, Lucian Bebchuk and Jesse Fried, provide many findings more consistent with a "board capture" view than a "shareholder value" perspective. In their telling, boards are typically so beholden to CEOs—who influence the nomination of board members and have substantial influence over those members' pay and perks—they offer little countervailing authority.[47]

The most revealing findings concern the design of executive compensation. Executive pay frequently departs from what would be expected to encourage good performance. Instead, corporate pay arrangements are shot through with what Bebchuk and Fried call "camouflage": features designed to mitigate public outrage rather than limit excessive pay or link it more closely to value. To cite a few examples: Stock options are designed so that CEOs gain the upside of bull markets but are protected from bear markets. A huge chunk of executive pay is hidden in so-called deferred compensation—pay that's put off to postpone taxes on interest and earnings—and in guaranteed-benefit pensions.

That's right. In an era in which most workers receive no defined benefit in retirement, CEOs still do. IBM's CEO, for example, was entitled to over $1 million a year in retirement benefits after about nine years of service to the company—an amount estimated to be worth about as much as he made while at the company.[48] The economic rationale for this guaranteed payout was nonexistent. Indeed, unlike ordinary workers' pensions, these massive executive benefits are not tax-free to the company (though they do shield *executives* from taxes on the interest that their pensions earn), and they can create staggering long-term liabilities for firms. But the camouflage they provided was substantial: IBM never had to report a cent of the payout as compensation.

The list goes on. Retired executives enjoy perks without parallel in the rest of the workplace. Guaranteed hours on corporate jets, chauffeurs, personal assistants, apartments, even lucrative consulting contracts— none has to be reported as executive pay. In 2001, executives at GE and Enron were guaranteed a rate of return on their deferred compensation of 12 percent, when long-run Treasury bills were paying out one-third of that. Coca-Cola's CEO was able to defer taxes on $1 billion in compensation and investment earnings—gains that did not have to be reported in the company's pay statements.[49] In 2008, while Wal-Mart workers lost an average of 18 percent of their 401(k) holdings, Wal-Mart's CEO, H. Lee Scott Jr., saw gains of $2.3 million in his $47 million retirement plan.[50]

Where were America's political leaders while all this was happening? For the most part, they were either freeing up executives to extract more or, like police officers on the take, looking the other way. This is in sharp contrast to the experience abroad, where there have been substantial efforts to monitor executive pay and facilitate organized pushback against managerial power.[51] In many nations, organized labor has served this countervailing role. But while American unions have tried to take on corporate pay, the broader challenges they have faced have severely hampered them. Another possible check on managerial autonomy, private litigation, was radically scaled back by mid-1990s legislation engineered by congressional Republicans. The bill had strong enough support from Democrats to pass over President Clinton's veto.

Washington also opened the floodgates for the rise of stock options, the main conduit for the tide of money streaming from corporate coffers to top executives. During the 1990s, stock options became the central vehicle for enhancing executive compensation, comprising roughly half of executive pay by 2001. These options were typically structured in ways that lowered the visibility of high payouts and failed to create strong connections between compensation and managerial effectiveness, even though instruments for establishing such links were well known and widely used abroad.[52] The value of options simply rose along with stock prices, even if stock price gains were fleeting, or a firm's performance badly trailed that of other companies in the same sector. In the extreme but widespread practice of "backdating," option values were reset retroactively to provide big gains for executives—a practice akin to repositioning the target after the fact to make sure the archer's shot hit the bull's-eye. But when the Financial Accounting Standards Board, which oversees accounting practices, tried to make firms report the costs of stock options like other compensation in the early 1990s, it was beaten back by a bipartisan coalition in the Senate galvanized by industry opposition.[53] This is a textbook example of drift.

Recent efforts to increase board independence and capacity tell a similar story. In the early 2000s, after a series of massive scandals in which CEO self-dealing wiped out the assets of shareholders and employees, elected officials faced strong pressure to reform corporate governance. Still, the bill that eventually passed, called Sarbanes-Oxley after its two congressional sponsors, would most likely have died but for the collapse of WorldCom as the 2002 elections approached. Even then, corporations were able to beat back the sorts of reforms that would have put the most effective checks on managerial autonomy.[54] Indeed, the nature of the compromise embodied in Sarbanes-Oxley is revealing. Managers accepted efforts designed to modestly increase transparency and regulate some of the most blatant conflicts of interest. At the same time, they quite effectively resisted efforts to increase the ability of shareholders to influence the governance of firms, including compensation practices.

Former chair of the SEC Arthur Levitt perfectly captures the political world that fostered ever-increasing executive payouts in his firsthand recollections of the unsuccessful battles over corporate reform in the 1990s:

> *During my seven and a half years in Washington . . . nothing astonished me more than witnessing the powerful special interest groups in full swing when they thought a proposed rule or a piece of legislation might hurt them, giving nary a thought to how the proposal might help the investing public. With laserlike precision, groups representing Wall Street firms, mutual fund companies, accounting firms, or corporate managers would quickly set about to defeat even minor threats. Individual investors, with no organized labor or trade association to represent their views in Washington, never knew what hit them.[55]*

Finance Rules: Heads I Win, Tails You Lose

With the pillars of Wall Street now battered, it is easy to forget how dramatic the rise of the financial sector has been. Between 1975 and 2007, wages and salaries in the industry roughly doubled as a share of national earnings.[56] The proportion of the economy comprising its activities exploded. Between 1980 and 2007, financial service companies expanded their share of company profits from around 13 percent to more than 27 percent. Even staid corporate giants got into the act. In 1980, GE earned 92 percent of its profit from manufacturing. In 2007, more than half of GE's profits came from financial businesses.[57]

In part, this is simply a chapter of the broader rise of executive pay just chronicled. But the other part is the runaway rewards that have flowed into the pockets of the rich from America's widening range of exotic new financial institutions. These rewards have involved the development of complex new financial products that, for most Americans, offered limited benefits and sometimes real economic risks. For the financial sector, however, the new instruments and expanding freedom to use them created astonishing opportunities: to increase the number of transactions (with intermediaries taking a cut on each one), to ratchet up leverage (and thus potential profits), and to increase the complexity and opacity in ways that advantaged insiders. Not coincidentally, all of these developments increased the risk to the system as a whole. However, that would be someone else's problem—or, as economists gently put it, an "externality." As Martin Wolf of the *Financial Times* observed acerbically in 2008, "No industry has a comparable talent for privatizing gains and socializing losses."[58]

At the very top, those privatized gains were mind-boggling. Wages in the financial sector took off in the 1980s. The pace of the rise accelerated in the 1990s, and again after the millennium. In 2002, one had to earn $30 million to make it to the top twenty-five hedge fund incomes; in 2004, $100 million; in 2005, $130 million (when the twenty-fifth spot was occupied by William Browder, grandson of Earl Browder, onetime head of the Communist Party of the United States). A year later, the average for the top twenty-five had nearly doubled to $240 million; in 2007, it hit $360 million. That year, five hedge fund managers made $1 billion or more, with the top three weighing in around $3 billion.[59] In the two years before they began reporting losses that dwarfed the profits of prior years and brought many of their stockholders to ruin, the venerable firms of Goldman Sachs, Merrill Lynch, Morgan Stanley, Lehman Brothers, and Bear Stearns paid their employees bonuses of $65.6 billion.[60] The home address of the winner-take-all economy has been neither Hollywood nor Silicon Valley, but Wall Street.

Until a few years ago, high finance was depicted as the purest of markets. When politicians and analysts referenced the preferences of "Wall Street," the phrase was taken (without irony) as a synonym for economic rationality itself, rather than as a set of specific interests. Yet financial markets, like others, are not pre-political. As Robert Kuttner detailed in his prescient 2007 book *The Squandering of America*, our financial system has always rested on an extensive set of government interventions.[61] The legal environment for financial transactions governs such crucial issues as what constitutes insider dealing or conflicts of interest, how much monitoring and transparency there must be in major financial transactions, and what levels of leverage and risk are acceptable. In response to market failures on all these dimensions, the New Deal ushered in extensive new federal regulations designed to ensure investor confidence and align private ambitions more closely with broad economic goals such as financial stability.[62]

Over the last three decades, these relatively quiet and stable financial markets have given way to much more dynamic and unstable ones with far more pervasive effects on the rest of the economy. Some of the shift was clearly driven by changes in the nature of economic activity and the possibilities for financial intermediation. Technological innovation made possible the development of new financial instruments and facilitated spectacular experiments with securitization. Computers helped Wall Street transform from million-share trading days in the 1980s to billion-share trading days in the late 1990s, magnifying the possibilities for gains—and losses.[63]

The shredding of the post–New Deal rule book for financial markets did not, however, simply result from the impersonal forces of "financial innovation." In Canada, for instance, government effectively resisted many of the efforts of financial interests to rewrite the rules—and Canada was largely spared the financial debacle of the past few years. The transformation of Wall Street reflected the repeated, aggressive application of political power. Some of that power was directed at removing existing regulations designed to protect against speculative excess and conflicts of interest. Some focused on thwarting would-be regulators who sought to update rules to address rapidly evolving financial realities. The net effect was not an idealized free market, but a playing field tilted in favor of those with power, connections, lack of scruples, and the ability to play the profitable but systematically risky new game.

Assessing the contribution of specific policy initiatives to the restructuring of financial markets is a matter of considerable controversy. That public action played a vital role, however, is less in doubt. A recent careful study by two enterprising economists, Thomas Philippon of New York University and Ariell Reshef of the University of Virginia, shows that regulatory restrictions on banking had been reduced below their pre–New Deal levels by the late 1990s.[64] The changes included deregulation of bank branching (facilitating mergers and acquisitions), relaxation of the traditional separation of commercial and investment banking (which was finally repealed by the Gramm-Leach-Bliley Act of 1999), removing ceilings on interest rates, and repealing the decades-old separation between banks and insurance companies.

Other policy efforts were geared at keeping regulators away from emerging areas of financial activity—a classic form of policy drift. Consider the case of Wendy Gramm, George H. W. Bush's chair of the Commodity Futures Trading Commission (CFTC). Only a few days before leaving office in early 1993, Gramm granted a "midnight order" that Enron had sought to allow it to trade in self-designed derivatives free of CFTC supervision.[65] A few weeks later, she received a seat on Enron's board. Her husband, Phil Gramm, was an even more prominent performer in the deregulation drama. As chair of the Senate Banking Committee, he was instrumental in laying down a little-noticed deregulatory milestone, the Commodity Futures Modernization Act. The 262-page bill—slipped into a far larger appropriations bill during the lame-duck fall 2000 session of Congress and signed into law by President Clinton—essentially exempted derivatives and other exotic instruments from oversight by the agencies that regulated more conventional financial assets.

Few now doubt that high finance profited at the expense of sensible regulations. But Philippon and Reshef's research indicates just how intertwined private rewards and public rules have been. For decades after the stock market crash of 1929, they find, finance jobs were neither all that glamorous nor all that lucrative, but pretty much run-of-the-mill white-collar positions whose compensation tracked the rewards available elsewhere in the economy to those with similar skills. As deregulatory fever took hold, however, all this changed. Suddenly, and increasingly, financial professionals were earning much more than similarly educated workers. Perhaps as much as half of their expanding pay premium, Philippon and Reshef calculate, can be linked to the deregulation wave.[66]

Economists have a name for such government-created rewards: "rents"—money that accrues to favored groups not because of their competitive edge, but because public policy gives them specific advantages relative to their competitors. The rents in zip code 10005 have risen through the roof.

We now know that the price tag for two decades of deregulatory excess will be unconscionably high. Yet in one respect the success of the deregulatory agenda remains undeniable and largely intact: the massive enrichment of an extremely thin slice of American society. In the eight years leading up to the collapse of Bear Stearns and Lehman Brothers in 2008, the top five executives at each firm cashed out a total of roughly $2.4 billion in bonuses and equity sales that were not lost or clawed back when the firms went under.[67] As one postcrash exposé explained the game, "Here's how it goes. You bet big with someone else's money. If you win, you get a huge bonus, based on the profits. If you lose, you lose someone else's money rather than your own, and you move on to the next job. If you're especially smart—like Lehman chief executive Dick Fuld—you take a lot of money off the table. During his tenure as CEO, Fuld made $490 million (before taxes) cashing in stock options and stock he received as compensation."[68]

Friends in High Places

The myth of America's winner-take-all economy is that government does not have much to do with it. Skyrocketing gains at the top are simply the

impersonal beneficence of Adam Smith's "invisible hand," the natural outcome of free-market forces. Listen to Sanford Weill, the former chairman
of Citigroup: "People can look at the last twenty-five years and say this is
an incredibly unique period of time. We didn't rely on somebody else to
build what we built."[69] Weill may not have relied on "somebody else" during this "unique period." He did, however, rely a great deal on government.
When Citigroup formed in 1998, one of the top bankers involved joked
at the celebratory press conference that any antitrust concerns could be
dealt with easily: "Sandy will call up his friend, the President."[70] Within a
few months, the financial industry had mounted a successful campaign to
repeal the Glass-Steagall Act, which since the 1930s had prohibited powerful financial conglomerates of the sort Weill now headed on the grounds
that they created conflicts of interest and impaired financial transparency
and accountability. Leading the charge against Glass-Steagall was, yes,
Sanford Weill.

The truth is that most people have missed the *visible* hand of government because they've been looking in the wrong place. They have talked
about the minimum wage, the Earned Income Tax Credit, Medicaid for
vulnerable children and families—in short, programs that help those at
the bottom. The real story, however, is what our national political elites
have done for those at the top, both through their actions and through
their deliberate failures to act.

We have our suspect. The winner-take-all economy was made, in substantial part, in Washington. Yet identifying the main suspect only makes
the core mystery more perplexing: How could this happen? No one ex-
pects the invisible hand of the market to press for equality. Yet there are
good reasons for thinking that the visible hand of government will. Indeed, as we shall see in the next chapter, a long line of thinkers has argued
that popular representation through democratic government creates
powerful pressures for greater equality, as less-advantaged majorities use
their political power to offset the economic power of those at the top.

That is clearly not what has happened in the United States over the last
generation. Where governments in other democracies worked energetically to offset increasing inequality, public policies in the United States

actively nurtured it. Why? How, in a country governed by majority rule, a country born of revolt against persistent differences in power and opportunity, could policy and government so favor such a narrow group, for so long, with so little real response? With the suspect identified, we now turn to the fundamental puzzle: What happened to American politics that precipitated these momentous changes?

This is not, it turns out, simply a question about contemporary American politics. In our search for clues regarding the transformation of American government since the 1970s, we kept coming upon striking parallels between our nation's present struggles and moments of political decay and renewal in the past. The winner-take-all economy described in the last two chapters is distinctively of our time. But the process by which it arose—and the prospects for its reform—can only be seen with clear eyes if we take a longer historical perspective.

American government has a rap sheet, if you will. Repeatedly in our nation's political history, Americans have found themselves buffeted by dislocating market forces while their government has seemed mired in gridlock and beholden to concentrated economic power. In the story of these past periods, we find the foundation of the answer to our central mystery.

Chapter 3

A Brief History of Democratic Capitalism

The rise of the winner-take-all economy represents a decisive break with our not-too-distant past. But the shifts in government's role chronicled in the last chapter are hardly the first of their sort. Indeed, our nation's public life has been marked by similar periods of gridlock and deference to economic power in the past. It has also been marked by dramatic moments of political renewal, in which seemingly immutable stalemate and rampant solicitousness toward the top have been overturned through the concerted efforts of political reformers.

The present chapter is about this historical back-and-forth. It is the necessary link between the identification of American government as our prime suspect and the explanation, in parts 2 and 3, of exactly *why* American government did it. For the history of America's particular form of democratic capitalism not only helps us better understand why elected politicians might choose to respond to the select top rather than the broad middle—contrary to the predictions of democracy's greatest theorists both ancient and modern. It also contains some big clues about what has happened to American politics since the 1970s.

"The Oldest and Most Fatal Ailment of All Republics"

It would be nice to think that the story of government-promoted enrichment of the rich that we told in the last chapter is a freak departure from the normally happy interplay of American democracy and American capitalism. It would be nice, but it would be wrong. Political and economic freedom do tend to go together, and American democracy and American capitalism have had many happy moments. But democracy and the market are in tension with each other, too—and American democracy and American capitalism are no exception.

The root of the tension is simple. Democracy is based on the ideal of political equality. Every citizen is supposed to have the same potential to influence what government does—even if, in practice, some may choose not to exercise that potential or exercise it poorly. Money should not matter in this calculus: the rich and poor are equal before government—"all men are created equal." In the marketplace, by contrast, money matters a great deal. Markets respond to what economists call "effective demand"— that is, preferences backed by dollars. The rich and poor may be equal politically. They are not equal economically.

The tension arises when the contrasting features of democracies and the market come into conflict, as they routinely do. Markets notoriously under-produce (or don't produce at all) "public goods" that are shared in common, such as unpolluted air, safe streets, a system of law, and well-paved roads. They falter in the presence of positive or negative "externalities," benefits or costs that accrue to those outside a market transaction (think toxic waste or the positive social effects of a child's education). And markets frequently trample on valued social priorities about which large numbers of citizens care deeply—from clean water to the just treatment of workers to, yes, the fair distribution of economic rewards.

When markets operate in damaging ways, the natural temptation is to turn to politics to correct the imbalance. And yet market participants have strong incentives to resist government regulation and democratic intervention. What's more, they usually have considerable resources to do so. Without strong protections of political equality, without firewalls between the market and democracy, those who have the most power in the market may also have the most power in politics, undermining the basic ideal on which democracy rests.

Since the first stirrings of democracy, virtually all its greatest theorists have recognized this. From Aristotle to Alexis de Tocqueville, from Plato to Thomas Paine, those who have contemplated what makes democracy tick have invariably expressed concern about its coexistence with sizable gaps in economic standing. The Roman priest Plutarch set the tone when he noted, "An imbalance between rich and poor is the oldest and most fatal ailment of all republics." Charles de Montesquieu, whose *The Spirit of the Laws* was a central text for many of our nation's Founders, identified "real equality" as "the very soul of democracy," though he conceded that in practice democratic republics could only "fix the differences to a certain point."[1]

To these thinkers, the danger of class divisions was the prospect of " 'perverted' forms of government," in the words of the political theorist Michael J. Thompson, in which "the few ruled over the many and the public good was trampled by the wealthy, powerful, and elite." As Thompson explains, the ancients and their Enlightenment heirs believed that preservation of democratic practices "required . . . not a utopian form of equality but a set of institutions and laws—and hopefully a civic culture as well—that would limit the excesses of wealth and property." No less an Enlightenment realist than David Hume observed that "[w]here the riches are in a few hands, these must enjoy all the power and will readily conspire to lay the whole burden on the poor, and oppress them still farther, to the discouragement of all industry." After noting the risks of great inequality to democratic institutions in *The Spirit of the Laws*, Montesquieu argued that "to men of overgrown estates, everything which does not contribute to advance their power and honor is considered by them as an injury."[2]

It should be little surprise, then, that in the late eighteenth century this risk had a profound effect on the deliberations over the construction of a new *American* republic. Despite their diverse views, the architects of American political institutions shared the assessment that deep class divisions threatened to undermine democracy. Madison famously justified America's fragmented constitutional structure as a means of curing the "mischief of faction," so it is notable that he believed "the most common and durable source of factions has been the various and unequal distribution of property."[3] Reacting against the feudal traditions of Europe, the Founders were acutely aware that differences in property engendered conflicting demands and differing capacities to achieve those demands. They feared the fledgling American republic could not long survive if class differences grew or hardened.

This was one reason why the Constitution included what were, at the time, extremely limited property qualifications for voters and—in a dramatic break with most states' practices—no property qualifications for elected representatives. In Federalist #39, Madison made clear that the new American republic would be a "government which derives all its powers directly or indirectly from the great body of the people," not aristocratic privilege or hereditary right.[4] As the constitutional law scholar Akhil Amar points out, "Although some modern readers have tried to stress property protection rather than popular sovereignty as the Constitution's bedrock idea, the words 'private property' did not appear in the Preamble, or anywhere in the document for that matter." (Indeed, Amar notes that the only reference to property is one reference to "*government property*.")[5] For all its limits as a democratic document, the Constitution embodied a broad rejection of property-based restrictions on citizen participation.

The Founders were not radical egalitarians by any means. Rather, they were keen students of political economy. They saw the new American republic as marked by a highly favorable starting point. The New World had land—the critical economic resource of their time—in abundance. This abundance produced a distribution of property much broader than that found in the class-bound Old World. And many of the Founders were convinced that preservation of this broad distribution was not just good in itself but essential to the institutional functioning of democracy. The risk was not just challenges to private property from below, but also challenges to democratic equality from above. These were the Scylla and Charybdis of democratic capitalism: on the one side, mob rule by propertyless democratic majorities; on the other side, oligarchic rule by the affluent. By understanding these twin perils, we gain a better sense of why American politics has veered toward the latter danger in recent decades.

Government of the Poor?

Will voting majorities use their political power to tax away the property of the wealthy? Or will the rich use their economic power to twist democracy to their own ends? Among the Founders, John Adams was perhaps the most clearly worried about the first possibility. If political equality was pursued too far, he warned, "Debts would be abolished first; taxes laid heavy on the rich, and not at all on the others; and at last a downright equal division of everything be demanded, and voted."[6] Yet it was the brilliant Frenchman Alexis de Tocqueville who made the point most articulately in his 1835 masterwork *Democracy in America*. As Tocqueville observed, "In all the nations of the world, the greatest number has always been composed of those who did not have property, or those whose property was too restricted for them to live in ease without working. Therefore universal suffrage really gives the government of society to the poor."[7]

And what would the less affluent do with "the government of society"? To Tocqueville, it was obvious: They would happily tax the rich to provide benefits to themselves. Echoing recent conservative complaints about the redistributive proclivities of those the *Wall Street Journal* has called "Lucky Duckies"—that is, voters so poor they don't pay income taxes and thus don't mind raising them—Tocqueville concluded: "The government of the democracy is the only one under which the power that votes the taxes escapes the payment of them."[8] In other words, the less affluent majority could use its political power to expropriate the rich.

Tocqueville's observation has received modern expression, with an optimistic twist, in leading theories of income redistribution offered by political scientists.[9] These theories are premised on the observation that the decisive swing voter in a democracy (the "median voter") almost invariably has an income lower than the average income in society. Yet this relative lack of material resources belies the median voter's political influence. As the last and decisive voter to join the majority in favor of a candidate or party, the median voter ultimately drives what politicians do. And because the median voter's income is below the average income, the theories predict that politicians seeking the median voter's all-powerful vote will redistribute income through government.

Of course, the median voter won't seek all the rich's riches. At a minimum, the median voter has to worry about removing the incentive of the rich to work—killing the goose that lays the golden egg, so to speak. Middle-class voters might also think it possible that they, too, will someday be rich—though, on the other hand, the rich also have to think about the possibility that they might someday be middle class. But the basic point holds true: When inequality in incomes goes up, these political-science models predict that the median voter will seek to reverse the balance. The dual dangers of runaway inequality and excessive redistribution will be held in check. Like a house's thermostat, whenever things get too hot (rising inequality) or too cold (poor economic performance), democracy's median voter will force a correction.

It is a decidedly optimistic view, but alas, optimistic does not mean accurate. Over the last generation, we have seen a massive increase in inequality. And this inequality has taken a form that's particularly puzzling from the standpoint of the theory: The vast majority of Americans have fallen further and further behind a tiny superrich segment of society. If people care about their relative economic standing in the way that these theories suggest they should, we should already have seen a major increase in government redistribution.

Yet, as we saw in the last chapter, the trends of the last generation have been exactly the opposite. Inequality in what people earn has skyrocketed. But instead of offsetting this rise, government taxes and benefits have actually exacerbated it, an outcome witnessed in virtually no other nation. And when we look beyond the highly visible redistribution that occurs through government taxes and benefits, the picture grows even starker. In a range of areas, from labor law to financial market regulation, public policy has reshaped the economy to favor those at the top. Far from "soaking the rich," elected political leaders have treated the rich more so-licitously than ever, even as the rich have grown massively richer at the expense of the majority.

To begin to grasp why the rich have had the political upper hand—contrary to the prediction of Tocqueville and his political-economy heirs—we need to travel back almost a century to examine the other side of the interplay between democracy and the market.

Progressives' Problems

Our generation is not the first in which the optimistic prediction that de-mocracy will naturally temper excesses of income and wealth has failed to ring true. In the early twentieth century, similar problems—and laments—were widespread. Financial and industrial titans commanded vast eco-nomic power that they used not just to despoil the environment, suppress workers' attempts to organize, and head off consumer protections, but also to buy off politicians who might stand in their way. The problem was particularly acute in the U.S. Senate, whose members were still appointed by state governments. The legendary journalist William Allen White portrayed the institution as a "millionaires' club," where a member "rep-resented something more than a state, more even than a region. He repre-sents principalities and powers in business. One Senator . . . represents the Union Pacific Railway System; another the New York Central; still another the insurance interests of New York and New Jersey." [10]

These problems did not go unnoticed—by citizens or by the reform-ers of the time, who called themselves "Progressives." Progressive think-ers had many concerns: environmental degradation, monopolies stifling competition, ill-treated workers. Yet what worried them most was the distortion of politics by private economic power. As Theodore Roosevelt summed up the critique in 1912:

The true friend of property, the true conservative, is he who insists that property shall be the servant and not the master of the com-

monwealth; who insists that the creature of man's making shall be the servant and not the master of the man who made it. The citizens of the United States must effectively control the mighty commercial forces which they themselves have called into being . . . The absence of effective state, and, especially, national, restraint upon unfair money-getting has tended to create a small class of enormously wealthy and economically powerful men, whose chief object is to hold and increase their power.[11]

Like the ancients' worries about oligarchy, the Progressive critique centered on the threats to political equality posed by the excessive concentration of property and economic power. And yet, by the early twentieth century, the concern took a new, more modern form: the classical fear of a hereditary aristocracy had been replaced by a concern with the depredations of large-scale industrial capitalism and the distortions created by financial speculation. By the time TR spoke of controlling "the mighty commercial forces," Progressives had zeroed in on bigness and the banks as the great challenges to democracy of the day.

Indeed, in the very year of Roosevelt's fiery speech, "the money trust" became the focus of highly publicized congressional hearings that revealed widespread abuses in the banking industry. It then became the subject of one of the most important muckraking works of the era, *Other People's Money, and How the Bankers Use It*—a damning indictment of the "financial oligarchy" that increasingly dominated industry and government.

The author of *Other People's Money* was Louis Brandeis, the towering legal thinker who would later become a Supreme Court justice and head of the American Zionist movement. In 1912, however, Brandeis was in his fifties (he would live into his eighties) and had already gained national prominence as a skilled legal advocate on behalf of Progressive causes. He had served as lead counsel for the plaintiffs in the landmark case *Muller v. Oregon*, in which the power of states to regulate the workplace to protect women workers was upheld. Brandeis jumped from cause to cause—he had a role in nearly every facet of Progressive social reform—but his activities were united by an abiding conviction that, in the words of his biographer Melvin Urofsky, "in a democratic society the existence of large centers of private power is dangerous to the continuing vitality of a free people."[12]

Other People's Money highlighted the perils of handing too much of that private power to those who controlled the lifeblood of capitalism. "The economic menace of past ages," Brandeis later told a journalist, "was the dead hand which gradually acquired a large part of all available lands"—the fear of feudal privilege voiced by the Founders. "The greatest economic menace today," he continued, updating the classical republican worry, "is a very live hand—these few able financiers who are gradually acquiring control over our quick capital."[13]

Brandeis's argument gained power from an early twentieth-century school of thought known as legal realism.[14] Legal realism challenged the common notion, frequently invoked by those advantaged by the economy, that the structure of the market and the division of its gains was a natural phenomenon, completely separate from politics and government, the result of free choice and unfettered competition that yielded a distribution of property based on merit and hard work. The legal realists countered that property and markets were instead deeply intertwined with politics and government. There are no pre-political markets. Markets are inevitably shaped and channeled by political forces, dependent on the rules that are created and enforced by those who control the coercive power of the state. The laissez-faire vision of the economy held up in the Supreme Court's 1905 decision in *Lochner v. New York* was a political choice, one with distinct, sometimes brutal consequences, and one that required a great deal of government intervention to emerge and survive.

That markets are constructed through public policies and shaped by politics—and therefore could be reshaped to produce better outcomes—was a central observation of Progressive reformers. It was also a central observation of our last chapter, in which we argued that government construction of markets remains among the most significant, and often least recognized, areas of public policy. So it is important to understand what the observation means and does not mean. It does not mean that democratic politics always produces well-functioning markets, or that government intervention is always justified or desirable. Rather, it means simply that, for good or ill, democratic politics makes markets. The debate should not be over whether government is involved in the formation of markets. It always is. The debate should be over whether it is involved in a manner conducive to a good society.

For the Progressives, the answer to that question in the early twentieth century was no. Policies passed in the name of free commerce frequently created markets that were mainly in the interests of a narrow economic elite. Efforts to address these inequities were blocked in legislatures highly attentive to business concerns. Where laws promoting social reform were passed, they were thrown out by the courts. Lest this critique be seen as deeply radical in spirit, it is worth quoting a little-noticed passage in Adam Smith's 1776 *The Wealth of Nations*, now viewed as the bible of limited-government free-market economics. "Wherever there is great property," Smith wrote, "there is great inequality . . . Civil government, so far as it is instituted for the security of property, is in reality, instituted for the defence of the rich against the poor, or of those who have some property against those who have none at all."[15] (Smith, a resolute skeptic about the rationality of unfettered financial markets, also authored the phrase "other people's money," which titled Brandeis's famous work.) A clearer statement of the legal realist view of a century and a half later would be hard to find.

In short, property and markets rest on government and law. And, in the Progressive critique, they had to be restrained and limited by government and law. Without such restraints and limits, greater economic inequality would lead to greater political inequality, which in turn would lead to government policies that reflected the interests of those at the top. Swamped by the tides of inequality, democracy would give way to oligarchy—the very concern that recent economic events have cast in stark relief.

The Politics of Drift

In 1914, the twenty-five-year-old Walter Lippmann summed up the intellectual foundations of the Progressive Era in a three-word book title: *Drift and Mastery*. The "drift" of which Lippmann wrote, like the drift of which we wrote in the last chapter, was the failure of government to respond to new economic realities.[16] The solution, according to Lippmann, was not to do away with modern industrial capitalism, with all its astonishing benefits as well as its dismaying costs. The answer was to tame it by asserting democratic supervision over its activities—to "master" it, in Lippmann's words. Lippmann knew this was an imperfect solution given the distortion of politics by money that was all around him. But it was the only solution. "That is the way democracies move: they have in literal truth to lift themselves by their own bootstraps," Lippmann wrote. "Those who have some simpler method than the one I have sketched are, it seems to me, either unaware of the nature of the problem, interested only in some one phase of it, or unconsciously impatient with the limitations of democracy."[17]

Lippmann's contrast of "drift" and "mastery" provides an apt dichotomy for the seesaw evolution of democratic capitalism in the United States. Since the emergence of modern capitalism, American politics has repeatedly oscillated between the politics of drift and the politics of renewal—between long periods in which curbs on economic inequality and market power remain largely off the agenda and dramatic periods of reform in which markets and inequality have come under intense scrutiny. In the first phase, economic dynamism outpaces the capacity of governing institutions. In the second, challenges to a political order that is viewed as corrupt and biased overcome, at least partially, the slow-moving structure of American governance to produce reform.

The main reason for this recurrent pattern is straightforward: In American politics, it is hard to get things done and easy to block them. With its multiple branches and hurdles, the institutional structure of American government allows organized and intense interests—even quite narrow ones—to create gridlock and stalemate. First, there is the famous division of governing authority into three separate branches with overlapping powers. Next, power is divided not just horizontally but vertically, with states and the federal government sharing and competing for authority. Add on top of this the high supermajority hurdles that legislation must sometimes clear. If the president vetoes a bill, for example, two-thirds of members of both houses of Congress must vote to override, a hurdle that requires unusual consensus among members of Congress about the need for change.

And then there are those two houses of Congress, with different election calendars, different constituencies, different procedures, and different numbers of members. The more clubby Senate, of course, bases its smaller membership on state boundaries, so sparsely populated Wyoming (population: 532,000) has the same number of senators as crowded California (population: 36.7 million). The results are predictable and have been well documented: The weight of rural interests—including the agricultural sector and extractive industries located in low-population states—is magnified. The weight of urban areas and ethnic and racial minorities—packed as they are into high-population states—is reduced.[18] Moreover, the need for agreement between two quite different chambers makes consensus over policy change significantly harder to achieve. Fragmented political institutions in which "ambition checks ambition," in Madison's famous phrase, are not designed to encourage dramatic social reform.

It is worth stressing that, in many ways, this system is far more convoluted than what the Founders intended. Many of the protections for sparsely populated states that thwart majorities were seen by Madison and others as a bug, not a desired feature. In a context where existing states needed to ratify the proposed Constitution, they were concessions to political practicalities. Indeed, as the political theorist Robert Dahl has stressed, the political leaders at the Constitutional Convention came very close to approving a design that would have allowed Congress to choose the president, an outcome that would have yielded something much closer to the more streamlined parliamentary systems used in most modern democracies.[19]

As we will see in the chapters to come, many of the biggest contributors to contemporary stalemate are not features of the original design at all, but have developed in conjunction with that framework as society has changed over the intervening centuries. The filibuster, which has become an increasingly prominent source of gridlock, is a Senate practice unmentioned in the Constitution. And partisan polarization, which has mixed with the filibuster to form a potent cocktail of political obstruction, is the outgrowth of a development—the creation of parties—that most of the Founders hoped to prevent.

Other hurdles, too, grew out of the evolution of American society since the time of the Constitution's creation. The malapportionment of the Senate, for instance, worsened dramatically over time as newer states with small populations were admitted to the union. In 1810, the minimum percentage of the population that could elect a Senate majority was 33 percent. In 1970, it was 17 percent, roughly where it is today.[20] In crossnational perspective, the U.S. Senate is one of the most malapportioned upper chambers in the world, ranking just behind Argentina, Brazil, Bolivia, and the Dominican Republic.[21] Needless to say, it is surely the most powerful upper chamber that is so skewed.

It is not just the capacity for obstruction that has grown over the long life of our democracy. So, too, have the consequences of that obstruction. The Founders designed the Constitution in an overwhelmingly agricultural society. At the time, the dynamism of an industrial economy—as well as the social challenges it would create—was difficult to imagine (although some key figures like Alexander Hamilton anticipated some of it and tried to harness a strong national state to bring it about). The potential failure of government to act decisively in the face of dramatic economic change was simply not at the top of the Founders' list of concerns.

And yet this very same institutional structure was designed to be highly democratic for its day—and it has become more and more democratic over time. Multiple venues create not just veto points at which change can be blocked, but also access points where a multitude of interests and groups can press their claims. The result is a system that simultaneously calls forth powerful demands from "We the People" and makes efforts to achieve those demands frustrating, halting, and sometimes impossible.

Indeed, perhaps no other period better captured these contradictory forces than the Progressive Era. Despite the ferment of reform, Progressives fell far short of bringing about Lippmann's "mastery." Important political reforms occurred, including a constitutional amendment requiring the direct election of senators. New regulatory agencies were created, and a number of key social reforms passed at the state level. But the reform movement split politically—literally so, when Theodore Roosevelt ran unsuccessfully for the presidency as the Progressive Party candidate, challenging Democrat Woodrow Wilson, a weaker champion of the cause.

Like the split within the Progressive ranks highlighted by TR's independent run, some of the Progressive reformers' wounds were self-inflicted. Elite-oriented political reforms that emphasized informed, independent political participation undermined the vibrant, though highly corrupt, party democracy of the late nineteenth century and gave cover to poll taxes and literacy tests for voting that gravely restricted the franchise. In the words of the sociologist Michael Schudson, Progressive Era reforms "helped free people from parties" deeply corrupted by patronage and private interests, but "also provided new means to exclude some people from voting altogether."[22]

Yet the greater source of injury to the cause was organized, entrenched opposition. On a host of fronts—workers' rights, health and unemployment insurance, old-age pensions—Progressive campaigns ran headlong into fierce counter-campaigns by business interests. At a time of weak, immobilized national government, opponents took advantage of America's decentralized federalism to play one state off against another.[23] Strong and intensely conservative courts struck down reforms on those infrequent occasions when Progressives succeeded in running the legislative gauntlet. The Progressive Era ultimately gave way to the Roaring Twenties of unbridled capitalism, market celebration, and industry-dominated politics.

It also, of course, gave way to the Great Depression—a sequence that now seems eerily familiar. And if the travails of the Progressive Era and complacency of the Roaring Twenties provide a series of powerful clues about why, since the 1970s, American government has proved so stalemated and complicit in the face of rising inequality, the reforms that emerged out of the crucible of the Great Depression provide the clearest indication of what it takes to bring about substantial reforms of governance to master new economic realities.

The Politics of Renewal

For too many of us the political equality we once had was meaningless in the face of economic inequality. A small group had concentrated in their own hands an almost complete control over other people's property, other people's money, other people's labor—other people's lives. For too many of us life was no longer free; liberty no longer real; men could no longer follow the pursuit of happiness.

Against economic tyranny such as this, the American citizen could appeal only to the organized power of Government. The collapse of 1929 showed up the despotism for what it was. The election of 1932 was the people's mandate to end it. Under that mandate it is being ended.

—Franklin Delano Roosevelt, accepting his renomination, 1936.[24]

The Great Depression represented the failure of a philosophy that said that the market, left alone, would right itself and that the pain inflicted on workers and their families was the necessary condition of recovery. The classical view of the market held by many economic elites at the time—and widely held again today—distilled Adam Smith's relatively nuanced view of markets and human nature down to its free-market vapors and then mixed it with a Calvinist social Darwinism that saw economic success as a sign of superior personal character (and the reverse as a sign of individual moral failing). The year after the stock market crash of 1929, Treasury Secretary Andrew Mellon was still calling for get-tough measures—"Liquidate labor, liquidate stocks, liquidate real estate"—to allow "enterprising people" to "pick up the wreck from less competent people."[25]

Meanwhile, as the unemployment rate climbed toward 25 percent, the president of the National Association of Manufacturers asked rhetorically of the growing numbers of jobless: "If they do not . . . practice the habits of thrift and conservation, or if they gamble away their savings in the stock market or elsewhere, is our economic system, or government, or industry to blame?"[26] (Echoes can be heard in the words of a CNBC commentator who, on the floor of the Chicago Mercantile Exchange in 2009, launched a tirade against "the government . . . promoting bad behavior" by helping out "losers" whose homes were in foreclosure; the surrounding traders cheered.)[27] The poverty of this view soon became abundantly clear, and with it, the limits of the relatively weak federal government and money-dominated politics that had previously reigned.

What emerged, of course, was the most concentrated burst of economic reform in American political history. The changes ushered in by the New Deal were neither as complete nor as unblemished as the most sympathetic chroniclers have suggested. (To cite one of the greatest blemishes, Roosevelt spent little of his political capital on the cause of civil rights, acceding again and again to the demands of Southern Democrats for accommodation of the region's embedded and elaborate system of racial hierarchy.) But collectively the New Deal reforms stand as the paradigmatic example of the politics of renewal. Banks were regulated and consumer deposits insured. The securities industry was placed under tight new restrictions. Taxes were levied on the rich and raised over time to fund public programs in support of the unemployed and destitute. A brief, ill-fated attempt at government-sponsored self-regulation in the form of the National Industrial Recovery Act—mercifully killed by the Supreme Court not long after its creation—gave way to more aggressive regulation of business.

Roosevelt's economic officials also gradually embraced increased public spending to boost the economy—the priming of the pump that the British economist John Maynard Keynes was simultaneously advocating, initially to deaf ears. Critically, they bolstered middle-class democracy by supporting measures that gave unions—stymied by the courts and a hostile federal government in the past—greater ability to organize and bargain. Programs of economic security, from old-age insurance to unemployment benefits, gave those newly empowered workers basic economic protections that few had previously enjoyed.

When the New Dealers reached for the rhetorical stars, they cast their program as part of a broader movement toward human flourishing and democratic liberty. (Secretary of Labor Frances Perkins went so far as to portray the social insurance breakthroughs of the 1930s as "a fundamental part of another great forward step in that liberation of humanity which began with the Renaissance.") [28] The end result was a new economic order—built on the conviction that the federal government had a responsibility to stabilize the economy, provide economic security, and ensure at least a modicum of redistribution from rich to poor.

The reforms were not just economic, but also political—a remaking of core constitutional understandings.[29] Though Roosevelt suffered politically when he threatened to "pack" the recalcitrant Supreme Court with new members sympathetic to an activist federal government, the Court relented in the face of his program. Roosevelt also recast the role of the president, building upon previous steps by Wilson (as well as the maligned Hoover) to expand the role of the executive in domestic policy. Federalism was similarly turned upside down, with the federal government assuming a more central role relative to the states. This transformation not only strengthened the capacities of public authority; it helped weaken the sway of business interests. They had long been the strongest voices in state capitols, thanks in part to fear on the part of political leaders that any new taxes or regulations would lead businesses to relocate to friendlier jurisdictions. At the national level, business lobbyists were weaker, and fears of capital flight were far less of an obstacle to economic and social reform.

And, of course, there were changes that did not rise to the level of new constitutional understandings. The Democratic Party captured Congress with overwhelming margins, where its majority status would become a near-permanent fixture for the next sixty years. Republicans were discredited and marginalized. Unions and other voluntary organizations flourished, with a new capacity to shape activity in the enlarging range of areas where government policy reached. In short, the New Deal came to describe not just a new economic order but also a new political order. This was fitting, because New Dealers were convinced, in the words of the historian William Leuchtenburg, that "the depression was the result not simply of an economic breakdown but of a political collapse."[30] Like the Progressives before them, what they sought was more than economic reversal; it was political renewal.

The words "breakdown" and "collapse" are not too strong because the starting precondition of the politics of renewal is crisis. The crisis can be massive and fast-moving, as it was during the Great Depression, or it can be deeper and slower to develop, as it was during the Progressive Era. But the large majorities required to bring about major reforms must be catalyzed. In addition, the politics of renewal demand leadership, and in the modern era that leadership has come from the White House. And finally, the politics of renewal require a political vacuum—a vacuum created by the loss of the opposition party in an election rout or the manifest failure of the governing regime (and usually both). By clinging, in fact or appearance, to a leadership stance out of touch with evolving realities—to gridlock and drift rather than renewal and mastery—the discredited regime catalyzes the reform movement that replaces it.

Waiting for Renewal

The health of American democracy has always depended on the politics of renewal, on periodic efforts to ensure that drift driven by economic changes does not cripple government and allow the powerful to steamroll the rest of us. The Progressive Era through which Lippmann lived was the first of three great reformist periods of the twentieth century. The New Deal marked the next. And we shall see in Part 2 that the "long 1960s"— which, for government, really stretches from 1964 to 1977—represents the third. Each of these moments of political renewal generated major public initiatives designed to address excesses, inequities, and failures associated with government's inability to keep up with rapid social and economic change. In each case, a dynamic democracy tempered and civilized a dynamic capitalism.

Since the late 1970s, however, the politics of renewal has been on long-term hold. Instead, the winner-take-all economy of the last generation has realized the fear voiced by democratic theorists from the ancients through the Founders that the balance of governance would tip toward those with the greatest resources and economic might. Armed with the clues from our investigation, we now are in a position to explain why that fear has been realized.

There can be little doubt that government deserves to be our prime suspect. The DNA evidence reveals that the inequality explosion has taken the form of a dramatic pulling away of the rich, an outcome largely inconsistent with other leading theories. We have seen that government surely had the means to bring about this outcome, and that public officials seized on those means—through direct interventions in the form of taxes and benefits, through deliberate failures to act in the face of rapid economic and social change, and through the public restructuring of private markets. And we have learned that this sort of activity is nothing new. It reflects powerful tendencies rooted in our political institutions that have, at crucial junctures in the past, overwhelmed the strong pressures for greater equality that democratic politics can create.

But we have yet to tell the full story of how American politics came to slam closed the long era of shared prosperity and usher in the winner-take-all economy. Parts 2 and 3 tell this story, and in them, we find yet more surprises. The political sources of rising inequality lie not in the culture wars of the 1960s, but in the forgotten economic clashes of the 1970s. The reform spirit of the 1960s was not extinguished when Republicans captured the Oval Office in 1968, just four years after a stunning defeat. Instead, it was during the unsettled economic environment of the mid-1970s that the drift of which Lippmann wrote sixty years prior re-emerged. And the source of the change was an organizational revolution few heirs of the New Deal saw coming—a revolution that would transform the rules of Washington seemingly overnight.

Part II

The Rise of Winner-Take-All Politics

Chapter 4

The Unseen Revolution of the 1970s

In the conventional telling of our modern political history, the 1960s represents the crucible—a cauldron of discontent leading directly to the divisions and debates of our present politics. In the words of historian Allen Matusow, the '60s represented "The Unraveling of America." Amid the turbulence of civil rights, Vietnam, and rising crime, liberalism crashed. Conservatives, led by Richard Nixon, seized the opportunity. Republicans successfully split the New Deal coalition that had reigned for a generation. White backlash became the cornerstone of GOP rule. To critics of this new order, Republicans pioneered the politics of resentment, turning the United States into "Nixonland"—to use the evocative title of historian Rick Perlstein's recent book—by realigning the South, rescuing the Republican Party, and road-testing the "us versus them" politics that came to characterize America's fiercely partisan debates.[1]

This near-universal narrative is colorful, easy to tell, and superficially appealing. Political threads connecting the '60s to the present are real enough: from the southern realignment prompted by LBJ's fateful fight for civil rights to the flight of working-class whites from the New Deal coalition. Nixon's politics of resentment paved the way for a new sort of campaign, one based on right-wing populism and anger, focused on culture rather than economics, and directed at Washington liberals rather than business. And these shifts directly contributed to two great political trends of our era: a strengthened and radicalized Republican Party and a growing chasm between the GOP and the once-dominant Democrats (or, to use the political science term of art, "polarization").

Yet despite the familiarity and appeal of this narrative, it has a serious problem: It misses the real story. The Nixonland narrative dates the moment of change in American politics ten years too early, and it fails utterly to explain the epochal transformation that would occur in the subsequent decade. 1968 was not the great switch point in American politics. 1978—a year that stirs no one's historical passion—was. Understanding why will bring us much closer to a true understanding of how Washington works and why it has turned its back on the middle class.

Watch What It Does

Suppose you tried to get a sense of American politics not, as journalists typically do, by looking at campaigns and election outcomes, but by examining *what the government was actually doing.* Would 1968 or 1972 emerge as a turning point? Absolutely not. Far from being moments of fundamental change, these elections that supposedly redefined America come smack in the middle of the great "bulge" of government activism that runs from, roughly, 1964 to 1977. When it comes to spending, taxation, regulation, and all the other things that government does, nothing unraveled during "The Unraveling of America." Washington just kept on doing what it had been doing.

We know that LBJ helped usher in a period in which the federal government greatly expanded its reach not just in civil rights but in broad areas of domestic policy ranging from social programs (Medicaid and Medicare) to consumer and environmental protection. What we often forget is that, in all these areas and more, Washington remained on course following the "crucible" elections of 1968 and 1972.

In fact, the surge of government activism actually accelerated under Nixon—exactly the opposite of what the conventional story would lead you to expect. Nixon, not Johnson, oversaw the most rapid increase in domestic spending since the New Deal. He signed on to a huge expansion of Social Security, as well as to the creation of a national food stamps program. Nixon also approved the transformation of Old Age Assistance into a much larger and fully national Supplemental Security Income program.

Nixon, not Johnson, signed into law the huge extensions of national regulatory policy that marked this period, creating the Environmental Protection Agency (1970), the Occupational Safety and Health Administration (1970), the National Traffic Safety Commission (1970), the Consumer Product Safety Commission (1972), and the Mine Safety and Health Administration (1973). And while Nixon had been forced out of office by the time that the massive Employee Retirement Income Security Act (1974) made it through Congress, his successor, Gerald Ford, signed the bill, which transformed the entire system of employer-provided benefits for workers.

Of course, Democrats ran Congress at the time. But Nixon was no mere bystander. Even as he moved to challenge Democrats from the right on matters of race, culture, and crime, he was convinced that competing for the center required a strong dose of economic populism and a willingness to use government to manage or moderate markets. Compared to leaders of today's GOP—or even many current Democrats—Nixon looks like a full-throated Social Democrat. Although he attacked George McGovern's position on welfare, he, too, supported a guaranteed annual income for the poor. His health-care proposals would look like very respectable Democratic fare today (actually, more ambitious than what President Obama proposed in 2009). Nixon actively cultivated the head of the AFL-CIO, George Meany, and enlisted liberal social policy experts like Daniel Patrick Moynihan.

The blueprint for this domestic strategy was laid out in Kevin Phillips's influential *The Emerging Republican Majority*.[2] Phillips (who ironically would emerge decades later as a fierce critic of Republican contributions to mounting inequality) dedicated his work to "the emerging Republican majority and its two principal architects: President Richard M. Nixon and Attorney General John N. Mitchell." Phillips argued for a coalition grounded in "middle-class *realpolitik*." He stressed that a Republican majority would need to be responsive to middle-class economic concerns and gave no hint of a platform challenging the New Deal economic agenda. For Phillips, it was liberals who had repudiated the New Deal by moving "beyond programs taxing the few for the benefit of the many (the New Deal) to programs taxing the many on behalf of the few (the Great Society)." The main obstacles to Republican inroads among northern blue-collar workers were "[f]ears that a Republican administration would undermine Social Security, Medicare, collective bargaining and aid to education." If a Nixon administration could "dispel these apprehensions," it would gain the political loyalties of the white working class.[3]

The Nixon we remember was the "law and order" president who cultivated working-class cultural anxieties. But Nixon cut a far different figure when it came to most of the essential aspects of domestic governance, especially those related to the economy and social welfare. On the lunch-pail concerns of Middle America, Nixon represented not backlash but broad acceptance of the liberal consensus. And while the Watergate scandal weakened Nixon and the Republicans more generally, it had surprisingly little effect on governance. As Nixon faltered, he acceded to some legislative items that he might not have supported earlier (and left his successor, Gerald Ford, facing tough times after the 1974 election, when Democrats added forty-nine House members and five new senators to their already significant majorities). Yet most of the big domestic expansions had already occurred. Nixon's fall brought a wave of new Democrats to Congress, but it did not change the fundamental contours of what government was doing.

Carterland

Indeed, once one looks past the continuities of Nixon and Ford to examine the Carter presidency, the puzzles associated with our traditional, election-focused narrative only multiply. In 1976, after an eight-year interregnum, a Democrat entered the White House. With the Republican veto threat gone, the opportunities for liberals to control the political agenda greatly expanded. Within his party, Carter was regarded as a moderate, but he had staked out liberal positions on a range of major economic issues, including health care, taxes, and labor relations. Equally significant, the new Democratic president could work with massive majorities in both the House and the Senate.

A view of politics that puts elections front and center would have expected policy to shift sharply leftward. Certainly, liberal activists of the day shared that expectation, sensing new opportunities for ambitious initiatives on taxes, industrial relations, the minimum wage, health care, consumer protection, and a range of other domestic issues. So cocky were Democrats that they rejected Nixon's (and later Ford's) overtures for compromises on a range of issues like welfare reform and health care, anticipating that they would be in a stronger position in 1977.

Oops. If one wanted a book title to capture the great turning point in modern American political history, it would be more accurate, if less catchy, to call it *Carterland*. 1977 and 1978 marked the rapid demise of the liberal era and the emergence of something radically different. Tax reform: defeated. A new consumer protection agency: defeated. Election Day voter registration: scuttled before reaching the floor of the House. Health-care reform: defeated. A proposal to tie the minimum wage to the average manufacturing wage to prevent its future erosion: defeated. An overhaul of outdated labor relations laws: successfully filibustered in the Senate, despite the presence of sixty-one Democrats and a Republican minority containing some genuine supporters of organized labor, not to mention far, far more moderates than in the GOP we know today.

It wasn't just the string of defeats for liberal policy initiatives, stunning as those were. By 1978, at a time of unified Democratic control of the House, Senate, and White House, the precursors of the Reagan revolution were already visible. Congress passed a tax bill whose signature provision was a deep cut in the capital gains tax—a change that would largely benefit the wealthy. This followed hard on the heels of a decision to sharply raise payroll taxes, the most regressive federal levy. These two initiatives—fully a decade removed from the supposed turning point of

Nixon's rise—marked the beginning of the pronounced reversal in federal tax policy we described in chapter 2. The United States began its long, dramatic move away from the established practice of using taxes as an instrument for tempering market-generated inequalities associated with the outsized earnings of those at the top.

At the same time, Congress and the president embarked on a major shift in economic policy, embracing the argument that excessive regulation had become a serious curb on growth. In the mid to late 1970s the call for deregulation was often bipartisan and narrowly focused. It centered on particular sectors of the economy (transportation, communications, energy). Equally important, it targeted a specific form of regulation that erected barriers to entry, enabling existing firms to raise prices and fostering cozy relationships between regulators and favored firms. Yet this deregulatory stream created an opening for broader action. It would not be long before it flooded over its narrow banks to become an ever-widening attack on the very idea of economic regulation. Here again the story begins in the 1970s, not the 1960s.

So we have a dominant narrative of contemporary American politics, "1968 as crucible," that fundamentally misses what actually happened in the corridors of power. Moreover, it misses what actually happened precisely when the winner-take-all economy began to emerge. We have tumultuous electoral waves, but the political fortunes of economic interests in Washington seem to be riding their own currents. Republicans win, and the contours of the Great Society continue to expand. Democrats win, and policy shifts sharply to the right. What can explain why Nixonland leaves the postwar governing order untouched, while Carterland turns it upside down?

From Electoral Spectacle to Organized Combat

We need to dig deeper to sort this out. After all, the conventional narrative of election-driven change not only dominates most accounts of our recent past; it also typifies most discussion of our current politics. What is the basic vision of politics that underpins this dominant view? Call it "politics as electoral spectacle."

At the center of this blinkered vision are the huge shows we call elections, circuses that bring together two broad groups under a red-white-and-blue tent. In the audience sits a fairly inchoate mass of voters. In the ring are the politicians, individual showmen who seek their favor. They succeed or fail in wooing a fickle electorate partly based on events—Vietnam, riots, an assassination, an economic downturn—and partly on their skill in managing the related challenges.

This view of politics is appealing and easily packaged. It's also reassuring: If politicians are doing something, it must be because voters want them to. There's just one problem: It misses the essence of American politics.

In particular, this near-universal perspective leaves out two critical things: public policy and organized interest groups. By policy we mean something very simple: what the government actually *does*. The main reason we care about politics, after all, is because we believe what government does matters. We think that the leaders who exercise political authority, and use it to tell citizens what they can and cannot and must do, make a difference for the quality of people's lives.

In the last two chapters, we saw that this belief is well founded. Especially in the modern era of activist government, those in positions of power can have an enormous influence over the economy, the distribution of income, and the life chances of citizens. This is most obvious when we think about the enormous system of taxes and transfer programs that all rich democracies operate. Yet, as we have seen, in areas far beyond the scope of taxes and transfers, the exercise of political authority is an extraordinarily powerful means of influencing the structure of "private" markets that determine the economy's winners and losers.

To take policy out of the picture is to reduce political conflict to the status of sports. Clashes between the "red team" and the "blue team" become no different from a game between the Celtics and the Lakers. This is no doubt why politics as electoral spectacle is so appealing to the media: It's exciting, and it's simple. Aficionados can memorize the stats of their favorite players or become experts on the great games of the past. Everyone, however, can enjoy the gripping spectacle of two highly motivated teams slugging it out.

Once we see policy, rather than electoral victory, as the grand prize of political conflict, we see politics for what it is: a contest with big and often enduring stakes—a contest more like the one that gladiators played in the Roman Colosseum than the one the Celtics and Lakers play in the Staples Center. And who are the contestants? Who are the political gladiators? They are not, for the most part, atomized voters. The main competitors, the ones in the ring from start to finish wielding their weapons and enduring each other's blows, are organized groups.

Call this vision "politics as organized combat." It is a perspective on American politics that provides a much better way to make sense of the remarkable transformation of the past few decades and of the political world we inhabit today. To see it clearly, we need to step away from the conflicts of the 1960s and 1970s for a minute, and move to a loftier height—say, about 29,000 feet.

Who Climbed Everest?

The story of Edmund Hillary, who died in 2008 at the age of eighty-eight, is usually told as one of heroic individual achievement. If the story comes with a twist, it's the modern one of identity politics—how to apportion credit between Hillary and Tenzing Norgay, the Sherpa guide who joined him at the summit of Everest. The story is rarely, if ever, told as a victory for organization.

But a victory for organization it certainly was. Arrayed below Hillary and Norgay on the slopes was a remarkable display of mobilization and coordination: a team of a dozen climbers, thirty-five Sherpa guides, 350 porters, and 36,000 pounds of equipment and supplies.[4] The reality of the first successful assault on Everest is less romantic than the conventional tale but no less impressive: It was a feat of modern management. Without that formidable logistical effort, there would have been no climb to the summit, and no one would ever have heard of Edmund Hillary.

That we tell the Everest saga, and so many others like it, as one of individual initiative is revealing. Such a view is deeply rooted in our culture. Observers of the United States have long identified the tendency to see the world this way as distinctively American. More than most societies, Americans believe that people rise or fall as a result of their own efforts, and therefore get what they deserve. Critically, when we say this is a nation of individualists, we don't just mean Americans embrace individualism as a social ethic. Underpinning this ethic is a tendency to *interpret* the world in highly individualistic terms. We distribute blame and praise to individuals because we believe that it is their individual actions, for better or worse, that matter. *People get what they deserve.*

Our media-driven culture of celebrity reinforces this individualistic outlook. Television, of course, is tailor-made for visual images of larger-than-life individuals. Building up (and tearing down) those who capture the media's fancy lends itself to the simple storytelling and morality tales that audiences crave. Never mind that, just like on Everest, massive organizational realities lurk behind the individualistic facade. New York and Hollywood are home to huge factories of organized activity that cultivate, produce, and then bloviate about the "individuals" who command our attention. The factories stay in the background, while breathless discussions of Brangelina's twins get the airtime.

This preoccupation with specific personalities and insistence on attributing everything that happens to the qualities of individuals is a form of blindness. We see individuals, but not the organizations that help to pool their resources and can vastly extend their range of social action. Remember the anguished kid in *The Sixth Sense*? His "gift," or curse, was an awareness of what others couldn't see ("I see dead people"). To understand our politics, and the remarkable transformation it has undergone, we need to cultivate a different sixth sense: a deeper awareness of the powerful role of organizations.

The Organizational Edge

Look carefully, and organizations come into focus. In every walk of life, huge institutions link together individuals, provide standard operating routines, impart and sort valuable information, and allow isolated individual actions to add up to cohesive systemic effects. Most obviously, in the realm of business, idealized as the territory of individual entrepreneurs, giant organizations rule. We extol scrappy upstart competitors even as we drive our Toyotas to Wal-Mart, pick up remodeling supplies from Home Depot, grab fast food at McDonald's, and check our Bank of America online accounts with software from Microsoft running on an Intel chip.

The clout that huge organizations wield in American life is real, and it is neither accident nor conspiracy. Organizations have formidable advantages, and modern life is unimaginable in their absence. They can marshal vastly greater resources than can any individual. Organizations permit specialization and thus the development of expertise—a critical advantage in a world of staggering and ever-increasing complexity. They allow many different kinds of talent to be combined and directed toward some big task. They can operate simultaneously in many different arenas. Perhaps most important, they are durable, even relentless, where individuals are flighty and, of course, mortal. Organizations can learn from experience. They can sustain a focus for decades if need be: watching, waiting, planning, and then seizing opportunity when the time is right.

At one level, of course, people know this. They talk about "big oil" or "special interests" or "Wall Street," and overwhelmingly decry their perceived influence in Washington. Yet these generally remain distant abstractions, vaguely malevolent but obscure. They pop up in campaign ads. They are grist for a faux-populist discourse that works great in movies like *Michael Clayton* or *Erin Brockovich*. The ironies of these populist epics are rich. Each is the product of a huge media factory, each stars a celebrity carefully cultivated by these factories, and each tells the tale of a heroic individual. Through grit and savvy, George Clooney and Julia Roberts ultimately triumph over a faceless, malevolent organization.

Despite our tendency to sneer at "special interests" however, attention to organizations rarely features prominently in respectable punditry or political analysis. Indeed, the tendency to see the world in highly individualized, organization-free terms may be even stronger in political commentary than it is in the way we discuss other parts of the social world. Popular accounts of politics focus on the Hillarys (Clinton, not Edmund). We endlessly analyze the great personalities who dot the political landscape, their psychologies and strategic acumen, their personal appeal and personae, their eloquence (even if manufactured for them by a stable of speechwriters) and gaffes (even if substantively trivial).

No sign of this individualistic focus is more telling than the American media's fixation on elections—and, within their treatment of those political contests, their preoccupation with the "horse race" elements. This intense concentration on the most circus-like aspects of political life is now so thoroughly institutionalized that we hardly notice it. But we should.

As political circuses go, of course, there is nothing like a rip-roaring election. Unlike just about everything else in politics, elections are made for TV. They involve head-to-head competitions between dueling personalities. For most Americans, and, it seems, for more and more reporters, the day-to-day business of governing is frankly boring. Policy can be mind-numbingly complicated. One night after the first televised presidential debate between Bush and Gore in 2000, Ted Koppel was on *Larry King Live* talking about the heated disputes between the two candidates over tax policy. Gore had complained that Bush's proposals simply didn't add up and would lead to massive deficits. "You know, honestly, it turns my brains to mush," Koppel admitted. "I can't pretend for a minute that I'm really able to follow the argument of the debates. Parts of it, yes. Parts of it, I haven't a clue what they're talking about."[5] This is not some local news intern speaking. It's Ted Koppel, the host of the former late-night wonkfest *Nightline*. And he's not speaking about rocket science, or even climate science, but a subject where relatively definitive answers can be reached without much technical heavy lifting. But no heavy lifting at all is required to say who's up and who's down in an election.

Worse for media executives constantly looking to attract "eyeballs" to their product, government policy is excruciatingly slow to develop. Headline: "Obama's Tax Proposals Are the Same As They Were Yesterday!" The great health-care debate of 2009 was one of the most important domestic policy discussions of a generation—more important even than the debate over President Clinton's health plan in the early 1990s given how much further it progressed in Congress. And yet, to many in the news industry, it was, in the candid words of MSNBC host Dylan Ratigan, "bad for ratings." When health care is under discussion, Ratigan fretted, "cable networks' ratings go off a cliff." "It's not only not a cable TV–friendly story," agreed John Harwood, chief Washington correspondent for CNBC. "It's not a journalism-friendly story."[6] For all the changes in Americans' lives that health-care reform could produce, to many in the news business, it looked like something that was very hard to understand happening too slowly.

By contrast, elections are fast-moving and easy to follow. Even better, they can be covered and dissected in a manner that closely resembles the way the press covers sports (Was that ad effective? Who will he pick as a running mate?) or entertainment (Where is Obama going on vacation? Does that backdrop make McCain look old?). For the media, governing often seems like something that happens in the off-season. Even then, much of the conversation focuses on how it sets things up for the next election. For too many reporters, the struggle to shape life-or-death decisions in the corridors of Washington is treated as the political equivalent of training camp. Campaigns can still generate ratings. Health-care reform can't.

Organized interests see the world the other way around. Elections are training camps; daily action in Washington is the regular season. Let's pursue that tax reform example a little more. When pundits and columnists feel like singing a hymn to American government, one of their favorite examples is the Tax Reform Act of 1986. Two skilled reporters at the time dubbed this the "showdown at Gucci Gulch."[7] Gucci Gulch is the gauntlet of well-heeled lobbyists that lawmakers have to run in the corridors outside the House and Senate chambers where tax legislation gets written. Somehow, against all odds, the Erin Brockoviches won. The showdown ended with the good guys celebrating as the Gucci gang fled town.

The law Reagan signed was hailed as a bipartisan triumph of public-spiritedness over the special interests. It sharply reduced tax breaks—aka corporate welfare—for the Gucci Gulch folks in order to finance lower tax rates for the vast majority of Americans without increasing the deficit. Economists of very different stripes lauded the new law as a triumph for transparency and efficiency over pork. Voters, not special interests, seemed to come out ahead.

Seemed to. Moving forward a few years, the story looks very different. If you take a good look at the tax code now, you'll see that it is chock-full of new tax breaks, far more expensive than the ones eliminated with such fanfare. In hindsight, the venerated Tax Reform Act of 1986 resembles the ill-fated Roanoke colony in early Virginia. Like that colony, visitors returning to the act after a long absence would find it had vanished without a trace.

In contrast to the mystery surrounding the settlers of Roanoke, however, we know what happened. The attention of voters and the press wandered elsewhere. Gucci Gulch, the lobbyists' hunting ground, remained. The organized groups who had taken such a political hit in 1986 simply went back to work. Year after year, out of the spotlight, they lobbied to advance their interests. Year after year, they succeeded in adding back loopholes—one unnoticed provision at a time. They could do so not because public opinion had drifted rightward (it hadn't), but because they were organized and their opponents were not. Backed by organizations, they pushed politicians to respond to their concerns. And nobody pushed back.

Organization Matters

The story of organizational triumph over popular concerns has been repeated time after time, especially in the last thirty years. A possibly apocryphal story about FDR has him responding to a delegation imploring him for action: "Fine, you've convinced me. Now make me do it." What he meant was, "Get some organized pressure behind you, so that I will be rewarded for doing the right thing and punished for doing the wrong thing." Struggles over policy—over what the government actually *does* for and to its citizens—are almost always long, hard slogs. They involve drawn-out conflicts in multiple arenas. They involve extremely complicated issues where only full-time, well-trained participants are likely to be effective. They involve stakes that can easily be in the tens or even hundreds of billions of dollars. Inevitably, organized groups are crucial actors—and often *the* crucial actors—in these fights.

Against these forces, voters often find themselves in the position of the farmer in that famous scene in John Steinbeck's *The Grapes of Wrath* when a man on a tractor arrives to destroy the homes of tenants. The farmer comes out and threatens the man with a gun, but the tractor driver says he is not at fault; he is just doing his job. The farmer responds that in that case he will shoot the driver's boss, only to hear that that man, too, is just following instructions. And so the conversation goes, back and forth, up an endless chain of command. The helpless farmer ends up standing there as his home is destroyed, asking, "Who can we shoot?"[8]

Those who see politics as electoral spectacle frequently assume that it's easy for voters to figure out who to "shoot"—that is, which policies to support or oppose, which politicians to vote in and out of office. But to form grounded views and votes, citizens need important resources that are too often lacking. Perhaps the most important is knowledge: knowledge of the problems that concern them, knowledge of what politicians do—or don't do—to address these problems, and knowledge of what those actions mean for citizens. If voters don't have this knowledge, then they need to get signals from figures they trust that give them a reasonable prospect of rewarding or punishing politicians as necessary. In short, they need access to reliable organizations.

Optimists about American democracy too often presume that all this is relatively straightforward. The truth is much more unsettling—so unsettling that even in serious political discourse it is usually considered bad manners to point it out. The truth is that most citizens pay very little attention to politics, and it shows. To call their knowledge of even the most elementary facts about the political system shaky would be generous. To take just a few examples, less than a third of Americans know that a member of the House serves for two years or that a senator serves for six. In 2000, six years after Newt Gingrich became House Speaker, only 55 percent knew the Republicans were the majority party in the House—a success rate only a little superior to a random guess. Just two years after he presided over Bill Clinton's impeachment trial in the Senate, only 11 percent of those surveyed could identify William Rehnquist as chief justice of the United States.[9]

Crucial and basic matters of political process are equally opaque to most voters. In early 2010, as Republicans brought Washington to a halt as effectively as the unexpected winter snowstorms, most Americans had no idea that not a single Republican senator had voted for health-care reform (two-thirds either put the number at between five and twenty or said they didn't know), and less than a third could correctly identify the number of votes needed to overcome a filibuster (sixty). Well over half of Americans either said fifty-one votes were sufficient, or confessed they had no idea.[10]

About policy, most voters know even less, and are prone to staggering mistakes. Roughly half of Americans think that foreign aid is one of the two top expenditures in the federal budget (in reality, it consumes about 1 percent of the budget). In 1980, in the midst of the Cold War, 38 percent of Americans surveyed believed that the Soviet Union was a member of NATO—the anti-Soviet defense alliance. Two years after the huge 2001 tax cuts, half of Americans were unable to recall that there had been tax cuts at all.[11] Most of the famous "swing voters," whom journalists tend to idealize as standing above the fray, carefully sorting among the strengths and weaknesses of each party's offerings, are actually the *least* engaged, *least* well-informed citizens, reaching a final decision (if at all) on the flimsiest grounds.

This is the dirty little secret of our profession. Among political scientists, that most voters are woefully ignorant about politics is completely uncontroversial, and has been for decades. The survey evidence on this subject is overwhelming. Yet it is not something widely disseminated, and a good deal of effort in the discipline is devoted to scrounging for reasons why the severe knowledge deficits of voters don't matter all that much, and why Washington will be attentive to voters' demands even if most voters are not very well informed and not paying all that much attention.[12]

What does it take for weakly informed and aware voters to attract Washington's sustained notice? It takes organization. To be more than bystanders in American politics wondering whom to shoot, voters need strong organizational mooring and consistent cues to recognize and respond to changes in public policy. Yet, on economic matters, this mooring and these cues have eroded just as they have become more crucial. This erosion hasn't just made it harder for voters to know whom to shoot. It has also dramatically undermined voters' confidence in government and politicians, especially their sense that elected officials are looking out for their interests. Trust in government has plummeted, and cynicism about the effectiveness of the representative process has grown. In the mid-1960s, less than a third of Americans agreed that "government is pretty much run by a few big interests looking out for themselves." Over the last couple decades, more than two-thirds have. In 2008, the share was more than 70 percent.[13]

Unrepresentative Democracy

These polls reflect an underlying reality. New research by political scientists suggests that there is plenty of reason to question the clout of ordinary voters, especially those who have most clearly been on the losing end of the winner-take-all economy. Two professors working separately at Princeton University, Larry Bartels and Martin Gilens, have been studying the correspondence between what politicians do and what their constituents of differing economic backgrounds say they want them to do in opinion polls.[14] Are the opinions of wealthier Americans more likely to be heard and heeded than those of less affluent Americans?

The answer, perhaps unsurprisingly, is yes. But the scale of the disparity may shock those used to thinking that everyone's opinion counts. Bartels looked at how closely aligned with voters U.S. senators were on key votes in the late 1980s and early 1990s. It turns out there is a pretty high degree of congruence between senators' positions and the opinions of their constituents—at least when those constituents are in the top third of the income distribution. For constituents in the middle third of the income distribution, the correspondence is much weaker, and for those in the bottom third, it is actually negative. (Yes, when the poorest people in a state support a policy, their senators are *less* likely to vote for it.) Bartels also found that while senators in both parties were more likely to vote for a policy when it was supported by better-off voters, Republicans were much more responsive to high-income voters than were Democrats. Senators may pledge to represent everyone in a state, but they do not, Bartels's analysis suggests, represent them equally—or sometimes at all.

Gilens took Bartels's investigation a step further. In a truly mammoth research undertaking, he collected almost two thousand survey questions fielded since the early 1980s that ask people to say whether they wanted government policy to change. Then he looked at whether government policy actually *did* change. Like Bartels, Gilens did not just look at people in general, but broke the population down into income groups. Did it make a difference, Gilens asked, whether a policy had strong support among the poor (in Gilens's analysis, someone with income greater than just 10 percent of the population), the middle class (the median income), or the well-off (income greater than 90 percent of the population)?

It turns out it makes a huge difference. Most policy changes with majority support didn't become law—itself an important reminder of how hard it is to change policy in our fragmented and increasingly polarized politics. But they only stood a good chance of becoming law, Gilens found, when they were supported by those at the top. When the opinions of the poor diverged from those of the well-off, the opinions of the poor ceased to have any apparent influence: If 90 percent of poor Americans supported a policy change, it was no more likely to happen than if 10 percent did. By contrast, when more of the well-off supported a change, it was substantially more likely to happen.

But what about the middle class? They did not fare much better than the poor when their opinions departed from those of the well-off. When well-off people strongly supported a policy change, it had almost three times the chance of becoming law as when they strongly opposed it. When median-income people strongly supported a policy change, it had hardly any greater chance of becoming law than when they strongly opposed it. As Gilens concluded acerbically, "Most middle-income Americans think that public officials do not care much about the preferences of 'people like me.' Sadly, the results presented above suggest they may be right. Whether or not elected officials and other decision makers 'care' about middle-class Americans, influence over actual policy outcomes appears to be reserved almost exclusively for those at the top of the income distribution."[15]

The apparent weakness of the link between what elected representatives do and the opinion of middle- and working-class Americans reminds us that there is nothing automatic about democratic responsiveness—even in a nation, like the United States, where formal political equality is more or less universally guaranteed. Gilens's and Bartels's results suggest a startling disconnect in American politics, a chasm between voters and policymakers.

Yet this only deepens the mystery, since neither has much to say about what creates that chasm. Opinion surveys are largely devoid of information about the lobbying and organizational activities that really make politics tick. And they don't reach many of the truly rich, so they are not going to help us understand the political activities and positions of the small slice of Americans who've made out so well in the winner-take-all economy. To figure out what has been happening, we need to unpack the politics of organized combat.

The Politics of Organized Combat

Where "politics as spectacle" concentrates on voters and politics, "politics as organized combat" focuses on groups and policies. Voters are hardly powerless. But their attention to what government actually does is limited and typically brief. And given the complexity of our political institutions, they can have a devilishly hard time determining whom they should hold accountable when they are discontented. In our fragmented political system, victories without enduring organization are almost always fleeting. To influence the exercise of government authority in a modern democracy generally requires a range of formidable capabilities: the capacity to mobilize resources, coordinate actions with others, develop extensive expertise, focus sustained attention, and operate flexibly across multiple domains of activity. These are the attributes of organizations, not discrete, atomized voters.

The peculiar institutions of American democracy that we looked at in the last chapter reinforce the exceptional advantages of organized groups. Our institutions were designed to fragment power among multiple sites of political authority—local, state, and federal; legislatures, presidents, and courts. Stasis rather than change is the natural expectation. Moreover, leaders with limited time and resources face many competing demands. They will generally make something a priority only if they see big opportunities, or expect to face substantial risks if they do nothing. Moving the mountain of our huge, complex government typically requires coordinated action on a broad scale. Stopping government initiatives, by contrast, often requires not mass support but only effective mobilization at one point in the complicated and mostly invisible chain of decision-making. The ear of a crucial committee chair may suffice.

Don't get us wrong: Organized groups care deeply about elections, and they try very hard to swing them their way. But they are also shrewd enough, and experienced enough, to place the competition for votes in proper perspective. For most organizations engaged in politics, the fruit of all this effort is not the winning of office for its own sake but influence over policy. Fundamentally, what interest organizations care about is not the trappings of office but the substance of governance. Elections are only a means to the true end: control over political authority and, with it, the capacity to make policies.

We know what groups care about because of what they do, and especially because of what they spend money on. Organized interests convey their priorities and their sense of how politics works most clearly when they reach for their wallets. And in recent decades they have been reaching a lot deeper into their wallets—but not principally to shape elections. Of the billions of dollars now spent every year on politics, only a fairly small fraction is directly connected to electoral contests. The bulk of it goes to lobbying—sustained, intense efforts to shape what happens in Washington. Officially, over $3 billion is now spent every year by lobbyists. This figure has nearly doubled in just a decade and almost certainly dramatically understates true expenditures to influence policy. For powerful groups the center of action is in Washington, not the swing states. And more and more over the last thirty years, Washington has become their playground.

"Who Are Those Guys?"

We've always had a fondness for buddy flicks, and one of the best captures the central message of this book. Really.

Butch Cassidy and the Sundance Kid is a film about the West. Like many of the great westerns, it is really about the death of the frontier. Butch (Paul Newman) and Sundance (Robert Redford) are charming rogues of moderate talent. With good humor, they exploit the disorganization of frontier life. Fronting a gang of ne'er-do-wells, they pick off isolated banks, or trains steaming alone through the prairies. Relying on little more than guile (mostly Newman) and bravado (mostly Redford), they find a market niche, and without breaking much of a sweat they build a nice little business.

Initially played mostly for laughs, the mood changes midway through the film. What looks like simply the gang's latest prey turns out to be a trap. Their motley crew dispatched in shockingly rapid fashion, the two heroes beat a stunned and rapid retreat, with a mysterious and sinister team in hot pursuit. Newman and Redford employ every escape trick they know, and they know quite a few. But each one fails. After each failure they watch their relentless pursuers close in and, with growing apprehension, repeat the same question: "Who are those guys?"

"Those guys" are a modern, efficient organization—bringing with them the death of the old West, and more specifically the death of amateur thieves like the film's heroes. Butch and Sundance eventually learn that the banks and railroads have grown tired of the nagging interference of the Hole-in-the-Wall Gang. In response, they have recruited, equipped, and deployed a team of superb specialists (trackers, sharpshooters, and so on) to bring the source of the corporations' modest irritation to an end.

Hopelessly cornered and desperate, Butch and Sundance make a spectacular, death-defying escape. Given a chance to regroup, they conclude that their only bet is to find a new frontier, and they head for Bolivia. There they repeat some of their earlier successes against disorganized targets, reprising the light tone of the film's first scenes. But it is only Indian summer. Even in Bolivia, the machinery of modernity is advancing. Before long, the charismatic bandits are literally outgunned—spectacularly so—by another organization, composed of what seems like half the Bolivian army.

"Who are those guys?" is, in a sense, the underlying question of this book. Why has Washington made the rich richer and abandoned the middle class? Because of the relentless effectiveness of modern, efficient organizations operating in a much less modern and efficient political system. Our story begins when these organizations were built, during the tumultuous years in which the unexpected liberalism of Nixonland turned into the unexpected conservatism of Carterland.

Chapter 5

The Politics of Organized Combat

In the fall of 1972, the venerable National Association of Manufacturers (NAM) made a surprising announcement: It planned to move its main offices from New York to Washington, D.C. As its chief, Burt Raynes, observed:

> We have been in New York since before the turn of the century, because we regarded this city as the center of business and industry. But the thing that affects business most today is government. The interrelationship of business with business is no longer so important as the interrelationship of business with government. In the last several years, that has become very apparent to us.[1]

To be more precise, what had become very apparent to the business community was that it was getting its clock cleaned. Used to having broad sway, employers faced a series of surprising defeats in the 1960s and early 1970s. As we have seen, these defeats continued unabated when Richard Nixon won the White House. Despite electoral setbacks, the liberalism of the Great Society had surprising political momentum. "From 1969 to 1972," as the political scientist David Vogel summarizes in one of the best books on the political role of business, "virtually the entire American business community experienced a series of political setbacks without parallel in the postwar period." In particular, Washington undertook a vast expansion of its regulatory power, introducing tough and extensive restrictions and requirements on business in areas from the environment to occupational safety to consumer protection.[2]

In corporate circles, this pronounced and sustained shift was met with disbelief and then alarm. By 1971, future Supreme Court justice Lewis Powell felt compelled to assert, in a memo that was to help galvanize business circles, that the "American economic system is under broad attack." This attack, Powell maintained, required mobilization for political combat: "Business must learn the lesson . . . that political power is necessary; that such power must be assiduously cultivated; and that when necessary, it must be used aggressively and with determination—without embarrassment and without the reluctance which has been so characteristic of American business." Moreover, Powell stressed, the critical ingredient for success would be organization: "Strength lies in organization, in careful long-range planning and implementation, in consistency of action over an indefinite period of years, in the scale of financing available only through joint effort, and in the political power available only through united action and national organizations."[3]

Powell was just one of many who pushed to reinvigorate the political clout of employers. Before the policy winds shifted in the '60s, business had seen little need to mobilize anything more than a network of trade associations. It relied mostly on personal contacts, and the main role of lobbyists in Washington was to troll for government contracts and tax breaks. The explosion of policy activism, and rise of public interest groups like those affiliated with Ralph Nader, created a fundamental challenge. And as the 1970s progressed, the problems seemed to be getting worse. Powell wrote in 1971, but even after Nixon swept to a landslide reelection the following year, the legislative tide continued to come in. With Watergate leading to Nixon's humiliating resignation and a spectacular Democratic victory in 1974, the situation grew even more dire. "The danger had suddenly escalated," Bryce Harlow, senior Washington representative for Procter & Gamble and one of the engineers of the corporate political revival was to say later. "We had to prevent business from being rolled up and put in the trash can by that Congress."[4]

Powell, Harlow, and others sought to replace the old boys' club with a more modern, sophisticated, and diversified apparatus—one capable of advancing employers' interests even under the most difficult political circumstances. They recognized that business had hardly begun to tap its potential for wielding political power. Not only were the financial resources at the disposal of business leaders unrivaled. The hierarchical structures of corporations made it possible for a handful of decision-makers to deploy those resources and combine them with the massive but underutilized capacities of their far-flung organizations. These were the preconditions for an organizational revolution that was to remake Washington in less than a decade—and, in the process, lay the critical groundwork for winner-take-all politics.

Businessmen of the World, Unite!

The organizational counterattack of business in the 1970s was swift and sweeping—a domestic version of Shock and Awe. The number of corporations with public affairs offices in Washington grew from 100 in 1968 to over 500 in 1978. In 1971, only 175 firms had registered lobbyists in Washington, but by 1982, nearly 2,500 did. The number of corporate PACs increased from under 300 in 1976 to over 1,200 by the middle of 1980.[5] On every dimension of corporate political activity, the numbers reveal a dramatic, rapid mobilization of business resources in the mid-1970s.

What the numbers alone cannot show is something of potentially even greater significance: Employers learned how to work together to achieve shared political goals. As members of coalitions, firms could mobilize more proactively and on a much broader front. Corporate leaders became advocates not just for the narrow interests of their firms but also for the shared interests of business as a whole.

Ironically, this new capacity was in part an unexpected gift of Great Society liberalism. One of the distinctive features of the big expansion of government authority in the '60s and early '70s was that it created new forms of regulation that simultaneously affected many industries. Previously, the airlines might have lobbied the Civil Aeronautics Board, the steel companies might have focused on restricting foreign competitors, the energy producers might have gained special tax breaks from a favorite congressman. Now companies across a wide range of sectors faced a common threat: increasingly powerful regulatory agencies overseeing their treatment of the environment, workers, and consumers. Individual firms had little chance of fending off such broad initiatives on their own; to craft an appropriately broad political defense, they needed organization.

Business was galvanized by more than perceived government overreach. It was also responding to the growing economic challenges it faced. Organization-building began even before the economy soured in the early 1970s, but the tumultuous economy of that decade—battered by two major oil shocks, which pushed up inflation and dragged down growth—created panic in corporate sectors as well as growing dissatisfaction among voters. The 1970s was not the economic wasteland that retrospective accounts often suggest. The economy actually grew more quickly overall (after adjusting for inflation) during the 1970s than during the 1980s.[6] But against the backdrop of the roaring 1960s, the economic turbulence was a rude jolt that strengthened the case of business leaders that a new governing approach was needed.

When he penned his influential memo, Lewis Powell was chair of the Education Committee of the Chamber of Commerce. The Chamber was one of a number of business groups that responded to the emerging threat by becoming much more organized. The Chamber doubled in membership between 1974 and 1980. Its budget tripled. The National Federation of Independent Business (NFIB) doubled its membership between 1970 and 1979.[7]

The expansion of the Chamber and the NFIB signaled not only a rise in the collective capacity of business; it brought a harder-edged form of mobilization. Composed disproportionately of smaller firms, these organizations were especially livid about the rise of government regulation. Big companies had an easier time absorbing the administrative costs of complying with new rules, and more opportunities to pass the costs on to consumers. Moreover, business associations based on a multitude of small firms proved especially capable of mobilizing mass outrage, which would turn out to be a very effective political weapon.

Of course, big business fought back as well. In 1972, three business organizations merged to form the Business Roundtable, the first business association whose membership was restricted to top corporate CEOs. In part at the urging of Bryce Harlow, lobbyist for Procter & Gamble, this new organization combined two groups focused on relatively narrow business issues with an informal organization called the March Group. The March Group had grown out of a meeting with top Nixon admin-istration officials and prominent executives and was designed to bring together many of the nation's most powerful CEOs. Within five years the new mega-organization had enlisted 113 of the top *Fortune* 200 compa-nies, accounting for nearly half of the economy.[8]

The Business Roundtable quickly developed into a formidable group, designed to mobilize high-level CEOs as a collective force to lobby for the advancement of shared interests. President Ford's deputy treasury secre-tary Charls Walker, a leading corporate organizer about whom we'll say more in a moment, later put it this way: "The Roundtable has made a lot of difference. They know how to get the CEOs into Washington and lobby; they maintain good relationships with the congressional staffs; they've just learned a lot about Washington they didn't know before."[9]

Keeping Up With the Naders

The role of the business community not only grew but expanded, shift-ing into new modes of organization that had previously been confined to its critics. Recognizing that lawmaking in Washington had become more open and dynamic, business groups remade themselves to fit the times. The expanding network of business groups would soon be ca-pable of hoisting the public interest groups on their own petards. Using rapidly emerging tools of marketing and communications, they learned how to generate mass campaigns. Building networks of employees, share-holders, local companies, and firms with shared interests (for example, retailers and suppliers), they could soon flood Washington with letters and phone calls. Within a few years, these classically top-down organizations were to thrive at generating "bottom up"–style campaigns that not only matched the efforts of their rivals but surpassed them.

These emerging "outside" strategies were married to "inside" ones. Business organizations developed lists of prominent executives capable of making personal contacts with key legislative figures. In private meetings organized by the Conference Board, CEOs compared notes and discussed how to learn from and outmaneuver organized labor. In the words of one executive, "If you don't know your senators on a first-name basis, you are not doing an adequate job for your stockholders."[10]

Business also massively increased its political giving—at precisely the time when the cost of campaigns began to skyrocket (in part because of the ascendance of television). The insatiable need for cash gave politicians good reason to be attentive to those with deep pockets. Business had by far the deepest pockets, and was happy to make contributions to members of both parties. Clifton Garvin, chairman of both Exxon and the Business Roundtable in the early 1980s, summarized the attitude toward partisanship this way: "The Roundtable tries to work with whichever political party is in power. We may each individually have our own political alliances, but as a group the Roundtable works with every administration to the degree they let us."[11]

The newly mobilized business groups understood that Democrats and Republicans could play distinct but complementary roles. As the party with a seemingly permanent lock on Congress, Democrats needed to be pried away from their traditional alliance with organized labor. Money was key here: From the late 1970s to the late 1980s, corporate PACs increased their expenditures in congressional races nearly fivefold. Labor PAC spending only rose about half as fast. In the early 1970s, business PACs contributed less to congressional races overall than labor PACs did. By the mid-1970s, the two were at rough parity, and by the end of the decade, business PACs were way ahead. By 1980, unions accounted for less than a quarter of all PAC contributions—down from half six years earlier. The shift was largest among Democrats, who were of course the most reliant on labor money: Nearly half of Senate incumbents' campaign funds came from labor PACs in the mid-1970s. A decade later, the share was below one-fifth.[12]

By this time, however, business PACs were shifting away from their traditional focus on buttering up (mostly Democratic) incumbents toward a strategy that mixed donations to those in power with support for conservative political challengers. Such a pattern was evident in the critical election year of 1978. Through September of the election season, nearly half of corporate campaign contributions flowed into Democrats' coffers. In the crucial weeks before the 1978 election, however, only 29 percent did. By the end of the 1978 campaign, more than 60 percent of corporate contributions had gone to Republicans, both GOP challengers and Republican incumbents fighting off liberal Democrats.[13] A new era of campaign finance was born: Not only were corporate contributions growing ever bigger, Democrats had to work harder for them. More and more, to receive business largesse, they had to do more than hold power; they had to wield it in ways that business liked.

PACs were, of course, not the only means by which business leaders gave to politicians. They also contributed individually—which, thanks to a practice known as bundling, often meant coordinated donations by large numbers of a firm's executives. Another form of coordination was the formation and strengthening of business organizations devoted to directing PAC contributions to targeted races, such as the Business-Industry Political Action Committee (founded in 1963 but greatly expanded in the 1970s) and the National Association of Business Political Action Committees (founded in 1977).[14]

Employers and wealthy families also poured vast new resources into efforts designed not just to fund candidates or lobby on particular bills but also to shape the broader political climate. Especially prominent in this effort were wealthy conservative activists, such as the beer magnate Joseph Coors, metal and ammunitions industrialist John Olin, and newspaper publisher Richard Scaife. Staunch economic conservatives, they were fiercely critical of the basic contours of the post–World War II domestic settlement between labor and industry—and willing to put their money where their ideology was.

Establishment figures, like financier and former Ford treasury secretary William Simon, played a central role as well. Simon, who moved from Treasury to head the influential and deeply conservative Olin Foundation, was convinced that conservatives were losing the war of ideas. To win, they needed to nurture a generation of conservative idea merchants. And to do *that* they needed to build idea factories, rapidly and on a massive scale.

Simon and allies like Irving Kristol (father of current conservative idea merchant William Kristol) worked with corporations and wealthy conservative families to build an industry of new foundations and think tanks. Some, like the American Enterprise Institute (AEI), sought to create a mirror image of traditional policy shops like the mildly liberal Brookings Institution. Others, however, were built to contrast with an organizational model they saw as naive and old-fashioned. Brookings strove to provide what it considered "objective" policy advice—the best expert thinking on a particular subject. New outfits like the Heritage Foundation explicitly saw their mission as shifting public opinion and policy in a conservative direction, to persuade rather than investigate. They sought to set the political agenda, to provide argumentative weaponry for the conservative cause, and to train and house reliable policy specialists who could staff business-friendly administrations.

Over the course of the 1970s, this project was enormously successful. The AEI, which had one-tenth the budget of Brookings in 1970, was roughly the same size by 1980. The Heritage Foundation was born in 1973. Backed by money from beer magnate Joseph Coors and the Sarah Mellon Scaife Foundation, it equaled the size of AEI and Brookings by the early 1980s. Arguably, the reach of an outfit like Heritage was far greater, for it devoted far more energy than its traditional counterparts to proselytizing. Brookings spent less than one-twentieth of its budget on public relations and outreach; Heritage, around a fifth.

And that spending was unabashedly directed at pushing conservative ideas into the mainstream and, specifically, into the hands of the GOP. Brookings' mission statement reads like a university brochure ("an independent, nonpartisan organization devoted to research and public education"); the Heritage Foundation's, a manifesto ("a think tank . . . whose mission is to formulate and promote conservative public policies based on the principles of free enterprise, limited government, individual freedom, traditional American values, and a strong national defense"). The Heritage Foundation is, like Brookings, officially nonpartisan. But, unlike Brookings, its creators saw their goal as supporting the activities of a particular party, the GOP. "We realized that we not only needed a Republican Study Committee on the inside [of Congress] to help the congressman with internal staff," one of its founders later recounted, "but we needed something on the outside to promote ideas and do the longer-term research, but still research that is policy relevant. Hence Heritage."[15]

Walker, Texas Lobbyist

No one personified the organizational revolution better than Charls Walker, the former deputy treasury secretary we met earlier. A crusty, cigar-smoking, deal-making Texan—with a PhD in economics—Walker built a group to advocate business tax cuts that put together all the pieces: the coordination of many companies toward shared goals, the emphasis on being proactive and shaping public discourse and the political agenda, the spearheading of grassroots campaigns, and the careful cultivation of important figures in both political parties. The new name of Walker's organization, the American Council for Capital Formation, was an artful rechristening of the "American Council for Estate and Gift Taxation." The name change signified the focus of Walker's efforts: to sell the proposition that what was good for America's richest corporations and individuals was good for America.

By 1975, when his group was formed, Walker had had ample opportunity to ponder the declining political fortunes of business. He had moved from his post as executive head—essentially chief lobbyist—of the American Bankers Association to positions in the Treasury under Nixon and Ford. There Walker had a front-row seat as business lost the legislative battles of the early 1970s. He participated in the conversations that led up to the formation of the Business Roundtable. When he returned to lobbying, he turned the American Council for Capital Formation into an umbrella group to advocate for reduced taxes on businesses, especially large, capital-intensive ones.

Walker's strategy exemplified the new capacity of business to launch multi-faceted campaigns in Washington, and to work not only to block unwanted changes but also to achieve wanted reforms. He built a *coalition*—not seeking specific breaks for a single company but bringing together a large number of firms (over three hundred by the early 1980s) behind a common agenda. He signed up a team of impressive conservative economists (including three who would later be heads of the Council of Economic Advisers in Republican administrations) to help make the case that what he advocated was in the public interest. He put boots on the ground to demonstrate constituency support. As the journalist John Judis writes, "Walker pioneered the tactic of getting local company officials, armed with local job loss and gain figures, to meet directly with their House or Senate member."[16] And, along with all this, he cultivated individual contacts in both parties that would prove critical in closed-door deliberations. Democratic lions like Clark Clifford and Edward Bennett Williams sat on his board. He had the ear of the powerful Democratic chair of the Senate Finance Committee, Louisiana's Russell Long.

All over Washington, the formidable new capacities that characterized Charls Walker's organization were being replicated, and bridges connecting these organizations were being constructed. In a remarkably short time, Lewis Powell's urgent plea for a savvier, proactive, well-funded—in short, *organized*—business presence had been answered. On every significant economic matter that came to the public agenda, business was now prepared.

The timing, however, seemed inauspicious. In January 1977, business was to face unified Democratic control of Washington for the first time in a decade. Congress's crowded docket included major items like establishing a consumer protection agency, labor law reform, and taxes, where only the threat of a presidential veto had stymied the liberal agenda. Walker, for one, was not intimidated. "There's a fiction around," he said, "that you can't do anything with Congress, particularly if it's a Democratic Congress. But that is not true. You can get things done over there if you know how to do it."[17] It was time to take the new organizational machine for a test-drive.

The Corporate Stamp on Carterland

When elections produce a swing of political power in Washington, there are usually several items that have languished for years but are ready for rapid passage. The new President Clinton, for instance, quickly signed the Family and Medical Leave Act, which had been blocked by Republican vetoes. Similarly, Congress was able to race popular bills expanding children's health insurance and strengthening protections for gender equity in pay to Barack Obama's desk within days of his inauguration.

When Jimmy Carter's election gave Democrats unified control of Washington, the first action item was a bill to establish a new Office of Consumer Representation. The agency would have consolidated consumer issues in a single place and given consumers an organized advocate in rule-making activities throughout the federal bureaucracy. For Ralph Nader and his public interest allies, it would represent the culmination of their remarkable success in expanding federal regulatory protections for citizens whose interests had failed to find organized representation in Washington before the late 1960s. There was every reason for confidence: Polls showed that voters backed the idea of such an agency 2–1. The Senate had already passed versions of the bill in 1970 and 1975, and the House had done so in 1971, 1974, and 1975. Gerald Ford's veto had been the only thing standing between Nader and the birth of the new agency, and now Ford was gone.

This time, however, the new apparatus of business organizations was prepared. The Business Roundtable helped assemble a huge coalition of other leading umbrella organizations (such as the Chamber of Commerce) as well as hundreds of firms. Together, these groups launched a diversified attack—one that House Speaker Tip O'Neill would describe as the most intense he had seen in twenty-five years.[18] Business organizations worked on public opinion—orchestrating a campaign of op-ed pieces and magazine articles designed to frame the proposed $15 million agency as a massive expansion of government authority. The coalition unveiled its new capacity for grassroots mobilization, flooding Congress with calls, letters, and visits from influential constituents. Finally, it targeted moderate Democrats elected in 1974 and 1976—many of them representing suburban districts that had traditionally been Republican.

These efforts turned an anticipated easy victory for consumer advocates into an unexpected rout. The bill barely emerged unscathed from committee, and stalled in the House. Compromises designed to water down the legislation in return for broadened support had little effect. When, after much delay, the bill finally came up for a vote in February 1978, it went down in a stunning defeat, 189–227. Fully three-fifths of the new class of Democrats in the House voted against the proposal. Swing voters in Congress deserted reformers, adopting what might be called the "Scarlett O'Hara defense": *oh, yes* they supported reform, but *this* specific bill had too many problems. They would think about it tomorrow. Of course, tomorrow would never come. Over the next few decades, the Scarlett O'Hara defense would become part of the standard repertoire of obstruction, a rhetorical cornerstone of the politics of drift.

Labor Rules No Longer

Far more devastating and consequential in the long run was the fate of industrial relations reform. Like Nader's Raiders, organized labor felt emboldened by the new electoral math. Seeing a rare opportunity, it made an all-out push to enlist government support in its struggle to reverse its slowly but steadily declining place in the American economy. As we saw in chapter 2, U.S. laws governing industrial relations were becoming dramatically less effective in supporting union organization due to two linked challenges faced by organized labor. The first was a rise in capital mobility, which enhanced the capacity of businesses to use the famous 14(b) provision of the Taft-Hartley Act to shift their operations to right-to-work states, where unions were barred from making union membership a condition of employment in a firm or industry.

The second threat, as also discussed in chapter 2, was the rise of much more aggressive employer tactics to block union organizing. Between 1960 and 1980, there was a fourfold increase in charges of unfair labor practices, a threefold rise in charges of unlawful termination, and a fivefold increase in workers awarded back pay or granted reinstatement orders.[19] These stunning figures suggest that employers increasingly saw such practices as simply a cost of doing business, and far preferable to successful unionization. Moreover, the shift in climate was almost certainly greater than the massive rise in violations suggested, since they took place at a time when employers (backed by the new industry of union-avoidance consultants) were deploying increasingly sophisticated techniques to punish organizers without appearing to violate the law.

Labor began its efforts to regain lost ground by reintroducing the Common Situs Picketing Bill, which would have legalized common-site picketing for construction labor (picketing of an entire site over a grievance held against a single subcontractor). Since the bill had passed both chambers of Congress, only to be vetoed by Ford the previous year, labor expected an easy win that would set the stage for bigger initiatives. Instead, in March 1977, the bill went down to unexpected defeat in the House, 217–205. Business organizations effectively targeted freshmen representatives who were, in the words of a Chamber of Commerce official, "truly open-minded, not committed on the issue."[20] Tony Beilenson, a California Democrat, noted that he had received 248 pieces of mail opposing the bill, and only one in favor. Ultimately freshmen voted 68–37 against the legislation, including seven northern Democrats and thirteen freshmen who had been supported in their 1976 campaigns by the main labor PAC, the AFL-CIO's Committee on Political Education.[21]

The setback forced labor and its allies to reassess their ambitions.

Common Situs had been regarded as just a mood-setter. The unions' true goal was a labor law reform bill designed to facilitate organizing practices and deter some of the aggressive antiunion strategies deployed by management. Labor had originally sought its Holy Grail—repeal of the 14(b) provision of the Taft-Hartley Act. But the debacle over the Common Situs Picketing Bill led union leaders to trim their sails. As their strong ally Tip O'Neill said: "I have no intention of scheduling 14(b). It's an old rule of politics that you should not field the team unless you can win."[22]

Labor still pinned its hopes on the first major revision of industrial relations law since passage of the Landrum-Griffin Act of 1959. The bill's target was the increasingly aggressive tactics of firms like textile manufacturer JP Stevens. Unions were convinced that the modest and long-delayed penalties typically imposed by the National Labor Relations Board encouraged companies to employ any means to hold off organizing efforts. Defying the law was far cheaper than risking any prospect of unionization. The reform bill would have streamlined and accelerated NLRB decision-making and increased penalties for violators. As both labor and its opponents recognized, the stakes were far higher than the particulars of the bill itself. The fate of labor law reform would reveal the true balance of political power. Passage would represent union triumph in an intense battle of wills, and watchful political observers would absorb the lesson for future conflicts.

Chastened by the earlier defeat, labor redoubled its efforts. AFL-CIO head George Meany announced: "We are going to fight harder for this bill than any bill since the passage of the Wagner Act."[23] In the short run, the efforts paid off. In October 1977, the legislation passed the House by a strong vote of 257–163.

With the Senate housing sixty-one Democrats and many sympathetic Republicans as well, an opponent later said there "didn't seem to be any way to stop it."[24] The bill's adversaries, however, received a critical boost from the Business Roundtable. Many capital-intensive or already unionized companies advocated neutrality, but the Roundtable voted 19–11 to join the Chamber of Commerce, National Association of Manufacturers, and an army of small businesses in opposition. Where previously busi-

ness had been on the defensive, the time now seemed ripe for confrontation. Robert T. Thompson, chairman of the labor relations committee of
the Chamber of Commerce, observed that the result was that "business
is more unified in [seeking] outright defeat of this bill than in any other
labor issue I've observed over the past 25 years."[25]

In the late spring of 1978, an epic showdown took place in the Senate
chambers. Ironically, all three of the main legislative actors would still be
in the Senate thirty years later, when the full ramifications of the long, dramatic shift in the American political economy were to hit with full force.
The Democratic majority leader was Robert Byrd. At President Carter's
behest, he had squandered labor law reform's momentum by dedicat-
ing the winter and early spring to the long fight over the Panama Canal
Treaty. Nonetheless, Byrd was eager to show the priority the Democratic
leadership placed on industrial relations reform. He chose not to use the
"two-track" system under which part of the Senate's day is allotted to a
filibustered bill and parts to other bills. All other legislative activity was
to stop while senators wrangled over the future of American industrial
relations.

The opposition was led by two youthful Republican senators who
personified the newly aggressive conservative wing of the party, Utah's
Orrin Hatch and Indiana's Richard Lugar. (Revealingly, neither would be
considered particularly conservative within the Senate Republican caucus a generation later.) They decried the bill as a power grab by big labor.
Hatch insisted that the bill "makes it mandatory that businesses organize,
or they will be clubbed to death."[26] Today, we have become accustomed
to "pocket" filibusters, which require nothing more of obstructionists
than an unwillingness to vote to end debate. Hatch and Lugar's stall on
the labor law reform bill looked more like Jimmy Stewart's in *Mr. Smith
Goes to Washington.* The two junior senators organized their supporters into three teams, which took turns leading the filibuster. Day after
day, while legislative activity stayed frozen, they offered amendment after
amendment—eventually totaling roughly one thousand in all.

The fight on the Senate floor was to last almost five weeks. After three,
Byrd made two attempts at cloture, which failed badly. Consultations

with organized labor led to a decision by the bill's sponsors (New Jersey Democrat Harrison Williams and New York Republican Jacob Javits) to accept a series of compromise amendments. Most of these were aimed at restricting the bill's potential application to small firms, a move that reflected the prominent role of small businesses in the intense mobilization against reform. The compromises succeeded in winning over a number of Republicans (including Ted Stevens of Alaska), but not enough. In three cloture votes in mid-June the bill reached its high-water mark of support, 58–41—two votes short. On June 22, after a sixth failure, Byrd surrendered. The Senate voted to recommit the bill to the Committee on Human Resources. It would never return.

A remarkably unified and organized business coalition had won a stunning victory. Outspending labor 3–1, it had flooded Congress with eight million pieces of mail and filled the halls with angry small-business owners from every state and district. "It's a different type of lobbying," reported one aide to an uncommitted senator. "I'm seeing people on this bill that I wouldn't ordinarily see." An aide to Florida Democrat Lawton Chiles agreed: "I can't remember when we last experienced a lobbying effort like this. It is so well-structured, so well-organized, and I don't think they missed a single possible opponent of that bill in our state."[27]

Picking through the rubble of defeat, the longtime United Auto Workers leader Douglas Fraser had had enough. Fraser was serving on President Carter's Labor-Management Group. Led by Harvard economics professor John Dunlop, a longtime advocate of union-business cooperation, the Labor-Management Group was intended to foster an improved industrial relations climate. In the eyes of union leaders, it was now revealed as nothing more than a talking shop. Three weeks after the death of the labor law reform bill, Fraser penned his resignation letter.

I believe leaders of the business community, with few exceptions, have chosen to wage a one-sided class war... against working people... and even many in the middle class of our society. The leaders of industry, commerce and finance in the United States have broken and discarded the fragile, unwritten compact previously existing during a past period of growth and progress... The latest breakdown in our relationship is also perhaps the most serious. The fight waged by the business community against that Labor Law Reform bill stands as the most vicious, unfair attack upon the labor movement in more than 30 years... It became an extremely moderate, fair piece of legislation that only corporate outlaws would have had need to fear... At virtually every level, I discern a demand by business for docile government and unrestrained corporate individualism. Where industry once yearned for subservient unions, it now wants no unions at all... Our tax laws are a scandal, yet corporate America wants even wider inequities... The wealthy seek not to close loopholes, but to widen them by advocating the capital gains tax rollback that will bring them a huge bonanza... For all these reasons, I have concluded there is no point to continue sitting down at Labor-Management Group meetings and philosophizing about the future of the country and the world... I cannot sit there seeking unity with the leaders of American industry, while they try to destroy us and ruin the lives of the people I represent.[28]

Fraser understood the full import of what had just transpired. Labor was on its own.[29] If the unions couldn't win with Democratic control of Congress and Democrat Jimmy Carter in the White House, they couldn't win at all. Businesses would have a freer hand in the workplace, knowing that they would face no backlash in Washington. Legislators in marginal districts took note too; they would need to reassess whether they were making the right friends.

The impact of that reassessment was not long in coming.

Capital's Capitol

Jimmy Carter had been in office for little more than a year, and already most of his domestic agenda was in tatters. With everyone scrambling to adjust to the new realities, business was ready to go on the offensive. The prime target was Carter's tax initiative. Carter had campaigned on tax reform, calling the current code "a disgrace to the human race." His initial proposals were a combination of standard Democratic calls for more progressivity (a hike in the capital gains tax; the elimination of some high-end deductions like the "three-martini lunch") and a reformist dose of greater simplicity.

By the time administration officials were ready to present a plan to Congress in January 1978, they had already scaled back their ambitions. The bill was far less progressive than had been anticipated; while it still included a hike in capital gains taxes, the change was modest and was tempered by various carrots for industry. Charls Walker and his allies were pleasantly surprised. In the account of a Washington insider: "They were braced for an attack; when the attack never came, they decided to invade!"[30]

Walker understood the change in mood: "The consensus is cohering on a different basis than the consensus Lyndon Johnson had. There's a crossover of party lines, an ignoring of party lines. The American people deep down understand about capital."[31] Walker was correct that popular disgust with taxes and government was on the rise, crystallizing in revolts against rising property taxes in a number of states amid the difficult economy of the late 1970s. But, as two of the leading experts on the tax revolts observed in 1982, after carefully reviewing years of opinion data, "there was little evidence as President Reagan took office that the public's preferences concerning the government's activities in the economic and social domains had substantially changed."[32] Certainly, there was no widespread shift in public views that could explain why increased concern among homeowners whose property values had climbed, or middle-class Americans thrust into higher tax brackets due to inflation, was translated into a frenzy of tax-cutting for corporations and the wealthy.

More powerful than any shift in the public mood was a shift in who was driving the legislative train. Quickly realizing that the perfect vehicle was now moving through an increasingly cooperative Congress, Walker's coalition, and a more select group that came to be called the Carlton Group (after its regular meeting locale in the Ritz-Carlton), seized the wheel. Working with sympathetic members in both parties and both chambers of Congress, they successfully placed an amendment in the House bill that *cut the capital gains tax rate in half.* Only modest compromise was needed with the Senate. Before the year was out, a Democratic Congress overwhelmingly passed, and a Democratic president signed, a tax bill whose centerpiece was a reduction of the top rate of capital gains taxes from 48 percent to 28 percent.

As much as the outcome of labor law reform, the 1978 tax bill signaled a dramatic shift in governance in Washington. Three years later, Walker and his allies were to duplicate their victory on a much larger scale. Reagan's election, of course, galvanized the possibility for dramatic change in taxes, but the Carlton Group literally wrote many of the key provisions influencing business in the new president's proposals.[33] By then, Democrats in Congress were desperate to show some love to the business community. In a revealing development, the tax debate rapidly degenerated into a frenzied bidding war as both parties attempted to shower the most tax cuts on business. As Reagan's budget director David Stockman summarized the situation, "the hogs were really feeding."[34] Reagan ultimately won, wooing conservative Democrats (including soon-to-be-Republican ones like Phil Gramm) to his side.

By historical standards, the 1981 Economic Recovery and Tax Act (ERTA) was an astonishing acceleration of the 1978 formula of big tax cuts for business and the affluent. Extremely generous new depreciation rules and a vast expansion of tax loopholes sharply reduced overall taxes on corporations. Top income tax rates came down sharply, as did the capital gains tax (again). The top rate of taxation on the estate tax was cut from 70 percent to 50 percent, and the level of the individual exemption was raised substantially.

ERTA was Ronald Reagan's greatest legislative triumph, a fundamental rewriting of the nation's tax laws in favor of winner-take-all outcomes. But in a deeper sense it was the nature of the conflict that had changed the most. *Both* parties were now locked in a determined struggle to show who could shower more benefits on those at the top.

On Top of the World

In 1899, Congress passed the Height of Buildings Act, prohibiting any new building from exceeding the height of the U.S. Capitol. This makes it a little difficult for even the greatest power broker to gain the kind of perspective Edmund Hillary and Tenzing Norgay had on Everest that day in May of 1953. But imagine if you could take to the top of the Capitol one of the trailblazers who envisioned a world where business could not only speak with a loud, clear voice in Washington but have its message of free markets and lower taxes heard—Lewis Powell, or William Simon, or Charls Walker, or Irving Kristol, or a dozen others. Like Hillary and Norgay, they would see below them the clear signs of a formidable organizational triumph.

Stretching out before their eyes would be their own regularly spaced base camps—the stepping-stones to their new position atop the political world. From the lowest level, where private communications among business leaders had fostered a new collective strategy, to the highest level, where new teams of industry lobbyists plied the corridors of power, a once-improbable path to influence had been charted. At every step, organizational innovations marked the tracks of progress, tracing the rapid rightward movement of economic debates. It was a map that organized business interests would turn to again and again in the coming years, as the winner-take-all economy continued to intensify.

From their perch atop the great white dome of the nation's legislative body, the pioneers of the transformed world would also notice something else. Their competitors in the race to the summit were struggling. The trailblazers in business's organizational revolution had bested the consumer, labor, and environmental advocates who had galvanized them into action in the early 1970s. Some of these antagonists would return to wage a vigorous fight again. Others would not so easily spring back. Corporate America's most enduring competitor, organized labor, was left gasping for air far beneath the peak of power, leaving the route to unchallenged influence much clearer. And it was not just organized labor that had fallen behind. A whole host of organizations that had provided political leverage to working- and middle-class citizens, allowing them to make their own assaults on the heights of influence, were losing the clout that they had once enjoyed. The story of their downward transit—a much less triumphant journey—is our next subject.

Chapter 6

The Middle Goes Missing

A Democrat was in the White House. Democrats had control of both houses of Congress. But the president was hesitant to push for major economic reforms that would strain his mandate. The economy was delicate, the national debt large, right-wing opposition to his agenda strong. He also had conservatives to contend with in his own party. In the end, the president did not retreat—the challenges were far too great for that—but he trimmed his sails and sought reforms that fell well short of his and his party's grand ambitions.

It sounds like the story of Carterland told in the last chapter (or, to fast forward to the next Democrat in the White House, of President Clinton's first term). But, in fact, these words describe how FDR, the lion of liberalism, approached the thorny problem of managing the expected return of tens of millions of soldiers after World War II—a return that many worried would plunge the nation back into depression. This was no idle worry: A stunning 80 percent of American men born in the 1920s were or would be military veterans, and few believed the once-fragile labor market could handle the fifteen million returning veterans and ten million war-industry workers who would need new jobs if and when the war came to a close.[1]

And yet, despite the immensity of the challenge, the president's seemingly strong political position, and his demonstrated progressive commitments, FDR backed an anemic agenda for integrating veterans into the postwar economy. The president forwarded to Congress a plan for short-term educational support coupled with the prospect of continuing education for a relatively small number of soldiers who, in the words of a Roosevelt administration committee set up to formulate the plan, showed "unusual promise and ability."[2] Needless to say, this was not a new New Deal.

What happened next, however, will come as a shock to those used to seeing Democratic presidential initiatives get whittled down in Democratic congresses. A broad grassroots movement led by the American Legion (a veterans' organization with three million members in the mid-1940s) demanded that returning soldiers receive a broad range of generous social benefits, including up to four years of taxpayer-funded college or vocational education.

To achieve this bold goal, the Legion harnessed its vast nationwide structure, with local posts throughout the country, to rally Americans to the cause. Mailings, petition drives, entreaties to local journalists, even a motion picture clip promoting the bill—all fostered a broad public movement that members of Congress could not ignore. Within months, the Senate had approved the generous GI Bill backed by the Legion. In the House, southern conservatives managed to hold up the bill, which they feared would provide African Americans with new rights and benefits. But the Legion flexed its grassroots muscle again, harnessing its vast voluntary network to round up the last votes. In one case, quite literally: A local Legionnaire found a pivotal congressman who was ill at home in Georgia and drove him to the airport to catch a plane to Washington—where, not long thereafter, President Roosevelt made the GI Bill the law of the land in June of 1944.

The origins of the GI Bill illuminate a hopeful side of the politics of organized combat. We have seen in the past few chapters how the organized can, and frequently do, run roughshod over the disorganized. Organization often stands as an impediment to democracy—a source of disproportionate power for the wealthy and resourceful few that severely limits the sway of ordinary voters in politics.

And yet, as the American Legion's shepherding of the GI Bill through Congress suggests, organization is not always an impediment to voters.

On the contrary, it can serve as an essential conduit for effective citizen action. The capacities we have described—the ability to pool and concentrate resources, develop expertise, and sustain focus—are critical preconditions for political influence. When these capacities are exercised on behalf of the deep concerns of large numbers of ordinary citizens, they represent a fundamental component of a thriving democracy.

But there is nothing automatic about such amplification of ordinary citizens' voices—and, unfortunately, it has became increasingly rare on economic matters. The last chapter described one dramatic shift in the American political landscape: the mobilization of corporations to tilt the battleground of organized combat in their favor. This chapter looks at the other side of the landscape: the decline of the mid-century political world that we call "middle-class democracy." Behind the declining responsiveness of Washington to those outside the winner's circle is a complex tale of battered unions, distracted public interest groups, politically ascendant evangelicals, unmoored voters, and a compromised, and increasingly endangered, news media. The conclusion of the tale, however, is simple: ordinary citizens have lost the cues and clout that made their voices so loud amid the civic universe that reigned when the GI Bill passed.

Labor's Fall

No group better captures the mid-century influence of voluntary organizations representing middle- and working-class Americans than organized labor. The historically conservative American Legion may have been an unlikely ally of social reform. American labor was certainly not. Unions were on the front lines of every major economic battle of the mid-century—from the successful struggle for an expanded Social Security program in the 1950s to the passage of Medicare in 1965. Labor leaders even lent critical support to the civil rights movement, leading one congressional champion to observe that "we would never have passed the Civil Rights Act without labor. They had the muscle; the other civil rights groups did not."[3]

That "muscle" was yet another legacy of the New Deal. Aided by the 1935 Wagner Act, unions rapidly expanded in the tight labor market of World War II. By the mid-1950s, more than a third of private-sector workers were unionized. Historically fractious, unions created nation- and industry-spanning organizations like the AFL-CIO (founded through the merger of the American Federation of Labor and the Congress of Industrial Organizations in 1955) to press a pro-labor agenda in Washington. "The future of labor," declared John Lewis, head of the CIO from 1935 to 1940, "is the future of America."[4]

America's leaders apparently agreed. Shortly after World War II, a popular president stated that "unions have a secure place in our industrial life. Only a handful of reactionaries harbor the ugly thought of breaking unions and depriving working men and women of the right to join the union of their choice."[5] That president was Republican Dwight Eisenhower—and his affirmation was a sign that a labor movement increasingly aligned with the Democratic Party had plenty of clout among Republicans as well. In 1954, for instance, Eisenhower chose to expand Social Security despite fierce attacks on the program from business groups and conservative Republicans.[6] He did so in part because of the strong campaign waged by organized labor. At hearings on the expansion, AFL chief George Meany declared that in supporting a broader Social Security program, his union stood for "every person in America who works for a living."[7]

Meany's words were part rhetorical flourish, of course. But unions at the height of their power did indeed do more than simply bargain for a better deal for unionized workers. Nonunionized employers also felt heavy pressure to match union benefits and salaries—not least as a way of heading off labor drives.[8] Even more important, organized labor brought workers into sustained engagement with politics, often for the first time. Unions helped members identify common issues of concern, informed those members about politics and policy, and pressed those members' demands in political debates. And they also reached out to citizens outside the movement, sponsoring radio and television advertisements, launching voter registration drives, and involving union households in canvassing and mobilization within their communities.

By far the most visible effects could be seen as Election Day approached. Between 1936 and 1968, the combined political contributions of unions increased from less than $2 million to more than $7 million (after adjusting for inflation).[9] Most of this money, of course, went to Democrats—who were heavily reliant on labor contributions to finance their campaigns. But labor's biggest contribution to elections was not in dollars but in volunteers and voters. Union members engaged in voter mobilization on a scale previously unknown in national politics. In the razor-tight presidential contest of 1960, union members distributed ten million leaflets on congressional voting records and five million circulars comparing Kennedy's and Nixon's record on labor issues. As one clearly awed political scientist wrote in 1963, "The most fundamental postwar change in the structure and process of political parties has been the entrance of organized labor into electoral activity at the precinct level and on up."[10]

At the time, labor's influence was only expected to grow. As late as 1970, two distinguished students of American industrial relations, Derek Bok and John Dunlop (who would later work for both Nixon and Ford before heading Carter's ill-fated Labor-Management Committee), were confidently predicting that union voting drives would transform the American electorate.[11] Channeling the conventional wisdom of the day, Bok and Dunlop argued that unions—by bolstering the share of Americans who went to the polls—were destined to continue bringing less affluent Americans into the electoral fold. "The effect need not be to give the Democratic Party a perpetual majority, even though the bulk of nonvoters seem normally disposed toward the Democrats at the present time," they reflected. "Instead, the more likely result will be to shift both parties to the left toward a new equilibrium more responsive to the economic and social needs of less affluent segments of the population."[12]

A new equilibrium did indeed emerge, and unions helped bring it about. But as we have seen, that equilibrium was one more responsive to the economic and social needs of *more* affluent segments of the population, and the way unions brought it about was by losing ground in the face of an unprecedented mobilization of business. We have already told the story of labor's decline. We will only emphasize here one crucial element of it, documented in chapter 2: The precipitous fall in union membership occurred even though workers continued to voice strong—and, after 1984, increasing—public support for unions and their goals. Working Americans lost an important form of representation even as a rising share said they wanted it.

Declining union representation in the workforce directly increased inequality, as chapter 2 discussed. Yet the biggest way in which the decline of unions bolstered the winner-take-all economy had to do with labor's role in American politics. As unions shifted from confident involvement in politics to embattled defense of their ever-smaller pocket of the workforce, they also ceased to be able, or always willing, to play the role as champions of the broad middle class they had carved out in their heyday. Desperate to regain its membership, often torn by internal factions, and increasingly focused on the one place it continued to have strong success—the public sector—the labor movement came to look more and more like just another interest group, and an embattled interest group at that.

Unions had wielded power, after all, not just because they could spend on elections and lobbying, but because they had the ability to bring people out—out to the polls, out to the streets, out in their communities. Political scientists have long debated why voter turnout declined in the 1970s and 1980s, even as educational achievement—one of the strongest predictors of voting—rose. A key answer, it appears, is the decline of unions.[13] Fewer union members meant fewer union voters motivated to get to the polls and vote for candidates favorable to organized labor. More important, it also meant fewer get-out-the-vote drives, fewer voter education pamphlets, fewer pro-union advertisements, and fewer unionized workers in communities talking with friends, family, and neighbors about how they might vote. When membership was high, it served as something of a positive contagion, engaging union households *and* nonunion households in politics. As it declined, the contagion receded, reducing engagement more broadly.

To be sure, organized labor still had a strong grassroots presence compared with many groups. Nor did unions suddenly lack resources to deploy in campaigns and national policy debates. But, increasingly, organized labor was severely outgunned. In many economic debates, it was the major interest group representing the poor and the middle class, and often the only one with real clout.[14] In most of these debates, however, unions faced fierce enemy fire from a powerful array of corporate and trade groups. And they faced it with their own ammunition badly depleted. Middle- and working-class Americans lost a powerful, vigorous champion on pocketbook issues.

From Membership to Management

Organized labor was not the only mass membership organization to lose ground in the 1970s and beyond. Another victim of the organizational transformation of these decades was the association that pressed for the GI Bill, the American Legion—which lost more than 40 percent of its membership between 1955 and 1995. Even harder hit have been fraternal organizations, such as the Elks, Masons, and Eagles, and their female partner organizations. The membership rolls of all these groups have plummeted—by more than 60 percent in raw numbers and by nearly three-quarters as a share of the population.[15]

It is easy to dismiss old-line membership groups as men with funny hats, or women meeting for society lunches, forgetting how crucial they once were in America's voluntarist civic culture. As the political scientist Theda Skocpol observes in a landmark study, *Diminished Democracy: From Membership to Management in American Civic Life*, membership federations "complemented and rivaled political parties in setting the course of politics and government."[16] These organizations were a central feature of the dense web of civic connections and extensive bonds of trust and reciprocity that Robert Putnam has called "social capital."[17] And what was perhaps most remarkable about this social capital was that its distribution was so distinct from the more traditional form of capital, namely, money. Middle- and working-class Americans without much to spend to influence politics were deeply involved in American civic life in a way that they had not been in previous generations—or would be in subsequent ones.

Indeed, when the political scientists Gabriel Almond and Sidney Verba launched the first detailed survey of civic activities across nations around 1960, the foundation for their pioneering 1963 book *The Civic Culture*, they found that Americans were unusually engaged in and proud of their nation's political system.[18] And, perhaps most striking of all given present public cynicism, they also found that Americans were unusually confident they could shape local and national public affairs for the better.

Almond and Verba did not know it, but they were writing at the end of an era. Most of the newest groups on the American political landscape are very different from the American Legion or American labor. They are professional advocacy groups with mailing-list members, or no members at all. Some are "Astroturf" organizations, purporting to be broad-based but in actuality run by industry lobbyists. There is, for example, the curious case of the Alliance for Worker Retirement Security—a populist-sounding title for a front organization of the National Association of Manufacturers set up to push for the privatization of Social Security. Faux-grassroots groups have proliferated since the 1980s, and they have become much more sophisticated (in the old days, some would have a post office box as their mailing address). The American Petroleum Institute (API) joined forces with a number of conservative and industry associations to form Energy Citizens, which curiously lacked many citizens—though this did not stop the group from organizing API members to attend "citizen" rallies in key congressional districts.[19]

Other groups on the new political landscape are neither true grass nor Astroturf. They may have memberships in the hundreds of thousands. But the participation of these largely upper-middle-class members is more or less limited to writing a check in response to expertly designed solicitations from headquarters. The environmental movement stands out as the most successful example of this model. New and nimble environmental groups adept at attracting members through the mail burst onto the scene in the 1970s. Meanwhile, old-line groups like the Sierra Club and the National Audubon Society greatly expanded their membership in the years after 1970—though they have never come close to the size of old-line membership groups, and rely largely on centralized recruitment rather than bottom-up engagement through local chapters.

The vast majority of new advocacy organizations of the last generation, however, have no members at all. They are Washington-based, wholly professionalized, and funded not by dues-paying members but by nonprofit foundations, large donors, and government grants. In the words of Marshall Ganz, a legendary organizer for progressive causes, these groups are "bodiless heads."[20] They have national offices, engage in legislative and administrative advocacy, but have few members propelling the "head" in one direction or another.

The Postmaterialist Moment

The expansion of advocacy groups is often taken as an unqualified boon for liberalism, and, indeed, most of these new advocacy groups are on the left of the political spectrum. To take one prominent example, the group EMILY's List—a national political action committee with no state or local chapters that supports women candidates for elective office—has become one of the single largest sources of financial support for Democratic candidates, filling some of the gap left by the declining fortunes of organized labor. (EMILY stands for "Early Money Is Like Yeast," a playful reference to the importance of initial fund-raising for raising "dough.")

But, as the political scientist Jeffrey Berry has convincingly argued, the liberal groups that burst onto the scene in the 1970s and 1980s are best understood as elements of a "new liberalism," one that is quite distinct from the traditional bread-and-butter focus of older groups on the left, such as organized labor.[21] Berry aptly casts the contrast as a shift from "materialism" to "postmaterialism," from the pocketbook concerns of middle- and working-class voters to the social concerns of more affluent ones. EMILY's List, for example, bills itself as "building a progressive America by electing pro-choice Democratic women," suggesting a fairly narrow definition of a progressive America.[22] The short mission statement on the group's Web site makes two references to supporting pro-choice candidates (including one in the first sentence) but no reference to any other policy.

As organized labor declined in clout, the growing bevy of advocacy groups formed a powerful new liberal force—for a certain kind of liberalism. These groups proved skilled lobbyists on the issues they cared about, such as environmentalism, women's rights, and civil liberties. And yet, they almost never focused their attention on the economic issues that most powerfully affected the working and middle classes. The result was a boon for the postmaterialist causes of more affluent liberals, but it left traditional material causes with only a handful of energetic backers. "As the new left grew and grew," Berry concludes, "the old left was increasingly isolated."[23]

Even where the potential for a strong focus on economic disadvantage seemed evident, as with advocacy groups advancing the concerns of minorities and women, D.C. organizations tended to give such matters surprisingly low priority. The authors of a recent comprehensive study of lobbying marvel at "the relative paucity of issues relating to the poor and to the economic security of working-class Americans" on the lobbying agenda of even public interest groups. They find that while lobbyists for the wealthiest "do not always win, corporate, professional, and trade interests have a distinct advantage in setting the lobbying agenda" and that "the inequities of social class are sharply exacerbated by the organizational bias of interest-group politics."[24] This is by no means a new feature of America's pluralist interest-group environment. The political scientist E. E. Schattschneider observed in 1960 that "the flaw in the pluralist heaven is that the heavenly choir sings with an upper-class accent"—but the "upper-class accent" has grown far more pronounced in the era of winner-take-all inequality.[25]

The Grass Roots Grow on the Right

There is one big exception to the trend away from grassroots organizations with a solid footing in the working and middle classes: Christian conservatism. Yet, ironically, it is an exception that has strongly reinforced the broader trends that we have charted so far.

Amid the rise of "bodiless head" advocacy organizations, Christian conservatism is a striking anomaly. Starting at the grassroots and expanding largely outside of political sight in the 1970s, organizations mobilizing white Christian conservatives tapped into the social networks surrounding churches and evangelical denominations.[26] These groups benefited from the ability to mobilize the transferable civic skills that church participation fostered, like community engagement and knowledge of public affairs—skills that, thanks to the decline of civic America, were not nearly as widespread among less religiously engaged voters of the same background. In doing so, they helped bring large numbers of moderate-income voters into politics as an organized force, making them one of the few successful examples of sustained grassroots mobilization of the era.

Like the public interest groups on the left, however, the Christian Right has engaged voters on nonmaterial grounds. Moral values issues like abortion and gay marriage are the focus. And this concentration on moral issues has had a paradoxical consequence: It has aligned a large bloc of evangelical voters whose incomes are generally modest with a political party highly attuned to the economic demands of the wealthy, that is, the Republican Party. It has done so, moreover, in an era in which, over the entire electorate, economic issues divide the parties more sharply along class lines than in the past, with Democrats favored by less affluent voters and Republicans by more affluent voters.

Yes, you heard right: Evangelicals notwithstanding, economic issues divide the parties more sharply along class lines than in the past. If you listen to political pundits—particularly those on the right—you would think the exact opposite. David Brooks, Tucker Carlson, and others have expended much ink and airtime arguing that American politics had realigned around social and consumer values, rather than material issues: a less affluent red America filled with NASCAR-loving, gun-toting GOP traditionalists who oppose gay marriage versus a richer blue America filled with sushi-loving, *New Yorker*–reading Democratic cosmopolitans who want abortion on demand. In this common view, Republicans are the party of the working Joe (or "Joe the Plumber," to cite the unemployed, unlicensed plumber whom John McCain held up as the nation's every-man during the 2008 campaign); Democrats are the party of affluent liberals ("Joe the Professional"?). "Rich people vote liberal," Carlson opined in 2007. "I don't know what that's all about."[27]

The problem with this common view, however, is that it is wrong. Class remains highly relevant at the ballot box—indeed, more so than in the past. Since the 1950s and 1960s, the partisan allegiances of Americans have grown markedly more polarized by income. Republicans now draw their support more consistently than in the past from the top of the income distribution, while Democrats draw their support more consistently from the bottom. The gap is large—voters in the top fifth of the income distribution were around twice as likely to identify with the Republican Party in 2000 as voters in the bottom fifth.[28] Remarkably, given the common perception that this is a nation allergic to class politics, the divide is in fact larger than the income gap in support for conservative parties found in most other nations for which we have good evidence.[29]

Nor is it the case that economic issues no longer matter to most voters, as much of the commentary on evangelicals and other "values voters" might suggest. Far from it: Whether the measure is the frequency with which Americans cite the economy as their top concern, the number and prominence of mentions of the economy in party platforms, or the degree to which the economy as an issue appears to shape voters' choices in the voting booth, all available signs indicate that the economy has become more important to voters since the 1970s, not less.[30] Between 1946 and 1972, for example, voters named the economy "the most important problem" in only one-sixth of the frequent Gallup surveys asking voters to rank their concerns. Between 1973 and 2004, by contrast, economic concerns topped Gallup's list almost three-quarters of the time that the question was asked.[31] What's more, a huge body of research shows that economic issues continue to dominate the vote choices of a broad majority of Americans.[32]

All this makes it even more consequential that evangelicals have become such loyal GOP supporters. While Christian conservatives with high incomes are more likely to vote for Republicans than their poorer counterparts, evangelicals "tip" to the Republican Party at a much lower income level than do other voters—about $50,000 lower, according to statistical analyses. Put another way, an evangelical voter with $50,000 in annual income is as likely to be a Republican as a nonevangelical voter with $100,000 in annual income.[33] In a country where the typical household income is around $50,000, this is a huge effect, and it means that Republicans attract far more support from lower- and middle-class voters than they would otherwise. (In 2004, white evangelicals made up about a quarter of the electorate and about 40 percent of the GOP's electoral coalition.)[34] Evangelicals are "Sam's Club Republicans," as the conservative writers Ross Douthat and Reihan Salam have put it: Much more conservative on social issues, they are largely in line with the positions of other voters on economic issues (although evangelicals who have finished college are generally more conservative on economic issues than other Protestant voters).[35] These evangelical voters, unlike most of their working-class and middle-class brethren, *are* being mobilized—but by groups, and on terms, that activate their support on noneconomic grounds. They may be Sam's Club Republicans, but their party is shopping at Saks Fifth Avenue.

The Unmoored American Voter

Evangelicals have been organized into politics on nonmaterial grounds. Most voters of moderate means, however, have been organized *out of* politics, left adrift as the foundations of middle-class democracy have washed away. As the organizations concerned with the economic conditions of the middle class have eroded, so too has the engagement and leverage of the less affluent voters at the heart of American politics when the GI Bill passed.

Given the changes in the organizational terrain of American politics we have reviewed, this observation will come as no surprise. Yet it is a development that, on reflection, is as curious as it is troubling. The rise of winner-take-all inequality has disadvantaged the vast majority of Americans, and none more so than those on the lower and middle rungs of the economic ladder. As we saw in chapter 3, a long line of theorists and commentators, including such luminaries as Tocqueville, have argued that citizens on the losing end of inequality will use their power at the ballot box to rectify the imbalance. We might have expected, therefore, that the emergence of winner-take-all inequality would have galvanized Americans to become more involved in politics to demand a correction.

That has obviously not happened. Quite the contrary: The more experts on American politics delve into the transformation of American politics, the more they find the opposite. In 2004, a special task force of the American Political Science Association issued a report entitled "American Democracy in an Age of Rising Inequality." The product of more than a year's work and reflection by fifteen political scientists (including, full disclosure, one of us), the group's report offered a stark bottom line: "Our country's ideals of citizenship and responsive government may be under growing threat in an era of persistent and rising inequalities . . . Citizens with lower or moderate incomes speak with a whisper that is lost on the ears of inattentive government officials, while the advantaged roar with a clarity and consistency that policymakers readily hear and routinely follow." [36]

The decline in the reach and clout of organizations representing moderate-income Americans is the most fundamental aspect of this transformation. But it is not the only one. Voting has become more skewed by income, as the gap in turnout between the top and the bottom of the economic spectrum has grown. Even in 2008, despite substantial investments by the Democrats to turn out less affluent voters, more than a quarter of the electorate was made up of Americans with household incomes in excess of $100,000—a group that comprises about 16 percent of the U.S. population. [37]

Yet the vote is by far the most equally distributed of political resources, a resource that almost all adult citizens with a minimal commitment to politics have. On the other side of the spectrum is money, and money has become far more important in American politics. In response, parties and politicians have turned to affluent donors and organized interests as never before to finance their spiraling campaign costs. In recent elections, the parties have contacted nearly half of the richest third of Americans directly during campaign season, up from less than 15 percent of these voters in the 1950s.[38]

All this would matter less, of course, if better-off Americans had the same views as the less affluent on what government should do. And indeed there are many areas where Americans do not differ much on public policy by income group (when, that is, they have consistent and grounded views at all). But the role of government in the economy is not one of them. Wealthier Americans are less supportive of economic redistribution and measures to provide economic security. They are more supportive of free trade and deregulation. They are less supportive of Medicare and Social Security. They are more supportive of tax cuts, especially cuts in taxes on dividends and capital gains. They are markedly less supportive of health insurance expansions financed by an increase in taxes—in fact, income is a better predictor on this vital issue than party affiliation. Unlike poorer Americans, however, wealthier Americans can back their positions up with serious money.[39] As money has become more and more prominent, our politics has become more and more like the parable in Matthew 13: "For whosoever hath, to him shall be given, and he shall have more abundance."

"Misperceptions, Myopia, and Missing Connections"

Participation and money aren't the only political resources that are unequally distributed or lacking for many ordinary voters. So, too, is knowledge: knowledge of economic realities, of what politicians do to address them, and of what those responses mean for everyday citizens. And with few organizations to provide reliable guidance, inequalities in knowledge assume greater significance. As Larry Bartels argues in his magisterial *Unequal Democracy*, voters operating on their own have a hard time coming to clear judgments about what to demand from Washington and how to hold politicians accountable. They are prone to "misperceptions, myopia, and missing connections between values and interests on one hand and policy preferences and votes on the other."[40] This misunderstanding and confusion leaves politicians plenty of room to run (or hide) on many policy issues—especially when, as is often the case, "public sentiment is divided, unstable, confused, or simply nonexistent."[41]

These "misperceptions, myopia, and missing connections" can easily be found in public views of economic inequality, along with a healthy dose of ambivalence and a strong shot of cynicism. It is a myth that Americans are blithely unconcerned about inequality or uniformly resistant to government efforts to address it. Instead, as Lawrence Jacobs and Benjamin Page argue in their important book *Class War?*, Americans are best thought of as "conservative egalitarians."[42] On the "conservative" side, they worry about government waste and the dominance of special interests and do not trust public officials. This skepticism toward government has only grown as the winner-take-all economy has shifted into high gear. On the "egalitarian" side, they are concerned about inequality of income, wealth, and opportunity, and surprisingly (given how much we hear about their *in*-egalitarianism), are generally supportive of concrete measures to address inequality, insecurity, and hardship. Moreover, this is true at all points on the income distribution, though, yes, support is lower among the rich than among the poor.

To most pundits, it seems, Americans aren't "conservative egalitarians"; they're "conservative inegalitarians"—unconcerned about inequality, conservative to the core about economic issues, and certainly much more conservative than they were a generation ago. But thousands of relevant opinion polls and hundreds of opinion studies conducted in the last two decades directly contradict this view.[43] Yes, the share of Americans who identify as conservative has increased since the 1970s, from 25 percent when President Carter was elected in 1976 to 32 percent when President Bush was reelected in 2004. (The share who identify as liberal has increased from 16 percent to 23 percent over the same period.) Consistently, by far the largest group of Americans see themselves as moderates.[44] But survey questions regarding the role of government and key areas of public policy show little or no rightward shift—and perhaps even a leftward shift.[45] To be sure, all these results should be interpreted with serious caution, as opinion polls have difficulty capturing people's deeper attitudes toward government. But they offer not a whiff of support for the common presumption that a major right turn in American public opinion has driven the dramatic transformation of American public policy over the last generation.

Think Americans are unaware of runaway inequality? Think again: In 1988, the Gallup poll asked Americans whether the United States was "divided between haves and have-nots." One might have expected relatively few Americans to agree with this very stark description of the growing economic divide. But 26 percent of Americans did. But here's the more striking number: Two decades later, in 2007, the respected Pew Research Center asked the question again. This time, Americans were evenly divided, with 48 percent saying yes and 48 percent saying no.[46] That same year, another poll showed 72 percent of Americans agreeing that differences in income in the United States were "too large." This position gained majority assent even from the less than 4 percent of Americans who identified themselves as "upper class."[47] Americans don't know a lot about the dimensions of American economic inequality, as we shall see. But they know it's there and that it's been growing.[48]

Just as Americans seem to recognize (and dislike) rising inequality, they are also more realistic about their own economic situation than typically given credit for—though, here again, hardly immune to false or wishful thinking. Most describe their income as average or below average, with only 3 percent saying it is "far above average."[49] Contrary to popular mythology, not all Americans think they will become rich: In 2003, 31 percent said that it was "very" (10 percent) or "fairly" (21 percent) likely that they would "ever be rich"—virtually the identical level revealed by the same Gallup poll question in 1990.[50] Clearly, the dream of climbing to the top is alive and well. And clearly, Americans have greater faith in upward mobility than the facts reviewed in chapter 2 would seem to warrant. But that faith is hardly unlimited, and Americans have become no more likely to subscribe to it.

Despite all this, most Americans simply don't know all that much about economic inequality or the contours of economic policy, and understanding is weakest among those on the short end of the economic stick. Perhaps the most arresting illustration is provided by surveys on perceived inequality. In these polls—which, helpfully, have been done across a large number of nations—people are first asked what salaries workers in different occupations earn. What, for example, does a skilled factory worker earn? What does a lawyer earn? What does the chairman of a large national company earn? Then survey respondents are asked what people in these different jobs *should* earn. In other words, what's the proper pay level for a chairman or a lawyer or a factory worker? The size of the gap between the two sets of answers—between perceived and desired earnings—provides a rough measure of how much people want to reduce inequality.

So where does the United States line up on this score? Well, Americans *appear* to be relatively tolerant of inequality compared with citizens of other nations: The gap between what they think people should earn and what they think they do earn is smaller than the norm. But the reason Americans are tolerant is not because they support greater differences in what people should earn. Rather, it is mostly because they mistakenly think there is less inequality in what people *do* earn—even though the United States has far and away the highest level of actual inequality. In other words, Americans are no less egalitarian when it comes to their vision of an ideal world. But they are much less accurate when it comes to their vision of the real world.[51]

Revealingly, the greatest misperceptions concern the earnings of those at the top. Americans seem pretty good at figuring out what people in "normal" jobs earn. But when they try to estimate the earnings of wealthier workers, they start to really undershoot the mark. When it comes to the economy's big winners, Americans are like Dr. Evil in the *Austin Powers* comedies, who, after waking from a thirty-year sleep, threatens world leaders with nuclear blackmail to demand a ransom of *1 million* dollars. Asked in 2007 what a CEO of a national company earned, Americans come up with what must seem to them like a huge number: half a million dollars. Not quite: In 2007, the average CEO of an S&P 500 corporation earned over $14 million.[52] Although Americans aren't alone in under-estimating earnings at the top—people in all countries do—Americans underestimate earnings at the top much more than do citizens of other nations.[53]

Does this misperception matter? A clever question in the 2008 National Election Studies—the nation's premier election poll—suggests it does. Over the years, surveys have repeatedly asked whether "government ought to reduce . . . income differences." Consistently since the late 1970s, between a quarter and a third of Americans have agreed (choosing the two most positive positions on a seven-point scale). The 2008 poll, however, laid out how much people in the top and bottom portions of the income distribution actually earned. After this, the same basic question was asked. This time, *57 percent* favored reducing inequality.[54]

Of course, artificial interventions like these might not resemble what happens in the real world of politics, in which advocates are waging constant—if often highly lopsided—rhetorical battle. But among close analysts of American politics, there's little dispute about one big implication: In a world of declining citizen organization, in which political elites invest huge amounts of time and money to shape how Americans think about issues, most Americans find it very hard to link their broad economic concerns to the contours of specific policies. Indeed, policies today are arguably more complicated than ever, because government is relying more on private contractors and other nongovernmental entities, while doing more through tax breaks like the child care tax credit. In this environment, it's all the more important for ordinary voters to have reliable signals and the leverage to translate those signals into pressure on politicians—all the more important, but not all the more likely.

No News Is Bad News

We can be pretty sure of one thing: The help voters need is not consistently coming from the news media. The erosion of traditional interest organizations has meant that for many voters, the media are the only regular source of political information that once came from allied interest organizations and broad-based civic associations. And, indeed, many analysts (not least reporters themselves) have touted the media as the crucial watchdog for ordinary citizens who want to ensure that politicians do their bidding. As two veteran editors of the *Washington Post*, Leonard Downie Jr. and Robert Kaiser, summarize this widely held aspiration: "Our politicians know that informed voters can throw them out of office . . . Good journalism is a principal source of the information necessary to make such accountability meaningful."[55]

Yet the communications revolutions of the past few decades have not been kind to this watchdog role. Changes in the media environment, particularly the spread of cable and the Internet, have shifted news operations from relatively cozy monopolies into increasingly fierce competitors for a shrinking audience. The shifts have been especially dramatic for the major television networks, once the principal source of news for most Americans. Before cable, Americans who wished to watch TV during prime news hours had little choice but to be exposed to broad public affairs programming. That has ceased to be true. Television audiences have fragmented, and the viewership of network news has plummeted. When asked in 2000 to describe the mission of *NBC Nightly News*, Tom Brokaw's two-word answer was "to survive."[56]

The rise of the Internet has had a similar set of consequences, dividing the media audience into a hardy band of news junkies and a much larger pool of entertainment addicts.[57] While the best-informed citizens are better informed than ever, more and more citizens are consuming less and less news. And even for the news audience that remains, the media have faced increasing pressure to provide entertainment packaged as news. Stories have become shorter, and the emphasis has shifted to those that can best exploit the visual power of television: scandal, crime, celebrities, natural disasters, and "soft" news items like personal health and personal finance. What has been squeezed out is hard news, especially concerning relatively complex issues that require many words to explain and yield poor visuals. During the 1968 presidential campaign, candidates could expect to speak on camera for an average of forty seconds without interruption; two decades later, the average was just nine seconds. Not surprisingly, detailed discussions of policy that would allow voters to get a better sense of the stakes in ongoing political conflict fare especially poorly.

Even when the media cover public affairs, moreover, they tend to emphasize the "horse race" aspects of political life—who's up and who's down, who's the most captivating player in the electoral circus and who's not. This notion of politics as a contest of personalities and teams, coupled with dwindling resources for investigative work and the growth of more aggressive partisan monitoring of the news, has helped feed a style of political journalism that leans heavily on giving each "side" (all stories having exactly two) a platform for saying their piece. Even hard news consists mostly of dueling sound bites. Efforts to analyze the veracity or relevance of these claims, or to place them in context, are either left to the end or left out altogether.

The online and print news perform better, of course. But they have faced increasing competitive pressure as well. And even they provide surprisingly limited information related to the content of policy—the kind of information that is crucial for accountability for today's more atomized voters. Consider how *USA Today*, the nation's largest-circulation daily, covered the Bush tax cuts in 2001. For our 2005 book *Off Center*, we and a team of researchers examined every story written in the newspaper on the 2001 tax cuts.[58] The tax cuts were President Bush's top domestic priority, and the stakes for Americans were huge. Appropriately, *USA Today* printed seventy-eight stories about the tax cuts, many of them on the front page. But of those seventy-eight articles, only six were primarily about the content of the legislation. Only one was about the distributional effects of the proposed changes in policy—namely, the concentration of the tax cuts on higher-income taxpayers. Instead, the main focus of reporting was the political saga: the president's efforts to rally support, the tactics of opponents, and the slow but steady march of the Republicans' agenda through Congress.

What about the Internet? The first thing to note is that the minority of Americans who follow the news closely on the Internet is the same small and unrepresentative group that follow the news closely through print publications—educated, upper-income, and partisan voters.[59] What's more, only a tiny corner of the vast Internet world is devoted to hard news: news junkies can get their fix, but entertainment addicts are unlikely to become inadvertently informed by browsing the Web, as they were when they had to sit through the news to get to sitcoms. In the same way that the decline of mass-based organizations broke apart broad networks of shared interest that linked Americans of relatively diverse backgrounds, the decline of broadcast news in favor of "narrowcasting" through cable and the Internet have broken apart the shared media experience that once helped foster and sustain social capital.

To be clear, we are not arguing that more information about the details of policy or more statistics on the distribution of income would by itself revive middle-class democracy. Information must be tied to political action, understanding to leverage, and voters must feel this action and leverage can make a difference. The point is not that the media have become less capable of carrying out the task of informing and engaging citizens, though they almost certainly have. It is that this burden was always too great for them alone, and now they alone are trying to carry it.

Who's in Charge Here?

The problem for voters is not simply figuring out what or whom to support. It is also getting politicians to pay attention. As we noted back in chapter 4, Bartels (and, separately, his Princeton colleague Martin Gilens) found that even when lower- and middle-class voters are able to articulate clear views on policy matters, these positions—unlike the preferences of higher-income voters—have distressingly little impact on what elected officials do. To use the political scientists' term of art, politicians just do not seem to be very "responsive" on many issues.

Perhaps the most dramatic illustration is also one of the most maligned features of contemporary American politics: polarization. Scholars who have looked at the transformation closely—such as political scientists Nolan McCarty, Keith Poole, and Howard Rosenthal in their pathbreaking *Polarized America*—have concluded that the two parties are further apart ideologically than at any point since Reconstruction, just after the Civil War. As they put it, "Over the past thirty years, the parties [in Congress] have deserted the center of the floor in favor of the wings."[60]

In theory, the parties could be polarizing because voters are polarizing. Yet, puzzlingly, ideological polarization turns out to be mostly an elite affair. Most Americans, it turns out, are just not that far apart in their views.[61] Yes, voters are better "sorted" than they used to be, with liberals more likely to be Democrats and conservatives more likely to be Republicans. And, yes, activists within the parties have moved further apart. But the ideological polarization of the electorate as a whole—the degree of disagreement on left-right issues overall—is modest and has changed little over time. Polarization primarily reflects not the growing polarization of voters, but the declining responsiveness of American politicians to the electoral middle.

Lest you doubt this point, we offer a striking illustration of how elites can polarize even when they're responding to the same voters: Nevada— or rather, Nevada's two senators, Democratic Majority Leader Harry Reid and Republican conservative John Ensign. Though Reid is no liberal firebrand, the two are about as far apart on the issues as Republicans and Democrats can be—which is to say very, very far apart. But, of course, they both hail from the same state, and thus were elected by, and must seek reelection from, the same voters. If senators and Senate candidates were always seeking the lodestar of the swing voters within their states, we would expect little difference between senators from the same state with different party labels (at last count, thirteen states had a senator from each party). But, in fact, as with Reid and Ensign, what we see in state after state is a huge and growing divide between same-state senators of different parties—one that turns out to be almost as wide as the gap between the two parties within the Senate overall.[62]

No less puzzling, partisan polarization has been very one-sided: Republicans have moved substantially to the right, while Democrats have moved modestly to the left.[63] We see this even within those split-personality Senate delegations. Democrats from states that also elect a Republican are way more conservative than Senate Democrats as a whole. Republicans from states that also elect a Democrat are only modestly more liberal than Senate Republicans as a whole. Again, as a result, the center of ideological gravity has shifted substantially rightward among political elites. The same has not been true among American voters. Voters are about as likely to identify as conservative as they were a generation ago, and their views on left-right issues have—if anything, since measuring ideology is notoriously difficult—moved leftward.[64]

How can we explain this great disconnect? And what does it mean for winner-take-all politics? The convincing arguments of Bartels and other opinion experts about the difficulties that voters have calling the shots help us understand who *isn't* producing the politics of winner-take-all— the ordinary voter. But who is? If not the great electoral middle, who are political leaders responsive *to*? The answer takes us back to the politics of organized combat, and deep into the battle between America's two great political parties.

We have seen in the last three chapters that the organizational landscape of American politics has tilted dramatically. Ascendant business groups have gained ground, as has a mobilized evangelical movement that brings less affluent voters into unexpected alliance with these powerful economic interests through the GOP. But the broad set of organizations that once brought ordinary voters into politics, giving them knowledge and leverage and might, have lost ground. These fateful changes have transformed the playing field on which the parties struggle for supremacy. And as the field has shifted, the parties and the politicians within them have adapted. Republicans have been pulled sharply to the right, while Democrats have confronted new strategic dilemmas. The story of this imbalanced struggle—and how it has furthered the politics and economics of winner-take-all—is the next part of our saga.

Part III

Winner-Take-All Politics

Chapter 7

A Tale of Two Parties

If any political figure is associated with the post-1970s transformation of American politics and the rise of a new (and newly unequal) economy, it is surely Ronald Reagan. To detractors and admirers alike, he is the obvious leading man in the drama of the New Deal's demise. Reagan was simultaneously the conservatives' most eloquent advocate and their most successful candidate. He was, in a word, a game-changer. There was American politics before Reagan, and American politics after Reagan. Full stop.

Yet this familiar telling is profoundly misleading. Depicting Reagan as the personification of the modern Republican Party is twice mistaken: It overestimates the radicalism of Reagan's GOP, and it underestimates the radicalism of the GOP that was to come fifteen years later (and whose activities and impact we will discuss in the next chapter). The profound transformation of the Republican Party from its moderate roots into a force committed to the full reversal of a century of domestic policy took more than the eight years of Reagan's presidency to develop—indeed, the process continues to this day. Reagan was an inspiration and spur to this broader shift, but when he took office the ground was not yet prepared, and the party he governed was still a work in progress.

The image of Reagan as radical Republican conqueror is also misleading because it misses the organizational army that the GOP started to develop even before he took office and which Reagan only partially and temporarily directed. Reagan is the Edmund Hillary of the Republican revolution. His achievements were only possible because of the organization-building that took place beyond the sandstone walls of the White House.

Even before Reagan's electoral triumph, the Republican Party took advantage of the organizational shifts that we charted in the past three chapters to construct a formidable party structure that linked interest groups and candidates through the powerful bonds of campaign money and favorable public policy. Using new technologies and innovative organizational strategies, the GOP translated its mastery of an increasingly money-driven campaign world into durable and sometimes improbable election victories—victories that, in turn, allowed them to build on the policy foundations of the late 1970s supporting the emergent winner-take-all economy. With organized labor weakened and organized business strengthened, the Democratic Party struggled clumsily to respond. Between the growing demands for money and the rapidly expanding capacities of the GOP, Democrats found themselves caught in a financial arms race. Unfortunately for them, they got to play the part of the late–Cold War Soviet Union responding to Reagan's massive defense buildup.

The deep impact of this organizational imbalance revealed itself not at the high tide of the first-term Reagan revolution, but at its low point, the congressional midterm elections of 1982. 1982? Yes, here again our view of politics as organized combat points us to political turning points that a conventional telling of history ignores. We have already discussed how 1978 was important for what it brought—a conservative and business resurgence despite a Democratic Congress and President. 1982, by contrast, is important for what *didn't* happen: the collapse of Reaganism. How the Reagan revolution survived this near-death experience provides unparalleled insight into the political shifts that laid the groundwork for the emerging winner-take-all economy of this era—and the ascendant winner-take-all economy that was soon to take center stage.

The Rout Not Taken

Reagan is remembered as a political colossus, but our collective memories are highly selective. The Gipper's reputation as a political winner rests heavily on his exquisitely timed reelection campaign of 1984. Riding a brief economic boomlet ("It's morning again in America"), the President coasted to reelection, demolishing a dispirited Walter Mondale. Just two years earlier, however, Reagan had faced a near-certain electoral rout. The luster was gone from Reaganomics. In early October, the administration had to announce that unemployment had topped 10 percent, a level not seen since the Great Depression. An ill-advised trial balloon of cuts in Social Security had badly damaged the President's standing with elderly and blue-collar Americans. In the preelection Gallup poll, the president's job approval rating (42 percent) was the lowest at that stage of a presidency since Harry Truman's in 1946.[1]

Reagan and his advisers understood the gravity of the situation. Even under the best of circumstances, the first midterm election of a new presidency is typically a painful one, with an average loss in the postwar period of twenty-seven seats in the House. Under the grim conditions of 1982, Republicans could anticipate much worse. Through the summer and fall they watched as their candidates fell in the polls. As the executive director of the National Republican Congressional Committee (NRCC), Nancy Sinnott Dwight, later remembered, "It was a disaster facing us, of major proportions—55 to 60 seats."[2] Nor was this just ex post dramatics. Two prominent political science models, based on broad indicators of the political and economic climate, forecast Republican losses of fifty-eight and up to sixty seats respectively.[3] To put those numbers in perspective, the two biggest drubbings of the past fifty years were 1994, when President Clinton's party lost fifty-four House seats, and 1974, when Nixon's Republicans lost forty-eight. In short, Republicans were looking at a historic rebuke. With Reagan's domestic agenda resting on a shaky coalition of Republicans and conservative Democrats in the Democrat-controlled House, a loss of anything close to that magnitude would not just have placed the President firmly on the defensive for the duration of his term; it would have raised profound doubts about his brand of politics.

At the end of the day, House Republicans held their losses to twenty-six—a setback that was, by historical standards, extraordinarily ordinary. What saved the GOP, as political scientist Gary Jacobson has documented, was not the charm and skill of its leader, who was quite unpopular at the time. What saved the GOP was its pronounced organizational edge. The decisive races involved those where credible Democratic challengers confronted vulnerable Republicans. It was here that the organizational resources of the parties came into play. The Republican national committees—the RNC and the House and Senate campaign committees—were able to raise over *six times* as much as their Democratic counterparts, and they contributed almost six times as much to individual House and Senate candidates.

Democrats effectively had no organization. In July 1982, just months before the Democrats' best shot to derail Republican momentum, the Democratic National Committee (DNC) was so broke it was forced to lay off fifteen people from its ninety-member staff. Candidates had to rely on the money they raised for themselves. Much of it ended up being wasted by powerful incumbents who didn't need the help. As the opportunity for a "wave election" became clear in the late summer of 1982, party leaders begged these well-heeled incumbents to redistribute funds to under-financed challengers—to no avail. One exception was a young Charles Schumer, the New York Democrat whom we will see again in the story to come. Already demonstrating the fund-raising prowess that would mark his political career, he was one of only two House incumbents to offer funds to Democratic insurgents. At the end of the campaign thirty-two incumbent Democrats were left holding over $3 million in unspent funds. Had that amount been in the hands of the party, it could have doubled its contributions to candidates. These unspent funds were on top of the money incumbents unnecessarily spent on themselves. Nearly a third of all Democratic spending came in races involving a Democratic incumbent who won with over 70 percent of the vote (only 13 percent of Republican money was spent on such races).[4]

Retrospectives from both parties' leaders suggested that the NRCC's capacity to shore up its incumbents saved ten to twenty seats in the House. In the Senate, too, Republicans won the close ones; a mere 35,000 votes in the right places would have shifted control of the Senate from the Republicans to the Democrats.[5]

Nor was 1982 exceptional. Throughout the late 1970s and early 1980s, the GOP's massive organizational advantages helped it to get the maximum out of its electoral opportunities: In the four election cycles between 1978 and 1984, twenty-four U.S. Senate races ended with the winner enjoying just 51 percent or less of the vote. With their technological and strategic edge, the Republicans won nineteen of these tight races.[6]

In his previously discussed book *Unequal Democracy*, Larry Bartels finds an equally striking partisan impact of unequal finances in presidential elections. For fifty years, Republicans and their associated interest groups have had an edge in financing presidential campaigns. Using an elaborate statistical analysis, Bartels estimates the impact of that financial advantage on the GOP share of the presidential vote. It added about 1.5 percent in the 1950s and 1960s, over 3 percent in the 1970s, and almost 7 percent in the 1980s, before falling back to an average of about 3.5 percent in the 1992, 1996, and 2000 elections. This is an astonishing edge, easily enough by itself to have swung the presidential elections of 1968 and 2000 to the Republican candidate.[7]

The Hidden Life of the Parties

The huge organizational effect on display in 1982 belies the complacent way in which pundits—with their sustained depictions of out-of-touch Democrats and ascendant Republicans—simply equate election outcomes with popular will and the appeal of particular leaders. In the conventional view of politics as electoral spectacle, the two parties are seen as significant primarily because they provide the candidates for electoral contests. Attention focuses on those political celebrities, who battle like *American Idol* contenders for the fleeting affections of voters. The parties contribute further to the spectacle by giving political narratives the feel of sporting events. Which team is up? How big was the win? Who were the stars? What are the losers going to do now?

In this view, parties as powerful, durable organizational actors fade into the background. It is the voters who "send a message to Washington." In its extreme version (one that many analysts implicitly hold), whoever wins elections *must*, by definition, be responding to voters' wishes. Voters express their will through great electoral demonstrations. After that, Washington does their bidding. Or, if it fails to do so, it is because of the blunders or betrayals of the winning contestants—whose perceived missteps are dissected by a crew of pundits specializing in Monday-morning quarterbacking. As always, the focus is on individual politician-celebrities.

Parties, by contrast, often seem like an afterthought. Our House and Senate are not the British Parliament, where the victorious majority party provides the executive (the prime minister) and backbenchers are almost wholly dependent on the party. Trent Lott titled his memoir of his time as Senate majority leader *Herding Cats*. Lott's view echoes Will Rogers's famous depiction of the GOP's rival, "I'm a member of no organized political party—I'm a Democrat." But parties play a powerful role in American politics, and this role has been growing in strength since the 1970s. They do so precisely because they are *organizers*. Though very far from fully unified, the parties are nonetheless the great gatherers and coordinators in America's fragmented polity. Indeed, the very fragmentation of our government makes the parties all the more influential when they can translate their organization into sustained attention and activity along the lines that they—and supportive interest groups and voters—want.

For starters, the parties are central vehicles for setting the agenda in Washington. They generally decide what the main topics of debate will be. Sometimes, of course, events themselves thrust an issue to the forefront. Yet much of the time it is the majority party that allocates the scarce and unbelievably valuable space on Washington's docket. Republicans win and the subject is tax cuts. Democrats win and the subject is health care.

The parties don't just decide what issues get discussed. For those issues that make it to center stage, the majority party plays the leading role in deciding what kinds of proposals actually stand a chance of being adopted. If Washington is going to respond to global warming, or rising health-care costs, or a breakdown of financial regulation, *how* will it respond? If there is going to be a big tax cut, *whose* taxes are going to be cut, and by how much? As we stress throughout this book, when it comes to policy, the devil is most assuredly in such details—trillion-dollar details.

The coordinating role of parties takes several forms. On the one hand, parties bring together collections of politicians, both to fight elections and to try to agree on policy. Of course, bringing together a group of politicians—each with his or her own constituencies, interests, and overactive egos—is the kind of challenge that gives rise to depictions like Lott's. But party leaders have resources too: a range of carrots (like campaign funds or a good word with powerful interest groups) and sticks (like lost congressional committee chairmanships) that can advance or impede politicians' careers. In recent years, these powers have helped make the parties, and especially the Republican Party, much more unified and disciplined. Sometimes the cats *can* be herded.

Parties don't just try to round up politicians. Equally important, if less visible and less well understood, they try to bring together organized groups into successful coalitions. These groups can provide a party with critical financial and organizational support, in elections and beyond. Conversely, if powerful groups are sufficiently displeased, they can be a major threat. Of course, groups do not offer up support without certain expectations—expectations that overwhelmingly relate to the promotion of policies they favor. For this reason, parties face a dual burden: They simultaneously need to win over voters *and* please their most organized supporters.[8] Managing this trick successfully is the true art of modern party politics.

Because parties are coalitions of groups as well as coalitions of voters, the electoral environment is not their only concern. They must also respond to major shifts in the organizational landscape. A big change in the balance between organized groups can create powerful new incentives, cross-pressures, and challenges. One can usefully think of the process in Darwinian terms: A major change in the political ecosystem generates new competitive pressures. For both individual politicians and the party itself, those pressures carry a simple, insistent message: Adapt or die.

Over the past few decades, the organizational upheavals that we chronicled in the last three chapters have profoundly altered the political ecosystem in which America's two great parties compete. Each was pressed to adapt to this altered environment, and the way each adapted further transformed American politics—and the American economy— over the 1980s and 1990s. We begin, in this chapter, with the story of how the Republicans and Democrats scrambled to respond in the late 1970s and 1980s—a crucial period, as we shall see. The next two chapters show how first the Republicans embraced and then the Democrats accommodated the new realities of winner-take-all in the 1990s and beyond.

As the contrast between "embrace" and "accommodate" suggests, the evolutionary demands of America's new political ecosystem proved very different for Republicans and Democrats. Reflecting their deepening alliance with organized business, Republicans found it much easier to discover a niche that suited their ambitions as the economic winners gained ground. For Democrats, the new environment was decidedly less friendly to the traits they had evolved. And nowhere was the contrast more clear than in the unglamorous but critical corner of the new ecosystem known as campaign finance.

Money Changes Everything

William McKinley's campaign manager and all-around power broker, Mark Hanna, famously summarized his line of work: "There are two things that matter in politics. The first is money. I can't remember the second." Hanna knew what he was talking about. In one of the most famous and polarizing elections in American history, Hanna's candidate trounced his populist opponent, William Jennings Bryan—a victory facilitated by

McKinley's ability to double what Republicans had spent four years earlier and outspend Bryan 5–1.[9]

Hanna's joke usefully reminds us that money has always been a central feature of American politics. Yet here, as in other respects, the 1970s was a watershed. It was during this period that television emerged as the major conduit connecting politicians to voters. Television helped to generate a more "candidate centered" politics, oriented around individual politicians who knew how to use the new medium effectively and had the star appeal it favored. A second technology, modern polling, accompanied the rise of TV and had complementary effects. Polling helped individual candidates craft their own profiles and finely calibrated messages. It gave rise to a vast new profession of pricey political consultants who could conduct and interpret the polls and advise candidates on strategy.

These changes fundamentally altered the nature of running for office: who was favored and who was not, how candidates spent their time and crafted their messages, and how campaigns themselves were organized. Their most measurable effect, however, was to substantially increase the role of money in politics. In the decade stretching from the mid-1970s to the mid-1980s, average real expenditures by incumbents in the House roughly *tripled*.[10] In the new age of television, money became a prerequisite for electoral viability. Since it also served as a *signal* of viability, large war chests could be used to attract new contributions and deter possible rivals. Faced with these clear incentives, permanent, relentless fundraising became a fixture of American politics, even for seemingly secure incumbents.

Of course, this development fit well with the new landscape of organized interests. Beginning in the 1970s, first unions and then (on a much larger scale) business groups formed PACs and began to channel unprecedented amounts of money into campaigns. In 1976, there were 224 labor PACs, a number that would increase modestly to 261 a decade later. Over the same period, corporate and trade PACs increased from 922 to 2,182. Both sides ramped up spending over the period, but throughout the decade, trade and corporate PACs were able to outspend labor two or three to one.[11]

This imbalance played directly into the hands of the GOP, which had more natural affinities with business and the well-to-do. Democrats had historically focused more on mobilization than fund-raising; and they were hurt badly by the declining position of organized labor. But the Republican edge was not an automatic one, at least not the huge imbalance that emerged. It reflected a sustained organizational effort by the GOP to seize the advantage in the new political ecosystem.

The Republican Revival

Here again, the Carter presidency carries a surprising political significance. It marked the arrival of an active, innovative conservative organizer at the Republican National Committee (RNC), William Brock. Brock was an establishment political figure—a former congressman and cabinet member—and there was little indication at the time that his appointment as head of the RNC would be a significant one. Yet he turned out to be a gifted organizational reformer. During Brock's four-year tenure, stretching from Carter's first year in office to Reagan's, the RNC became a focal point for the remarkable resurgence of Republican organizational strength. Not coincidentally, this resurgence developed in tandem with rising business power—and with the first stirrings of the winner-take-all economy.

Brock took over at the low tide of the party's political fortunes. Not only had eight years of Republican control of the White House ended with Carter's victory over Ford, but the GOP held only 143 House seats and 38 Senate seats. Outside Washington, the situation was equally bleak. Republicans held only thirteen governorships and controlled just four state legislatures. Only a quarter of Americans identified themselves as Republicans.[12] Beyond the formal machinery of the parties themselves, Democrats seemed to have an organizational edge. Incumbents of the majority party could draw on their own staff, as well as volunteers from organized labor. Their candidates had the steady access to funds that came from their control of the levers of political power.

Republicans, in short, were in desperate need of a stronger party. They got one. In just four years, Brock remade a sleepy, demoralized organization into a robust and ambitious one. Brock vastly expanded and modernized the party's capacity to nurture and guide state-level and national activities. Most critical for the long haul, Republicans rapidly extended their natural financial advantage through cutting-edge fund-raising techniques. Brock's key innovation was the energetic expansion of direct-mail operations, which allowed the GOP to tap its strongest supporters and raise unprecedented sums. With Democrats controlling Washington, Brock could maximize the use of the negative appeals on which direct mail thrives. The number of donors more than quadrupled, from 250,000 to 1.2 million. RNC net receipts from direct mail increased from $12.7 million in 1976 to $26 million in 1980.[13] The preponderance of the new money came from small donations. But Brock's Republican Eagles program, consisting of those who had contributed $10,000 or more to the party, also grew—from 211 donors in 1978 to 865 in 1980. Overall, RNC hard money receipts (the regulated dollars used to explicitly support specific candidates) grew from $29 million in 1976 to $78 million just four years later.[14]

By the time he left the RNC, Brock had created what political scientist Gary Jacobson called "by far the strongest national party organization in American history."[15] Brock had a staff of 350 at GOP headquarters—up from 200 four years earlier and four times the size of the Democrats' operation. As the GOP's 1982 Houdini act would demonstrate, Brock had far more money to allocate to the critical races where the parties' candidates seemed evenly matched. Moreover, he was able to vastly outspend his rival on state and local party-building activities, candidate recruitment and training, and subsidized polling.[16] To give a sense of the scale of Republican efforts, by the 1981–82 cycle, rapidly growing PACs would contribute $83.6 million to congressional candidates. During that same cycle, the three Republican committees (the RNC and the House and Senate campaign committees) raised an astonishing $191 million.[17] As American politics shifted into a new era, Republicans were the first to make the crucial evolutionary moves that would allow them to capitalize on the new opportunities.

Democrats on the Defensive

The new political environment also had huge effects on the Democrats, for whom the shifting balance of organizational power and the growing role of money were far less favorable developments. Struggling mightily to compete with their more organizationally dynamic rival, they adopted a strategy of binge and purge, piling up debt in election years to try to give Democratic candidates a fighting chance. As a means of adjusting to the new political ecosystem, however, the binge-and-purge cycle only provided temporary respite from the inexorable pressure to adapt. Slowly, quietly, the resulting adjustments would bring a transformed Democratic Party into closer alignment with the emerging realities of money-driven politics.

Democrats failed to come close to raising the huge sums that the new GOP organization was hauling in. But even the lopsided revenue numbers understate the disparity. Much of the Democrats' spending had to go to repay old borrowing. In 1981, as Democrats grappled to respond to the new competitive threat posed by Reaganism, the DNC was still paying off bills from the *1968* election. Perennially saddled by election-year debt as it sought to stay in the game, the DNC had little chance of making meaningful investments in party-building.[18]

Thus the initial financial imbalance between the two parties fed on itself. Under Brock and his successors, the GOP used its impressive resource base to build long-term organizational capacity. The more it built this capacity, the more the Democrats were forced to repeat the painful process of binge and purge. According to the Federal Election Commission, the three Republican Party committees already outspent the equivalent Democratic groups by a little less than 3–1 in 1976. Things got markedly worse from there. Over the decade that followed, as the need for spending ramped up rapidly, the GOP advantage grew. By 1986, the GOP had almost quintupled its revenues and outpaced the Democratic committees by nearly a 5–1 margin.[19]

Those who view politics as electoral spectacle often dismiss the significance of such organizational details. What matters, they say, is whether particular candidates, or party appeals, resonate with the all-powerful voter. The fact that this view is almost universally held in the media doesn't make it any less flawed. Organization matters. As the 1982 election shows, sometimes it matters a lot.

Admittedly, much of the impact is hard to track. The financial imbalances allowed Republicans to invest in a wide range of activities that Democrats, scrambling simply to keep up the pace on costly campaign ads, could not hope to match. Republicans could invest in recruiting and training candidates, and bankroll more sophisticated campaign operations, from polling to voter-targeting. They had resources to plow into such critical but low-profile activities as funding tightly contested state legislative races. Control of state legislatures could mean control over redistricting efforts, which could eventually translate into more seats in Congress. In 1980, for instance, RNC funds poured into five close races for the Ohio state senate. Republicans won four, giving them control of that chamber.[20]

More important, Republicans had the flexibility of channeling election resources where they were most needed because the party itself directed a much larger portion of available funds. Aggregate measures of spending by candidates—which showed the two parties fairly even—masked a huge organizational imbalance. As noted earlier, Democratic spending totals rested in the hands of individual incumbents who could translate their positions of power into huge campaign war chests. From the point of view of the party, however, padding the accounts of incumbents who faced little danger was simply a waste of money. Indeed, it reinforced the tendency of these incumbent barons to exercise their independence. Getting the money to where it could do the party some good required a strong, central organization. Republicans had that; Democrats did not.

Democratic officials were well aware that William Brock's efforts had spearheaded an organizational revival that had catalyzed and protected Reagan's initial successes. 1980 was a debacle for the party, with nine Democratic senators, including such liberal lions as Frank Church and George McGovern, accompanying Jimmy Carter into forced retirement. Republicans also picked up three open seats, for a stunning overall swing of twelve that gave the GOP control of a chamber of Congress for the first time since 1954. Reflecting on the carnage, Anne Campbell, former head of the Association of State Democratic Chairs, admitted, "We were outspent, out-targeted and outpolled. The RNC did a superlative job. The Democratic Party should hold its head in shame." House Speaker Tip O'Neill called for more attention to strengthening the national party organization by expanding fund-raising, direct-mail operations, polling, and advertising.[21]

In 1981, the party chose Charles Manatt as the new chief of the DNC. Manatt was a former head of the California state party and, crucially, had served as the chairman of the DNC's finance council. He was viewed as an organization man through and through, who could modernize the DNC's operations. "My goal," Manatt insisted, "is to do the kind of job that Bill Brock did." "We must institutionalize the Democratic Party," he admitted. "The Republicans are way ahead of us . . . For many years, things were so easy for us that we didn't have to set up our party in any institutionalized way."[22]

Confirming Mark Hanna's first rule of politics, Manatt saw money as key. Michael Steed, Manatt's special counsel at the DNC, remembers the challenge his boss faced: "On the day that Manatt was elected, the good news was that in the morning we had $250,000 in the bank. The bad news was that by that afternoon, the $250,000 in the bank had been attached and that other bills were still showing up."[23] Manatt worked hard to develop a long-run financial strategy, including investments in direct mail, even as he sacrificed the DNC's immediate organizational capacity. In 1981, the party's revenues failed to fully meet its basic overhead, debt, and fund-raising costs. It had to borrow more just to fund a pitiful $300,000 for political activities. Astonishingly, it had been forced to lay off a sixth of its staff in the crucial period before the 1982 midterm elections.

Slowly, though, Manatt began to build the party's financial capacity, turning direct mail into a significant source of funds for the first time. He also reached out to business, establishing a Democratic Business Council with (pricey) memberships available to both individuals and PACs. The Democratic Business Council contributed $1 million to the party in

1981, and was generating $3 million by 1984. All told, the DNC doubled the amount coming from large donations between 1980 and 1984—a major improvement but not enough to even begin to close the gap with the RNC.

Democrats, Business, and the Incumbency Card

At the same time that Manatt struggled to drag the DNC into a new political world, change was under way in the remaining citadel of Democratic power: Capitol Hill. Indeed, it is here that one can see most clearly how the new political ecosystem altered the thinking of leading Democrats. Forced to deal with a much more organized and assertive business community and facing powerful financial incentives to seek accommodation, the Democratic Party apparatus reached out to corporate donors as never before. Its appeals rested largely on Democrats' one remaining trump card: incumbency. Despite Republican electoral advances, Democrats retained sizable majorities in the House until 1994. The Democrats' seemingly permanent majority status helped to mitigate the GOP's natural financial advantage, earning them the campaign donations of access-oriented businesses and other lobbies.[24]

Tony Coelho, who became head of the Democratic Congressional Campaign Committee (DCCC) in 1981, was the most successful practitioner of the Democrats' financial counteroffensive. In 1980, as Coelho subtly put it, Democrats "had our access kicked." Many in the party were increasingly eager to identify themselves as "business Democrats"—an identity they reinforced by voting in large numbers for the massive business tax cuts of 1981.[25]

The strategy paid off. In the last cycle before he took charge, the "D-triple-C" raised only $2.9 million in "hard" (that is, unrestricted cash) contributions—less than a *sixth* of the revenues produced by its GOP rival. By 1986, Coelho had increased that amount fourfold—still less than a third of the NRCC's haul, but major progress. He did so largely through a clear-eyed assessment of the party's constraints and opportunities, which led to the vigorous cultivation of business PACs. Coelho presented a business-friendly face to potential contributors and hired a full-time PAC liaison. "We provide the PACs with information on our candidates," Coelho explained. "We say, 'Here's a candidate who's reasonable, a candidate who's taken a position that X PAC should be comfortable with." Coelho doggedly insisted that many contributions came from PACs because "they like our businesslike approach." Yet he wasn't shy about acknowledging that Democrats could make a different pitch: "Business has to deal with us whether they like it or not, because we're the majority." [26]

In short, Coelho kept Democrats in the financial game by developing a prototype of the money-for-access system that the GOP was to perfect in House Majority Whip Tom DeLay's K Street Project after 1994. Revealingly, in the Senate, where Democrats in the early 1980s lacked the majority status that was crucial to Coelho's strategy, the organizational imbalance remained massive. During the period when Republicans held the majority (1981–86), the Republican Senate Campaign Committee outraised its Democratic counterpart by roughly 10–1. [27]

Throughout the 1980s, Democrats struggled to modernize their organizational infrastructure and compete with the GOP financially. Manatt's successor, Paul Kirk, continued the financial renovation of the party. Kirk, a former Ted Kennedy aide (who would briefly fill the Senate vacancy left when Kennedy died in 2009), came to the position with strong backing from organized labor. Despite his ties to the liberal wing of the party, Kirk sought institutional reforms that would push the party in a moderate direction. At the same time, he redoubled Manatt's fund-raising efforts, expanding both the DNC's direct-mail operations and chasing the large donors who could provide "soft money" donations (that is, donations earmarked for party-building, which were not subject to the same restrictions as hard money). By 1988, he had helped to cut into the RNC's traditional financial advantage. [28] Yet despite the effort and accommodation, the Democrats' new initiatives still left them struggling to keep up, and dangerously dependent on the incumbency card.

Democrat, Heal Thyself

For Democratic politicians, of course, the stark organizational imbalance sent its own kind of Darwinian message: You're on your own. Each candidate needed to build an independent financial base to succeed. Like Willie Sutton's answer to the question of why he robbed banks, individual Democrats needed to go where the money was. In practice, this meant two things: the new breed of affluent activists, and the business groups that were gaining political prominence.

Understandably, Democrats sought to gain support from the new bastions of affluent activism we discussed in chapter 6—the advocacy groups that had burst onto the scene in the 1960s and 1970s to champion the concerns of upper-middle-class Americans about environmentalism, consumer rights, and other postmaterial causes. As the new liberalism eclipsed the old liberalism, Democratic politicians came to rely heavily on well-off social liberals to meet the increasing cost of electoral campaigns. By the mid-1990s, EMILY's List—the feminist group that bundles contributions to support pro-choice candidates—had become the single biggest PAC in the country, giving $12 million to Democratic candidates.[29]

Business was the other major source of new financial support, and Democrats as well as Republicans successfully sought its favor. Despite its bipartisan outlays, however, business was actually treating the two parties very differently. When business gave money to Democrats, it went almost exclusively to incumbents, especially moderate to conservative ones. Republican incumbents got money too, but the GOP also got large sums for party-building efforts. Democratic incumbents could finance their reelection bids, but meanwhile their party was falling further and further behind in the money chase.

The targets of business largesse in the two parties differed because the goal of the contributions differed. Financing the GOP was an investment. Business dollars nurtured a cadre of elected officials committed to advancing a deregulatory and tax-cutting agenda. Moreover, contributions to candidates were reinforced by generous institutional support. Business bankrolled an intellectual infrastructure committed to advancing the religion of free markets, refining messages for public consumption, and marketing them energetically. As we have seen, business also gave much more heavily to the Republican Party organization, helping the GOP to outperform Democrats in closely contested elections.

Money to Democrats played a different, if no less critical, role. It was a form of insurance. Revealingly, the money went largely to individuals rather than to the party as an organization. It was destined for the powerful and "moderates," with the goal of minimizing any prospect of distasteful legislation. Carefully targeted contributions could effectively exploit the multiple channels American political institutions make available for blocking, dilution, or delay. Even grudging or quiet support from a handful of Democrats—particularly well-placed ones—could make a huge difference. Such allies could help keep issues off the agenda, substitute symbolic initiatives for real ones, add critical loopholes, or insist on otherwise unnecessary compromises with the GOP. Willing Democrats could also provide valuable bipartisan cover for business-friendly Republican initiatives. Here, as in so many other ways, Democrats and Republicans could play distinct but complementary roles in supporting business interests.

Building a Business-Friendly Party

On economic issues, this increasingly visible cluster of business-friendly Democrats took organizational form with the creation of the Democratic Leadership Council in 1985.[30] The DLC began to take shape in the early 1980s in response to the Reagan juggernaut and the search for a more competitive (that is, electable) Democratic Party. Most of the push came from southerners in the party's conservative wing. Louisiana representative Gillis Long, cousin of the legendary southern populist Huey Long, and his aide Al From provided the initial impetus, but Walter Mondale's 1984 campaign debacle closed the deal.

The DLC officially formed in 1985, with Missouri congressman Dick

Gephardt as chair. He was joined by a group of prominent or rising figures, mostly southern, who included Charles Robb of Virginia, Sam Nunn of Georgia, Lawton Chiles of Florida, John Breaux of Louisiana, Al Gore of Tennessee, and Bruce Babbitt of Arizona (later fixtures would include Bill Clinton and Joe Lieberman). They sought to change the direction of the party, both by reforming its rules to diminish the weight of liberal activists and by retooling its message to make it culturally and economically more conservative. Both moves were designed to make the party more electorally competitive, especially in the South.

In this last ambition the DLC fell short. In that conservative region, Democrats would continue to cede ground to ascendant Republicans. In other respects, however, developments in the party more closely tracked the DLC blueprint—and by 1992 would emerge in full form in the "New Democrat" campaign of Bill Clinton. The party's appeals began to mute aspects of cultural liberalism on guns, affirmative action, and crime, and took a tougher line on national defense. Proposals for welfare reform were structured to send a reassuring message to moderate voters about work and family.

Yet the DLC's reformation project was clearly as much or more about economics. Most of the group's leaders had built careers on a business-friendly posture, and they pushed to make that stance more prominent in the Democratic Party. From the outset, the group built its organization by bringing wealthy individuals attracted by the DLC message into contact with prominent public officials. In the words of a sympathetic historian of the DLC:

> *The lure for most donors was the association with an individual elected official or the desire to cultivate relationships with a handful of the party's rising stars . . . The DLC consciously used this cachet to attract wealthy benefactors, offering, for instance, private retreats with DLC leaders for its most generous donors. Indeed, from the beginning, just as the DLC's membership was limited to elected officials, its base of support was similarly select . . . In that sense, the DLC was an elite organization in every regard.*[31]

The DLC's economic message stressed the need for adjustment to "the new realities of the postindustrial global economy." It emphasized that government should work with a soft touch to foster a strong business climate, promoting free trade and investments in technology, infrastructure, and training to enhance the productivity of the workforce.[32]

Perhaps most significant, the DLC placed heavy stress on deficit reduction as a key element of economic policy. Moreover, DLC leaders framed the deficit issue in a way that is now familiar but was at the time a substantial change, identifying "entitlements" as the biggest problem. The move involved a subtle but radical rebranding of entitlements from their traditional meaning of earned benefits to one reflecting a something-for-nothing mentality. In this new language, both welfare and Social Security were "entitlements," and Washington needed to replace "the politics of entitlement with a new politics of reciprocal responsibility." The DLC stressed the need for a "hard look at federal entitlements and subsidies." Strikingly, during the 1990 deficit reduction fight, it took a position well to the right of the eventual agreement between Democrats and the Bush White House, opposing any tax increases as a way of reducing deficits.

The DLC's economic posture gave organizational expression to a set of ideas and positions that came to anchor the party's conservative wing— a wing that took on special prominence given the financial realities facing Democrats and the difficulties of breaking through gridlock as GOP strength grew. It also pointed to a fundamental, revealing asymmetry between the parties—the Democrats had a strong, organized faction pulling toward the positions of the other party.[33] On economic issues, the GOP lacked anything comparable. This striking difference showed up in two powerful ways: the inability of Democrats to push effectively for reforms that challenged powerful economic interests, and the willingness of many Democrats to accede to, or even cosponsor, Republican initiatives to support the emerging winner-take-all economy.

Breaux-mancing the GOP

If the DLC gave organized expression to this dynamic, the remarkable career of Louisiana Democrat John Breaux offers a more intimate portrait. Breaux, a former aide to the spectacularly corrupt Louisiana governor Edwin Edwards, first achieved national prominence as a member of the House in 1981. Siding with the Republicans on critical budget votes in return for sugar subsidies helpful to local business, Breaux famously insisted that his vote could not be bought—but "it can be rented."[34] Over time, as Breaux became more prominent (eventually becoming a powerful figure in the Senate and, directly following Bill Clinton, chair of the DLC) he refined this posture into something more statesmanlike. Positioning himself as a broker between the two parties, Breaux repeatedly called for his own "bipartisan" compromises that either undercut progressive initiatives (most significantly by backing an alternative to the Clinton health plan) or advanced policies highly favorable to business (the Medicare Prescription Drug Bill of 2003) and the affluent (the Bush tax cuts of 2001). Breaux typified an emerging generation of Democratic barons who, in a context of increasingly conservative and powerful Republicans, virtually assured the failure of any significant initiatives on behalf of the middle class.

Breaux's career reveals another, more subtle impact of the massive new wave of money on the Democratic Party. The growing importance of financial connections resulted in an increasingly profitable set of career linkages connecting the Democratic Party apparatus to the world of lobbying. Movements from elected or appointed office, congressional or presidential campaigns, or important staff positions to lucrative lobbying roles proliferated.

To take one of many examples, Peter Kelly, a Connecticut lawyer who served as the party's finance chairman from 1981 to 1985, joined the powerful Republican lobbying firm of Black, Manafort, and Stone. Around the same time, the firm hired former aides to the Democrats' two top tax legislators, Senator Russell Long and Representative Dan Rostenkowski.[35] Of course, the value of lobbyists like Kelly rested heavily on their access to Democratic policymakers, which they continued to cultivate once they

settled in their new positions. Like a rapidly increasing share of his colleagues, Breaux would end his career as an elected official by moving to a
lucrative post on K Street.

Whose Party Is It?

Increasingly during the 1980s, the Democrats lost their capacity to speak
to the economic concerns of the little guy. The shift in the interest group
basis of the party (toward nonmaterial upper-middle-class issues), combined with the stark moderating pull exerted as business support became
more critical, diminished the momentum toward policy activism on economic issues. Democrats faced less and less demand to present a sharp,
populist economic message, and more and more pressure to refrain from
such a position. They responded with a crouched economic posture that
offered little of appeal to the middle class.

Most notoriously, this involved a decade-long effort to reposition
the party as the advocates of deficit reduction.[36] Unable to compete with
Reagan's tax-cutting largesse, Mondale famously, and disastrously, fashioned himself as the "eat your peas" candidate by openly acknowledging
the need to raise taxes. Time and again, Democrats returned to the same
argument—in part because the conservative wing of the party made it all
but impossible to agree on any alternative.

Democrats also showed surprising receptivity to the widening deregulatory agenda. Recall that in the late 1970s the Carter administration,
backed by Democrats like Ted Kennedy, had encouraged deregulation
of sheltered industries like trucking and airlines. From there, however,
deregulation spread. Spurred by lobbyists seeking new opportunities,
the effort morphed from a careful, sector-by-sector analysis of the costs
and benefits of regulation to something more like a free-for-all. Old ideas
of a mixed economy based on checks and balances gave way to a simple
mantra: Economic regulation was outmoded and market self-regulation
should be the new norm.

Without a serious organizational counterweight, deregulation fed on itself. As new sources of competition emerged, they gave rise to new demands from still-regulated companies for yet more freedom from oversight. Alfred Kahn, the architect of Carter's initiative, could only shake his head decades later. Banks, he insisted, "were a different kind of animal . . . They were animals that had a direct effect on the macroeconomy. That is very different from the regulation of industries that provided goods and services . . . I never supported any type of deregulation of banking."[37]

Yet plenty of Democrats did. In 1980, they passed legislation freeing savings and loans from restrictions on the interest rates they could charge. Two years later, the bipartisan Garn–St. Germain Depository Institutions Act introduced sweeping deregulation that allowed the savings-and-loan industry to enter a wide range of new businesses with very limited oversight. Among the cosponsors were Democratic congressmen Steny Hoyer and Chuck Schumer. The reforms created a now-familiar set of perverse incentives, expanding opportunities to score big by betting with other people's money. The debacle that followed was an eerie precursor of the financial implosion of 2008, although this time the damage was largely contained within the S&L industry. The S&L crisis, which cost taxpayers over $125 billion in direct outlays, was a thoroughly bipartisan affair. Early efforts to correct the problems (at a time when the costs would have been minimal) were effectively blocked in Congress.[38] The whole sordid business was capped by a mostly Democratic (save for John McCain) scandal involving Charles Keating, the head of Lincoln Savings and Loan.

In sum, Democrats staggered through the 1980s on economic matters. With the party's new affluent base and stronger relationship with the business community, incumbents had sufficient resources to effectively counterpunch against Republicans in the White House. And the Democrats retained control over a critical citadel in American politics— the House of Representatives. Yet that control was increasingly unsteady, with the party leadership leaning precariously on the twin crutches of support from affluent social liberals and incumbency advantage. Worse for the Democrats, it was ever more clear that they had lost the capacity to create either an effective economic message or viable legislative coalitions for populist policies. These problems would only worsen in the following decade, as the pace of economic and political change accelerated, ushering in a new economic world.

The Emerging GOP Coalition

On the other side of the partisan aisle, the story was one of growing determination and focus, as the Republican Party marched steadily rightward. As conventionally told, this story has an obvious leading actor: Ronald Reagan. Yet during Reagan's presidency the political base for a sustained economic conservatism remained incomplete. In practice, Reaganism was a halfway house between the reluctant New Dealism of Richard Nixon and the winner-take-all enthusiasm of George W. Bush.

This is not to minimize the import of Reagan's election. In the watershed year of 1980, Reagan dispatched first the moderate, establishment Republican George H. W. Bush and then the Democratic incumbent Carter. In doing so, he dispelled any doubts about the electoral viability of a rhetorical economic conservatism that identified government as "the problem, not the solution." Only a few years before, Reagan was widely seen as out of the mainstream of American politics—an echo of the catastrophically failed candidacy of Barry Goldwater. Many analysts had a hard time taking him seriously as a national candidate. Yet he was a perfect fit for a time of economic turbulence when Democrats' control of all the levers of government provided an easy foil. Reagan was a master at targeting growing popular frustration and economic anxiety toward Washington. The term "Reagan Democrats" captures Reagan's success in winning white, working-class voters in both the South and the North—a crucial voting bloc that supported the charismatic candidate if not, yet, the GOP as a whole.

Nor was it just campaign rhetoric. Reagan's election accelerated Washington's shift to the right on economic issues. Deregulatory momentum got an additional boost. Reagan's famous showdown with the air-traffic controllers union, in which striking workers were summarily fired, was just the most visible face of an aggressively antiunion posture apparent in both the NLRB and the Department of Labor. Backed by a now much more organized conservative movement that fed the White House with a steady supply of policy ideas and personnel, Reagan stacked agencies with close allies of business. Once installed, these appointees proceeded to rewrite rules in corporate-friendly ways, while drastically slowing the pace and severity of enforcement actions.[39]

Reagan's signature policy move—supported by conservative Democrats as well as Republicans—was, of course, the "supply-side" tax cut of 1981. The 1981 tax bill combined large rate cuts, a variety of additional breaks for high-income households, and sharp reductions in business taxes. Crucially, if less prominently, the legislation also indexed tax brackets to inflation. "Bracket creep" had silently pushed up government revenues without legislators ever needing to vote in favor of taxes. Its elimination represented a major policy victory, ending one form of policy drift that had been hugely beneficial to liberals by allowing them to fund social programs without openly raising taxes.

The tax cuts of 1981 were a major policy landmark. Yet even more significant than their economic effects was their impact on the GOP's "brand" and its own self-image. In a move of lasting significance, Ronald Reagan placed lower taxes at the heart of the GOP agenda and economic message, supplanting the emphasis on budget balance and incremental change of a previous Republican generation.

Yet ironically, even as Reagan's tax cuts signaled a dramatic shift in policy and message, they also represented the legislative high-water mark of the Reagan presidency. Despite Reagan's electoral successes, the GOP never came close to capturing the House. Instead, Reagan was forced to assemble a working coalition from issue to issue and strike repeated compromises with his nemesis, House Speaker Tip O'Neill. By 1982, with the economy in recession, the deficit growing rapidly, and the president's popularity plummeting, Reagan had to accede to significant tax increases. He did so again in 1984. After stumbling badly over his apparent willingness to cut Social Security, Reagan tacked to the middle. Saved from irrelevance by Republicans' remarkable 1982 rescue, he participated in a bipartisan 1983 plan that shored up the classic New Deal program through a traditional combination of modest benefit cuts and, again, higher taxes.

Not even Reagan's landslide reelection could impart new momentum to the cause of economic conservatives. Indeed, the grand domestic policy initiative of Reagan's second term, the 1986 tax reform law, was the epitome of a rationalist, middle-of-the-road policy compromise. Negotiated with congressional Democrats, the legislation was carefully designed not to "starve the beast" in Washington but to be revenue neutral. It shifted the tax burden from ordinary citizens to firms by financing lower tax rates through the elimination of a variety of tax loopholes. It was, in short, a reform designed to improve the status quo rather than overthrow it (even though the new status quo it created was quickly undermined by the forces of winner-take-all politics).

Thus in practice, especially after its first year, Reaganism was not the conservative economic juggernaut that its critics and enthusiasts usually portray. After an initial flurry of activity, it devolved into a much more limited enterprise. Reagan did succeed in blocking new government programs, and his eight years in office inaugurated what would prove to be a generation of policy drift. Rarely, however, was the president able to mobilize sufficient support for ambitious initiatives of his own. In part, of course, this was because Republicans never controlled Congress. Almost invariably, the president found himself sitting across the negotiating table from traditional New Dealer Tip O'Neill, whose outlook on government was radically different.

It was in Congress, however, where the seeds for a true Republican revolution were growing. Even as Reagan faltered, a new version of economic conservatism—grounded not on fiscal rectitude but on tax cuts for those at the top and deregulation on an ever-widening scale—was gaining strength on Capitol Hill.

A House Divided

Congressional delegations are like multiple sediment layers. They reveal the long-term transformation of a party over time. Older members of the party embodying the circumstances and traditions of an earlier generation coexist uneasily with younger members more attuned to present organizational and electoral realities.

So it was when Reagan entered office. The Republican Party in Congress still featured a large bloc of traditional fiscal conservatives, as well as Eisenhower-style moderates from the Midwest, Northwest, and Northeast. These moderates had built successful careers by accepting the mixed economy and making peace with the most popular and durable elements of the New Deal. Like Nixon, they were skeptical of the economic radicals. Indeed, their views were nicely summarized by Dwight Eisenhower, Nixon's reluctant patron and the quintessential example of a successful Republican moderate. In a letter to his brother Edgar, written on November 8, 1954, Eisenhower signaled his disdain for those who sought to roll back the New Deal:

Should any political party attempt to abolish social security, unemployment insurance, and eliminate labor laws and farm programs, you would not hear of that party again in our political history. There is a tiny splinter group, of course, that believes you can do these things. Among them are H. L. Hunt (you possibly know his background), a few other Texas oil millionaires, and an occasional politician or business man from other areas. Their number is negligible and they are stupid.[40]

Under Reagan's watch, however, the ranks of those holding the views Eisenhower had scorned were growing. The "old" party was slowly giving way to a new one—a party that would spearhead a new economic conservatism. Large cohorts of conservative Republicans had entered the House in the late 1970s and early 1980s, including Dick Cheney and Newt

Gingrich in 1978, Vin Weber in 1980, and Dick Armey and Tom DeLay in 1984. Closely associated with the Reagan revolution, they saw the status quo as both unacceptable and vulnerable.

These younger Republicans were critical of a congressional GOP leadership that seemed comfortable with the art of compromise and reconciled to permanent minority status. Many of these members coalesced around Newt Gingrich and his Conservative Opportunity Society. Gingrich and his supporters were devoted to a strategy of full-out confrontation with the majority—a confrontation that they thought could topple the Democrats and remake the GOP at the same time. As a close ally would observe in the early 1990s, "It was [Gingrich's] understanding that political parties are cultures and that cultures are self-reinforcing and that a political party that had been a minority for as long as the Republican Party had been a minority party had learned all the habits of being a minority."[41]

Gingrich also knew something else: Sooner or later, politicians lose or leave office. If they fail to adapt to a new environment, they lose or leave office sooner. Two distinct processes transform congressional parties—"replacement" of old members by new ones and "conversion" as sitting members shift their positions to accommodate new pressures. Both processes were gradually strengthening the hands of the new conservatives.

Replacement itself has two distinct components. One form occurs when a particular House or Senate seat switches from one party to the other. By far the most important part of this process in the past generation has been the dramatic shift in representation in the South, which has moved from solidly Democratic to solidly Republican. Once the civil rights movement had clarified national partisan politics, it was only a matter of time before the nation's most conservative region aligned with the nation's more conservative political party. A few Southern Democrats, like Phil Gramm, caught the shifting winds and switched to the regionally ascendant and ideologically more palatable GOP. For the most part, however, they stayed Democrats. The electoral advantages of incumbency generally made it possible to hang on. Everyone could see, however, that the Southern Democrats were dead men walking. When they left office, their replacements were almost invariably far more conservative Republicans.

The second form of turnover that drove the party ever further rightward occurred within the GOP itself: the replacement of moderate Republicans by more conservative ones. This process was particularly pronounced in the South, where the new brand of economic radicalism sold especially well. As the party became more southern, the ranks of the most fiercely committed grew. Even outside the South, however, new members who replaced old ones were almost invariably more extreme on economic issues. They saw themselves as pursuing Reagan's agenda, yet they took positions well beyond anything Reagan had seriously tried to achieve when in office. And though the results would not show until the following decade, they were on the march. By 1989, their leader, Gingrich, had risen to the position of minority whip, and his conservative insurgents had turned up the heat so high that they had forced Democratic Speaker Jim Wright to resign.

The Death of the Old Guard

During the 1980s, thoughtful observers (like Thomas Edsall in his classic *The New Politics of Inequality*) could see that along with rising inequality a new kind of politics was emerging.[42] From the Reagan tax cuts, to the firing of striking federal workers, to the deregulation-induced S&L crisis, Washington was increasingly weighing in on the side of the have-it-alls. Yet compared to what was to come, all this was rather tepid. In fact, in the midst of the mild-mannered presidency of George H. W. Bush—Reagan's 1980 establishment foe who had derided supply-side tax cuts as "voodoo economics"—calls for radical change seemed to be receding.

George Herbert Walker Bush was an old-school Republican. He was an instinctive compromiser, trained in the establishment GOP habit of treading carefully around social and economic policy issues that were traditionally Democratic terrain. Anointed by Reagan, he had won grudging conservative support with his famous "read my lips, no new taxes" pledge during the 1988 campaign. In office, though, Bush proved willing to compromise with Democrats on big domestic issues such as the Clean Air Act Amendments of 1990 and the Americans with Disabilities Act. To disgusted conservatives, those bills suggested that he and other old-guard Republicans like Bob Dole might spout conservative rhetoric but would administer liberal programs in practice.

The unforgivable, however, was Bush's betrayal of his "no new taxes" pledge as part of his agreement to a huge deficit-reduction compromise in 1990. At the time, this deal seemed to be just one of what would be a long series of deficit-cutting packages that began in 1982 and would continue through 1997. Repeatedly, these agreements had combined tax increases (painful for Republicans) and spending cuts (painful for Democrats). Ronald Reagan had accepted similar packages, but only after he had established a record as an energetic tax-cutter. In retrospect, however, 1990 was a watershed, as important to the evolution of the GOP as the ambitious and politically more successful tax initiatives of Reagan in 1981 and George W. Bush in 2001.

1990's historic significance stems from the earthquake it triggered among Republican elites. Shifting structures of political influence are often virtually invisible for extended periods of time because they have not yet developed to the point where ascending groups can mount an effective challenge. Beneath the surface, as the journalists Daniel Balz and Ronald Brownstein ably show in their 1996 book *Storming the Gates*, a new Republican Party had gradually been taking shape, as an older generation of political moderates and fiscal conservatives gave way to an insurgent generation of hard-line conservatives and radical tax-cutters.[43] The new breed of conservative elites was gradually pushing up against the old. 1990 was the moment when this pressure finally burst.

The revolution was led by the new guard's leader, Newt Gingrich. In the face of a Republican president's appeal for compromise to reduce the deficit, Gingrich and his allies convinced well over half the Republicans in the House to inflict a humiliating defeat on their party's ostensible leader. In the short run, Bush was able to regroup and pass a revised (and, given the need to gain more Democratic votes in place of the rebels, more liberal) package. But the long-term effect on the Republican Party was profound. Bush's relations with the conservative wing were permanently damaged. As his son George W. observed firsthand, this damage was to prove very costly when Bush sought reelection two years later. Republican moderates never recovered. Gingrich's rebellion put House Minority Leader Robert Michel on notice: This was to be his last term at the top. When Michel announced his retirement, Gingrich and his allies swept into the leadership and rapidly signaled a much more aggressive and radical posture.

Republicans had long fought against higher taxes, but this goal had always been in tension with a commitment to fiscal conservatism. The traditional attitude was well captured in Gingrich's derisive description of Senate leader Robert Dole as "the tax collector for the welfare state." Gingrich's new-line Republicans reversed the priority between fiscal conservatism and tax cuts: Reducing taxes was paramount—a priority to be advanced at every opportunity. Even more important, they pushed for an energized and cohesive party dedicated to a radical restructuring of government's role to unleash the winner-take-all economy. The baby steps of the 1980s were ready to give way to something more ambitious.

Chapter 8

Building a Bridge to the Nineteenth Century

By all accounts, the 1980s was a great time to be rich. As chronicled in pop-culture movies like *The Bonfire of the Vanities* and *Wall Street*, it was a moment when capitalism's winners took center stage. And as they did so, they revealed the contours of a new capitalism. Deal-makers and financial gamblers were supplanting captains of industry as the biggest winners of all.

But the 1980s was just a warm-up act. The staggering paychecks that generated such wonder and bewilderment would have been dismissed a few years later as decidedly second-rate. In the following decade the extraordinary transfer of income to the top truly shifted into high gear. Year after year, under Democratic administrations as well as Republican ones, the rich pulled rapidly away from everyone else. During the expansion of the 1990s (1993–2000), the average pre-tax real income of the top 0.01 percent nearly tripled, increasing more than 16 percent a year after adjusting for inflation. During the expansion of the 2000s (2002–2007), it more than doubled again, increasing more than 17 percent a year after inflation and exceeding $35 million in 2007.[1] Broadland was dead. Richistan was born.

Not coincidentally, it was after 1990 that the full contours of winner-take-all politics came into focus. 1990, in fact, was a critical year. It was the year moderate Republicanism suffered its decisive, crushing defeat—at the hands of other Republicans. Its final standard-bearer, George H. W.

Bush, would hold office two more years. Yet his brand of politics, and his presidency, were over, definitively repudiated by the ascendant, Gingrich-led GOP. Ironically, this radical wing would ultimately achieve some of its greatest policy victories under the leadership of Bush's son and name-sake.

The Democrats, too, had changed with the times. True, the party never converted to the fervent tax-cutting religion of the GOP (although a substantial, often crucial, bloc was willing to support Republican tax cuts when they came up for a vote). Support for turbocharged, freewheel-ing markets was another matter. Those likely to raise doubts about these trends were still almost always Democrats. Yet Democrats at the com-manding heights of their party were increasingly eager to show their friendliness to business and, especially, Wall Street. Critical aspects of the new winner-take-all economy received sustained, enthusiastic bipartisan support not just under George W. Bush, but also under Bill Clinton.

The wonder years of the winner-take-all economy began with the re-cession that brought down Bush the elder. They ended with a recession of far greater magnitude that discredited Bush the younger—and powerfully showcased the new economy's true costs. Nothing better summed up the era, and its marriage of the economic and the political, than the résumés of the two men widely regarded as Clinton and Bush's most influential secretaries of the treasury, Robert Rubin and Henry Paulson. Different in many ways, including party affiliation, each nonetheless developed (for a time) a reputation for sophisticated economic management. And each derived much of that reputation from a previous career at a single com-pany, Goldman Sachs—the firm that, more than any other, came to sym-bolize the winner-take-all economy.

This chapter and the next chronicle how Republicans and Democrats each contributed, in different ways, to the new economic and political order. We begin with the GOP, which clearly merits top billing. More em-phatically than their opponents, Republicans saw the steep upward tilt of economic rewards as an indication that all was right with the universe—especially since they had good reason to think that they would be the po-litical masters of it.

Dr. Phil's Diagnosis

Of all the awkward moments in John McCain's failed 2008 presidential campaign—and there were many—perhaps the most tone-deaf of all was the day former Senator Phil Gramm, one of McCain's top economic advisers, dominated the news cycle. In early July, as storm clouds gathered over the American economy, Gramm gave an interview to the conservative *Washington Times*. In it, he said the American economy "had never been more dominant," dismissed the growing troubles as a "mental recession," and groused that the country was becoming "a nation of whiners."

A gleeful Obama campaign pounced, with its candidate responding that the nation's economic troubles were real, and that we hardly needed "another Dr. Phil," comparing Gramm to the popular TV psychologist.[2] Gramm had been a powerhouse in the Senate and was rumored to be a leading candidate for treasury secretary in a McCain administration. The two Republican titans were close. McCain had been chairman of Gramm's failed 1996 presidential run. Gramm, in turn, had stood with McCain in the dark days of 2007, when his campaign for the Republican nomination seemed doomed. He had played an important part in getting McCain back on track. Nonetheless, a week after scolding the American people for complaining about economic hardship, Gramm was forced to step down from the campaign.

If Gramm had a tin ear, it was for good reason. Few had such strong motivation to deny that the American economy was beginning to crumble. Like the character in Woody Allen's *Zelig*, Gramm would have shown up in almost every photo op during the thirty-year construction of the winner-take-all economy. Unlike Zelig, however, Gramm had been not just present, but an active participant throughout. Indeed, his career encapsulated the deep shifts in American politics that accompanied that construction, and his final years in the limelight revealed, in especially clear if unflattering terms, what elite-level politics had become.

In 1981, as a Democratic congressman from Texas, Gramm cosponsored the Gramm-Latta budget legislation that wrote many of Reagan's priorities into law. A decade later, having switched parties and legislative chambers, Gramm had become an ever more zealous and increasingly powerful advocate of tax cuts for the wealthy and full-throttle deregulation. By 1995, he was the Republican chair of the Senate Banking Committee. This lofty perch gave him enormous power to shape legislation that Wall Street favored and to block initiatives it opposed. Among his legislative triumphs was the 1999 repeal of the Glass-Steagall Act, the Depression-era law that erected boundaries between investment and commercial banking to limit systemic risk and conflicts of interest. Even more impressive was his successful effort, in the waning days of the 2000 legislative session, to insert the Commodity Futures Modernization Act within a must-pass budget bill. This act essentially prohibited regulation of derivatives—the emerging financial instrument that played such a critical role in ramping up leverage, speculation, and hence paydays on Wall Street.

As that preemptive action suggests, Gramm excelled at playing defense as well as offense. When concerns about lax lending standards and excessive risk-taking in the subprime mortgage market generated growing calls for a response, Gramm retorted that the real problem was not predatory lending but "predatory borrowers" who could not pay their mortgages. As Senate Banking Committee chair, he stymied reformers by simply refusing to hold hearings on proposed legislation. When Securities and Exchange Commission Chair Arthur Levitt sought to introduce tougher rules for accounting firms to prevent conflicts of interest—the kind of conflicts that played a pronounced role in the collapse of Enron and a spate of corporate scandals—Gramm threatened to cut the SEC's budget. Indeed, as the massive expansion of Wall Street strained the agency, Gramm repeatedly resisted calls to increase the SEC's funding. To Levitt, his message was blunt, if inadvertently and chillingly prescient: "Unless the waters are crimson with the blood of investors, I don't want you engaging in any regulatory flights of fancy."[3]

Gramm was perhaps second only to Alan Greenspan as a high priest of deregulation. "Some people look at subprime lending and see evil," he said during the fight over predatory lending. "I look at subprime lending and I see the American dream in action." "When I am on Wall Street," he said the previous year, "to me that's a holy place."[4] The tithing, however, went the other direction. From 1989 to 2002, Gramm was the top recipient of funds from commercial banks, and one of the top five recipients from Wall Street overall.[5]

Nor was corporate America simply a source of campaign funds. The Gramm family history is an impressive illustration of the increasingly lucrative rewards that could come from crossing the short bridge connecting Washington insiders to the winner-take-all economy. Gramm's wife, Wendy, had been a great friend to business as head of the Commodity Futures Trading Commission in the late 1980s and early 1990s. Under her leadership, the CFTC had adopted rules exempting some swaps and derivatives from regulations (the efforts of a later CFTC head, Brooksley Born, to undo this would prompt Gramm's legislative actions in 2000). After leaving the CFTC, Wendy Gramm joined the board of Enron—a company whose energy futures contracts had received exemption from federal oversight under the rules Ms. Gramm's CFTC had approved. In the following years, her Enron salary and stock income totaled between $915,000 and $1.8 million.[6]

Gramm himself would retire in 2003, executing his own take-the-money-and-run move. He accepted a high position at UBS, Switzerland's largest bank. Like Enron, UBS had utilized opportunities rooted in Gramm-led policymaking—in this case acquiring Paine Webber in a transaction made possible by the repeal of Glass-Steagall. Gramm's responsibilities at UBS included lobbying Congress and the Treasury on issues related to banking and mortgage finance. Gramm's total compensation at UBS is unknown. Nor is it known how much he lost when the firm suffered devastating setbacks during the financial crisis of 2008, forcing write-downs that offset the previous four years of earnings and prompting a massive financial bailout by the Swiss government.

The New GOP

Phil Gramm personifies the new Republican Party that emerged in the 1990s: exuberant cheerleaders of the winner-take-all economy. On economic issues, the modern GOP became astonishingly conservative—not just far more conservative than the party of Nixon or Gerald Ford but far more conservative than the party of Ronald Reagan. Or perhaps it's more appropriate to say that the party became astonishingly radical, for the new GOP bore little resemblance to the go-slow fiscal conservatism of its predecessor. Everywhere and always, the modern GOP called for the retreat of government from regulation and the provision of public goods. Everywhere and always, the modern GOP saw high-end tax cuts as the solution to any problem. Tom DeLay—"the Hammer," who served as House majority whip under Gingrich and then became an extremely powerful majority leader, before leaving office amid a widening scandal surrounding the business lobbyist Jack Abramoff—expressed the sentiment most succinctly in 2003: "Nothing is more important in the face of a war than cutting taxes."[7]

Of course, the Republicans had been clearly positioned as the conservative party on economic issues since 1980. Yet this seeming constancy is profoundly misleading. Here again, pundits err by focusing on the contests of the moment. Inattentive to the substance of policy fights or to slow shifts in organizations, they have generally missed the full extent and duration of the GOP's long rightward march. Reagan and George H. W. Bush had to contend not only with the Democrats, but with a Republican Party that was divided on economic issues. The result of the divisions, from the early 1980s to the early 1990s, was repeated compromise. No more. A twenty-year struggle, from the late 1970s to the late 1990s, ended with the decisive victory of economic hard-liners.

This internal struggle involved some great theater: a series of pitched battles as well as behind-the-scenes brawls. Much of the change, however, looked less like an earthquake and more like the drip, drip, drip of a melting ice cap. Over more than two decades, both the geographic and organizational bases of the party shifted in ways that reinforced its commitment

to an extreme economic platform. Eisenhower, Nixon, and, more ambiva-
lently, even Reagan had felt obliged to accept the New Deal while picking battles with Democrats elsewhere. Now many Republicans revealed a
thinly veiled desire to do more than combat LBJ's War on Poverty. Their
ambitions included repeal of huge swaths of not only the New Deal but
the Progressive Era: no Social Security, no effective minimum wage, no
progressive taxation, no support for employer-provided health care, almost no financial regulation. They sought, in short, to reestablish the policies of the Gilded Age to mirror the emerging Gilded Age economy.

Dixie Rising

These attitudes reflected a new Republican Party, defined both by the
sources of its voters and by the composition of its most organized voices.

In the electorate, two new pools of voters helped provide the preconditions for Republican radicalism. The first was the South. In 1974,
two-thirds of southern members of the House of Representatives were
Democrats; in 1994, two-thirds were Republicans. Moreover, a list of the
most powerful figures in the GOP during the period after 1994—Newt
Gingrich, Tom DeLay, Dick Armey, Mitch McConnell, Trent Lott, Bill
Frist, and, of course, George W. Bush—was almost monolithically southern (with only midwesterners Bob Dole and Dennis Hastert and semi-
renegade westerner John McCain making the A-list). The generational
transfer of power from the Bush of Kennebunkport to the Bush of Craw-
ford symbolized a deeper truth. Unlike the party of Reagan, the modern
GOP is a profoundly southern party.

The significance of the South's gradual shift from a Democratic to Republican stronghold is, of course, widely recognized. Yet two things about
it are not. The first is that it took a long time. The South had become,
by 1980, quite reliably Republican in presidential elections—even when
the Democratic standard-bearer was a southerner. In Congress, however,
the story was different. Aided by incumbency, and by their ability to separate their individual reputations from national party "brands," Southern

Democrats in Congress gamely hung on. For the most part, Republican gains occurred gradually as these Democrats retired. It was not until the 1994 election rout (itself aided by an unusually high number of Democratic retirements) that the southern realignment fully materialized.

The second underappreciated feature of the realignment is how much it has simultaneously radicalized the Republican Party and altered the dynamic between the parties. Southern Democrats anchored the right wing of their party, and their most natural allies were often northern GOP moderates. They were often the swing voters in Congress. The leaderships of both parties had to make plays for their support. The resulting dynamic of bargaining and compromise wasn't always pretty, but it was the opposite of radical.

The new southern Republicans were a different breed entirely. Theirs were the loudest voices for a fundamental restructuring of the American political economy. Grounded in an electorate (especially in primaries) far more conservative than the country as a whole, supported by activists who were more conservative still, they were least likely to see the appeal of compromise. Overwhelmingly, southerners came to populate the right edge of the modern GOP.

Consider the 2000 platform of the Texas GOP—the state party of George W. Bush, Tom DeLay, Dick Armey, and Phil Gramm. It called for a return to the gold standard, the abolition of the Federal Reserve, the elimination of the minimum wage, the gradual abolition of Social Security, the repeal of the Sixteenth Amendment (which created the federal income tax) and the elimination of the IRS.[8] As southerners have taken over the leadership of a party that was becoming more homogeneous and more centralized, the GOP's economic agenda crystallized and became more extreme.

Religious Reinforcements

The other big expansion of the Republican electorate came from the growing attachment of conservative evangelicals to the GOP that we briefly discussed in chapter 6. Again, this is something that everyone knows, but the same two points need to be emphasized. The attachment of evangelicals to the GOP has been a *gradual* process, and it has greatly promoted the party's radicalization on economic matters.

In 1960, even as evangelical Protestants voted for Nixon against the Catholic John Kennedy, they continued to identify with the Democratic Party and cast their congressional votes overwhelmingly for Democrats.[9] The move toward firm identification with the Republican Party was gradual, and slowed by the Democratic candidacy of a Southern Baptist, Jimmy Carter. Reagan's landslide reelection in 1984 represented a significant step toward a true attachment of most evangelicals to the GOP. Yet it was not until the 1990s—in part due to the intense backlash against Bill Clinton, rooted in disgust at his personal life and disagreement with his positions on controversial social issues—that the full contours of the evangelical realignment emerged.

The common view is that the Christian Right bubbled up from broad-based voter reaction to national social issues, like abortion. But that misses the critical organizational side of the story—which involved Christian organizations (and especially Christian schools) as much as Christian voters. For those who would come to lead the evangelical movement, the tax status of private Christian schools, placed in jeopardy by an IRS ruling, became a hot-button issue in the late 1970s. A vast network of these schools had developed in response to desegregation, and when a Carter-appointed IRS commissioner made the ruling—and the Carter White House proved unresponsive to the resulting fury of Christian conservatives—they turned increasingly to Republicans for support. Although the tax funding issue has received far less notoriety than the abortion issue, at the time it may have actually been a greater catalyst to political organization. In the words of Richard Viguerie, a legendary figure in the conservative counterrevolution, the tax ruling "kicked the sleeping dog . . . It galvanized the religious right. It was the spark that ignited the religious right's involvement in real politics." Along with evangelical churches, this "galvanized" network of Christian school associations formed the institutional backbone of a conservative political movement that would become increasingly partisan over time.

The most visible manifestation of this new mobilization was Jerry Falwell's Moral Majority. Its first executive director, Robert Billings Sr., came right out of the IRS–Christian school fight, and half of the first fifty state chairmen of the new organization were affiliated with churches sponsoring Christian academies.[10] During the 1980s, however, the Moral Majority's bark was arguably worse than its bite. It failed to fully exploit its grassroots potential, focusing instead on direct-mail fund-raising. Falwell's operation developed an ability to attract attention but limited capacity to mobilize. Even the financial resources it could generate were modest judged by the rapidly escalating expectations of Washington. By the end of Reagan's presidency, many viewed Christian conservatism as a declining political force.

Yet if the first wave had crested, a second, larger one was right behind it. In the late 1980s and early 1990s, as Falwell's efforts faded, the mobilization of Christian conservatism took on new life. This revitalization came through a combination of more decentralized, local efforts and a new national operation, Ralph Reed's Christian Coalition. Reed's effort, like Falwell's, proved to be mercurial—an important force in the critical 1994 election and for a time thereafter, but without staying power. At the local level, however, Christian groups continued to make quiet but crucial organizational gains. The magazine *Campaigns and Elections* makes periodic assessments of state parties, based on hundreds of interviews with informed political observers. In 1994, the journal listed thirty-one state Republican parties as under the "moderate" or "strong" control of Christian conservatives. By 2002, that number had increased to forty-four.[11] Moreover, the movement had increased its capacity to deliver dedicated volunteers willing to take on the unglamorous but essential work needed to get voters out on Election Day.

As we noted in chapter 6, the critical feature of this mobilization was that the realigning evangelical vote accompanied an increasingly politicized, organized Christian conservative movement that made common cause with the GOP. As with organized labor in its heyday, organized forces that brought voters into politics were central in deciding how political resources would be utilized—for what goals, and on behalf of which politicians—and in signaling to voters who should gain their allegiance or face their wrath, and for what. And what they decided is that conservative Christian voters should be brought into alliance with other forces in the GOP, trading support on the social issues the Christian Right cared most about for an economic agenda tailored to other interests.

It is sometimes argued—most entertainingly in Thomas Frank's *What's the Matter with Kansas?*—that Christian conservatives cut a bad deal. In Frank's telling, the religious right has served as the shock troops for a party committed to a business agenda. "They are massing at the gates," Frank writes, "hoisting the black flag, and while the millionaires tremble in their mansions, they are bellowing out their terrifying demands. 'We are here,' they scream, 'to cut your taxes.' "[12] For Frank, those focused on social issues have, effectively, transferred hard cash to Republican business interests in return for limp gestures.

We have no dog in this fight (though the role of social issue conservatism in shaping the judiciary strikes us as no small prize). Whether the market enthusiasts who receive the economic *quid* in this deal have had to concede to a meaningful social issue *quo* is of limited relevance to the politics of the winner-take-all economy. What is extremely relevant is the basic nature of the deal, rather than the specific terms. By the mid-1990s, tens of millions of middle- and working-class Christian conservatives were being brought into the GOP's electoral coalition. Even as voters in general lined up along the economic divide, evangelicals gave a big boost to GOP ranks. Crucially, this electoral army was being brought in on terms that required very little attention to their economic concerns. And the political figures, like Reed, who brokered this transaction could be relied upon to either deflect attention from economic issues or assure supporters that the threats to their economic security came from liberals and Democrats.

Market Mania, Inc.

If organization officiated the marriage of Christian conservatism to the GOP, the same could be said of the increasingly virulent economic conservatism that came to dominate the party in the 1990s. Again, "pro-business, antitax" is a label that one could very comfortably attach to the Republican Party circa 1980. But that doesn't mean the party was a finished product. Even as long-term trends were depleting the ranks of party moderates, two key organizational developments heightened the prominence of economic radicalism.

The first was the growing, organized presence of small business within the GOP. Small employers had long felt even more reason to complain about government than large firms. Although the regulatory demands emanating from Washington generally hit small and large businesses alike, large businesses had much broader shoulders to bear the costs of compliance. For a firm with thousands of employees, managing regulatory demands was often an irritant, but just a cost of doing business. Since competitors generally faced the same requirements, the expense could often be passed on to consumers. Sometimes large businesses were as concerned with receiving assurances that regulation would be uniform and predictable as with the level of regulation itself.

For small employers, however, the demands could be crushing. At a time of continuous, wrenching economic change, Washington became a major target for outrage. This was the milieu that would send the former owner of a pest-control company, Tom DeLay, to Washington, where he would target the Environmental Protection Agency as "the Gestapo of government, pure and simple."[13]

Those seeking to push the GOP rightward sought to amplify and harness this anger, and as it grew as a political force, it encouraged a continuous intensification of the party's anti-Washington stance. The National Federation of Independent Business (NFIB)—600,000 members strong at its peak—embodied the transformation. Traditionally the NFIB was something of an afterthought to organizations like the Business Roundtable, the National Association of Manufacturers, and the Chamber of

Commerce. In the 1990s, however, the NFIB came into its own, and its story epitomizes the deepening and radicalization of the business-GOP relationship.

For both sides of this emerging alliance, the battle over the Clinton health plan was a watershed. Part of the Clinton political strategy had been to "divide and conquer," splitting traditional opponents of reform by offering benefits to large employers and large health insurers. Indeed, large employer organizations like the Chamber of Commerce equivocated, uncertain whether to bargain for the best deal they could get or go into opposition. The NFIB didn't hesitate. For many of its members, the Clinton plan's mandate on employers to provide insurance was a clear loser, an especially egregious example of what NFIB president Jack Faris described as Washington's tendency to see business only "as the means to solve problem after problem facing our society."[14] Not only that, the NFIB leadership saw an excellent opportunity for organizational growth. Strident opposition to health-care reform helped the NFIB poach members from a Chamber of Commerce that claimed to represent small as well as large business but largely catered to the latter.

Encouraged by the most conservative Republicans, the NFIB mobilized heavily against the Clinton plan. In alliance with the Health Insurance Association of America—representative of the small insurers who had also been frozen out of reform, and who crafted the "Harry and Louise" ads attacking the initiative—the NFIB financed an aggressive campaign of negative ads and grassroots mobilization. It emerged successful, increasingly prominent (two thoughtful journalists opined that it had "surpassed more conciliatory big business organizations as a legislative force in Washington"), and with an experience that had "really cemented that relationship" with the GOP, according to NFIB's vice president.[15] The success helped energize radicals on both sides of the alliance. In a nice coda to their victory, and a sign of the intensified shift to the right that was under way, conservative business leaders and the House GOP successfully lobbied the Chamber of Commerce to oust its vice president, William Archey, who had orchestrated the Chamber's cautious stance toward the Clinton health-care plan.

When the GOP won a stunning victory in the 1994 midterm elections, the political connections binding it to business tightened further. Tom DeLay, in particular, seized the moment. He initiated what came to be known as the K Street Project, designed to bring lobbyists and corporations into a much closer, more coordinated relationship with the GOP leadership. "If you want to play in our revolution," he announced, "you have to live by our rules."[16] The K Street Project involved close and well-publicized monitoring of campaign contributions and hiring practices of lobbying firms and trade associations to make sure they were GOP-friendly. DeLay's efforts were so blatant that they earned that rarest of prizes: an admonition from the House Ethics Committee.

How much the arm-twisting mattered is hard to gauge—groups seeking Washington's favors have long had cause to help the majority party, and the GOP's agenda of deregulation and upper-end tax cuts was hardly a tough sell. Either way, the new political math was bad news for the Democratic Party. According to the Center for Responsive Politics, political donations from nineteen key industry sectors, which had been split roughly evenly between the parties a decade ago, shifted to a 2–1 GOP advantage.[17] This came, moreover, at a time when business was continuing to ramp up its political capacity in Washington. Accurate estimates of lobbying outlays before 1998 are unavailable, but once George W. Bush entered the White House, official lobbying expenditures skyrocketed, roughly doubling during his eight years in office.[18] The connections between business and the GOP had been strengthening for thirty years, but not since the early twentieth century had the two sides combined such formidable political resources.

RINO Hunters

The intensified connection of business to the GOP was reinforced by a second organizational development: the emergence of a cadre of activists devoted to making tax cuts the durable, unquestioned foundation of Republican doctrine.[19] Again, support for tax cuts was nothing new on the right. Now, however, conservatives left no doubt that tax cuts deserved clear priority over deficit reduction. Even more novel was the sustained, organized push of the antitax forces. Rather than simply advocate for tax rollbacks, they now focused on the recruitment and support of public officials devoted to the cause. And they backed up this recruitment and support with careful monitoring and the promise of swift retaliation to guard against any backsliding.

The new focus reflected tax-cutters' deep disappointment with the post-1981 Reagan presidency and the administration of George H. W. Bush: the acceptance of tax hikes in 1982 and 1984, the revenue-neutral tax reform of 1986, and, most infamous of all, Bush's betrayal of his "read my lips" pledge. The economic radicals, in Congress and out, seethed. Lip service from Republican moderates was not enough. As Richard Gilder, an influential stockbroker, philanthropist, and ardent supply-sider who would cofound the Club for Growth, put it, "We would hear these great growth ideas about how [the candidates] were going to cut taxes and push for growth, and then they'd get down there and vote to raise taxes."[20]

Out of this frustration emerged new organizations, heavily funded by the most affluent elements of American society. One of the many advantages of political organization is the capacity not just to learn from experience but to translate those lessons into renewed action. Antitax activists had learned some lessons from their prior disappointments. Their fervent commitment to tax cuts was not new, but their strategy was. Put crudely, their efforts shifted from creating broad public support to recruiting and monitoring politicians. These groups came to play a key role in producing like-minded candidates—or at least candidates who faced strong incentives to behave as if they were like-minded—and in radicalizing tax politics.

Two groups were at the heart of this effort: Grover Norquist's Americans for Tax Reform (ATR) and Stephen Moore's Club for Growth (CFG). ATR began as a Reagan White House operation, headed by Norquist, in the run-up to the (ironically, given ATR's evolution, revenue-neutral) Tax Reform Act of 1986. The Club for Growth really started only in 1999 (although formally it succeeded a virtually moribund predecessor). Moore founded the organization with backing from conservative think tanks and media figures, as well as Wall Street financial interests. His previous training reads like an extended boot camp for extreme economic conservatism: work at the hard right Heritage Foundation and the libertarian Cato Institute, along with a stint on Dick Armey's staff.

From the beginning, the objectives of these two groups were avowedly radical. Norquist described his goal as a 50 percent reduction in government as a share of GDP ("down to the size where you could drown it in the bathtub")—roughly the state of American government before World War II. Stephen Moore was a strong advocate of a flat tax—eliminating all progressivity from the tax code—an idea that was beyond the pale in the 1980s but would come to garner wide support within the GOP.

Both ATR and CFG were elite rather than mass operations. They had small memberships, and they relied heavily on large donations (including, in ATR's case, sizable contributions from the Republican Party). The "mass" element of these influential organizations was largely confined to electioneering rather than grassroots mobilization. Indeed, by the standards of mass membership organizations, CFG was Lilliputian, boasting around ten thousand members by 2003. Yet its affiliates were unusually well-heeled. During the 2002 midterm elections, the club's $10 million in contributions made it the leading source of campaign funds for Republicans outside of the GOP itself. In 2004, it spent a staggering $2.3 million on a single *primary* campaign, backing Pat Toomey in his almost successful effort to unseat incumbent Republican Senator Arlen Specter in Pennsylvania (six years later, the prospect of a rematch with Toomey would drive Specter out of the Republican Party altogether).

As CFG's assault on Specter suggests, these organizations targeted their energies on ensuring that the gradual process of replacement within the Republican Party promoted a relentless focus on tax cuts. For ATR, the central tool was the tax pledge. ATR asked elected officials and candidates for office to make specific promises not to support tax increases. Some Republican politicians, mostly moderate incumbents, resisted these pledges for a time. But the logic of contemporary Republican primaries quickly became clear. For nonincumbents, signing the pledge became a prerequisite for running for Congress (and, in many places, state office as well). Moderates wishing to protect their flank generally signed as well—if not, their successors did. By the end of 2003, ATR had pledges from 216 members of the House (just two short of a majority) and forty-two senators, as well as President Bush himself. Notably, signers of the pledge made up an absolute majority of members on the two crucial House committees (Ways and Means and Budget) that shaped the Bush tax cuts of 2001–2004.[21]

Like ATR, the Club for Growth also focused its energies on increasing the ranks of committed tax-cutters in Congress. The preferred technique was candidate recruitment for open seats, combined—strikingly—with efforts to take out RINOs ("Republicans in name only") like Arlen Specter. Club president Stephen Moore joked that when he threatened a primary challenge against wayward Republicans "they start wetting their pants." The club failed to take out a RINO until 2006, but it came close on several occasions and may well have hastened some retirements. More important, its efforts served to put moderates on notice. As club-supported House Republican Jeff Flake put it: "When you have 100 percent of Republicans voting for the Bush tax cuts, you know that they are looking over their shoulder and not wanting to have Steve Moore recruiting candidates in their district."[22]

Right All the Time

Of course, by the time Republicans took control of Congress in 1994, most of their members, at least in the House, needed little encouragement when it came to tax cuts. In 1990, there were still two Republican parties on economic issues. Within a few years, however, there was really only one: a party that relentlessly advanced the positions demanded by the right. After the revolt against Bush, aggressive conservatives consolidated control. With Newt Gingrich flanked by Dick Armey and Tom DeLay, the more confrontational stance of the leadership was clear. And Gingrich had the troops. Generational turnover, as well as the southern shift in the Republican caucus, had moved the bulk of the party well to the right. Monitoring groups could play a critical role in disciplining or punishing the stragglers.

The process took slightly longer in the Senate, where Bob Dole represented a continuing thread of Midwest, balanced-budget conservatism. There too, however, generational replacement was shifting the landscape. Moderates had an increasingly difficult time surviving Republican primaries. A large cadre of graduates from the Gingrich House brought their new version of hard-edged, polarizing conservatism to the clubbier Senate.[23] By the late 1990s, differences between the two conservative caucuses on economic issues had largely vanished.

The success of the leaders and their allies helped to assure that the party spoke with near-unity on economic issues—and that this unified voice articulated a consistently hard line. In doctrine, this new Republican Party was fervently antistatist. It was more than happy to make exceptions when it was advantageous—to use government money to enrich its strong supporters. But its message and most of its actions were geared to removing governmental constraints on those with economic clout. Regulation was to be rolled back whenever possible; where it couldn't be openly rolled back, it perhaps could be rendered ineffective. Tax cuts were the cornerstone of the party's philosophy, simultaneously contributing to its supporters' bottom line while cutting off the blood supply of government activism.

Why did the party become so radical on economic issues, so much more intensely focused on business concerns? In a fundamental sense, it did so because it *could*. The restructuring of the party over the course of the 1980s and 1990s helps explain how this shift to a position well to the right of previous practices, and of the center of public opinion, could occur. Attracting a huge new GOP voting bloc brought to the party largely for cultural reasons, reaping the extensive financial resources and organizational support that flowed from the economy's winners, and facing an opposition that was increasingly cross-pressured on economic matters, Republicans became confident they could take a radical economic stance and win.

"Reaganism at Warp Speed"

The imprint of this new Republican Party on governance—what Norquist enthusiastically dubbed "Reaganism at warp speed" was not long in coming.[24] 1993, with the party supposedly back on its heels following the defeat of a Republican sitting president, provided the first indication. President Clinton, facing strong pressure to confront the deficit, dropped his campaign ideas about social "investments" and proposed a combination of tax hikes and spending cuts. The legislation could hardly be called liberal. Indeed, Clinton's plan was astonishingly similar to the one his Republican predecessor had signed off on just three years earlier.[25] Clinton, however, attracted far fewer GOP votes. To be more precise, he received zero in the House, and an equally impressive zero in the Senate. It marked the first time in modern history that a budget had passed without a single vote from the minority party.

It also made clear that "split the difference" deficit-reduction packages were now off the table. No longer could moderates cobble together grudging bipartisan support for a combination of spending cuts and tax hikes. No longer would it be possible to attract GOP votes for any meaningful increase in revenues. To gain any GOP support, deficit-reduction bills—like the one warring Democrats and Republicans finally agreed to in 1997—now had to include spending cuts sufficient to not only reduce the deficit but allow additional tax cuts as well.

Indeed, nothing indicates so clearly the GOP's sharp turn to the right on economic issues, and its exuberant embrace of the winner-take-all economy, than the unrelenting priority placed on tax cuts for the wealthiest Americans. When DeLay said nothing was more important at a time of war than cutting taxes, he could easily have just said, "Nothing is more important than cutting taxes on the wealthy, period." In the new GOP's economic cookbook, all the pages bore the same recipe, whether there was war or peace, recession or booming growth, high deficits or low. When push came to shove, and the party was forced to indicate its true priorities—deficit reduction or tax cuts; tax cuts for the middle class, the well-off, or the truly rich—the answer always came back the same: tax cuts for the rich. Everyone else could get back in line.

At first, the GOP hard-liners faced constraints—especially the presence of Bill Clinton's veto pen in the White House. Through six years of fireworks, from government shutdowns to impeachment proceedings, the two sides jousted. Throughout, Republicans made clear the priority they placed on high-end tax cuts. In the highly touted 1997 budget deal that followed Clinton's reelection, the GOP obtained striking successes. In a compromise ostensibly geared to producing a balanced budget, and including extensive spending cuts, Republicans were still able to achieve very substantial tax cuts for wealthy Americans. They succeeded just as handsomely in demonizing the IRS, sharply diminishing the government's capacity to collect taxes that were legally owed. The Gipper would have been impressed.

Of course, Republican opportunities expanded greatly after the 2000 elections. Despite George W. Bush's loss of the popular vote and the GOP's narrow legislative advantage, the new president and Congressional leaders showed no hesitation in cashing in. One of the things that strengthened their hand was the so-called budget reconciliation process. Created in the 1970s, reconciliation allows a budget to pass with only fifty-one votes in the Senate (fifty, actually, when the president and the Senate are in the same partisan hands, since the vice president casts the tie-breaking vote). In previous years, the price for this no-filibuster process was deficit neutrality; bills that drove up the federal debt weren't allowed under reconciliation. But with the growing surplus that had occurred under Clinton due to the 1993 tax increase, the 1997 budget deal, and the gush of revenue produced by the dot-com bubble, these "pay-as-you-go" rules were allowed to lapse. This was good for the GOP that had universally opposed that 1993 agreement, because the party's most immediate goal was huge, unfunded tax cuts for the richest Americans.

We are well aware that this is ancient and well-known history. It is still worth pausing to remember, since here the marriage between the winner-take-all economy and winner-take-all politics was on full display. At a time when the country faced profound challenges—healing America's ailing health-care system, improving the nation's schools to face the demands of a new century, coping with the looming financial strains associated with an aging population—Republicans insisted that the country's top priority was big tax reductions for those at the top. They did so even though the incomes of the rich, and their share of national income, had grown faster in the previous decade than at any time in at least a century.

Republicans had criticized Democrats during the 2000 campaign for only supporting "targeted tax cuts." "Targeted" was GOP code for tax cuts that were smaller and more focused on the middle class. But the GOP's 2001 tax cuts were also targeted—on the rich. First, they focused only on the progressive income tax, rather than payroll taxes, which hit the working and middle classes much harder. Then GOP leaders said that an "across-the-board tax cut" meant that everyone should receive a proportional reduction in their tax rate, which meant in practice a much larger tax cut for people in the highest brackets. Then they insisted on the elimination of the estate tax, new incentives for high-income Americans to save, and the elimination of limits on itemized deductions for those at the top. (In 2003, they would add to these goodies for high-income taxpayers steep cuts in the capital gains and dividends taxes.) All told, more than a third of the 2001 tax cuts went to the richest 1 percent of Americans— a staggering $38,500 per household per year when all the tax cuts took effect. The average taxpayer in the bottom 80 percent of the income distribution received a slightly more modest $600.[26]

These tax cuts were popular in only the narrowest sense. Polls suggested that voters doubted that they would benefit personally, doubted tax cuts would have a positive effect on the economy, and overwhelmingly agreed that the tax cuts were unfairly distributed. If pollsters asked citizens to set tax cuts against other possible priorities, like spending on popular programs or deficit reduction, tax cuts typically finished last. Privately, the Bush administration acknowledged as much, with an internal Treasury Department memo warning bluntly that "the public prefers spending on things like health care and education over cutting taxes."[27]

Still, something beats nothing. If voters were asked, "Do you want a tax cut?" they were inclined to say yes. All this meant that the GOP needed to keep control of the conversation, making sure that tax cuts were not put in competition with other possible courses of action. Fortunately, the growing cohesiveness of the party in Congress, and the strong hand of its leaders, helped assure tight agenda control. The question would be kept simple: tax cuts, yes or no.

Tricks of the Tax-Cut Trade

Through the long deficit wars, Republicans and their organized allies had learned a second powerful lesson. Careful craftsmanship could make tax cuts look much smaller and more equitable than they actually were. Time and again, the GOP's tax initiatives were structured in ways that made sense only as a technique to mislead poorly informed voters. By employing phase-ins (gradually putting a provision in effect) and "sunsets" (declaring that a provision would be ended in the future, even if the chance of that happening was small), legislators could make the advertised cost of their proposals much lower than the actual cost was likely to be. By front-loading benefits to average Americans while back-loading benefits to the well-to-do, they could also camouflage the winner-take-all nature of the new laws. For example, the main benefit most Americans got from the huge tax cut of 2001 was a onetime tax rebate of $300, which appeared with a nice letter from Congress and the president just a few months after the bill was passed. In its first year, only 7 percent of the benefits of the tax cut went to the top 1 percent. Ten years later, when it was slated to fully phase in, that total was estimated to rise to an astonishing 51 percent.[28]

Features of the new legislation were designed not only to put the best initial face on these initiatives but also to prepare the way for further tax cuts down the road. The sordid (if mind-numbing) tale of the Alternative Minimum Tax is instructive. The AMT grew out of tax law changes of the late 1960s designed to ensure that high-income taxpayers could not avoid the income tax entirely. (It was prompted by the revelation that 155 people with incomes in excess of $200,000—around $1.2 million today—paid no income tax in 1967. Congress was inundated with public complaints, receiving more letters about the topic in 1969 than about the Vietnam War.) [29] As the name implies, the Alternative Minimum Tax required that certain taxpayers—those with income above a particular level or who claim specific sorts of deductions—figure out how much they owed under the AMT and pay that amount if it was greater than their regular income tax obligations. What made the AMT a sleeper issue, however, was that the level of taxpayer income at which it kicked in was not pegged to inflation. Year after year, in a contemporary version of 1970s "bracket creep," the AMT snared more and more Americans below the upper reaches of the income ladder. Indeed, the AMT hit hardest upper-middle-class families that claimed a large number of deductions—such as those living in areas with high home prices who deducted their mortgage interest.

By the time Bush took office, it was widely understood that something needed to be done about the AMT. So the GOP responded—sort of. The 2001 tax cuts, remarkably, included a "time bomb" that would make the Alternative Minimum Tax much *worse*, more than doubling the number of Americans who were expected to be hit with it by 2007 (from 10 million to 23 million). The time bomb resulted from the fact that the bill reduced the normal income tax rates for high-income taxpayers but did not alter the AMT to reflect this. As Senator Charles Grassley, chairman of the Finance Committee, noted in a rare moment of GOP candor about the provision, "President Bush's plan [will] bring millions more Americans into the AMT process." [30]

Why did the GOP's legislative architects intentionally exacerbate a problem that, by 2004, was estimated to require a further $800 billion to fix? Simple: By actually expanding the reach of the AMT, Republicans could use the money it was projected to raise to "finance" more tax cuts. And they could set the stage for further rounds of tax cuts as the AMT pinched more Americans, when Republicans would claim that the AMT was an unanticipated problem beyond their control. (Here's Senator Grassley in 2007: "It's ridiculous to rely on revenue that was never supposed to be collected in the first place ... It's unfair to raise taxes to repeal something with serious unintended consequences like the AMT.") [31]

Essentially, the GOP held upper-middle-class Americans' feet to the fire to finance tax cuts for the super-wealthy and to crank up pressure for yet more tax cuts. Tellingly, while the Republican-engineered expansion of the AMT would have a major impact on many of those in the upper 20 percent of the income distribution, potentially offsetting all their gains from the Bush tax cuts, it would have no impact on those in the top 1 percent, who were already in the income range where the AMT was a threat.

The massive 2001 tax cuts were just the beginning. With the strengthening of "supply-side" advocacy groups and a more radicalized Republican caucus, tax cuts became the essential priority regardless of whether they produced deficits or not. Casting off the shackles of fiscal conservatism that had moderated the impulses of Bush Sr., Bob Dole, and even Reagan himself was enormously liberating. The contrast between the aftermaths of 1981 and 2001 could not be more striking. Republicans in Congress had eagerly embraced the Reagan tax cuts, but many of them were willing to change course once large deficits appeared. Twenty years later a ballooning deficit had nothing like the same effect—Republican politicians were more committed than ever to holding the line on taxes. As red ink began to flow, they continued to work energetically to push the revenue line lower.

The biggest of the post-2001 bills, the tax revision of 2003, was perhaps the most remarkable of all. Roughly as tilted toward the affluent as the 2001 bill, its estimated price tag exceeded $1 trillion over ten years— at a time when budget projections signaled huge and growing deficits. According to his treasury secretary, Paul O'Neill, even George W. Bush wondered if this was too much: "Didn't we already give them a break at the top?" In private meetings, however, Dick Cheney offered a chilling defense: "Reagan proved that deficits don't matter. We won the midterms. This is our due."[32] Sizable tax cuts were introduced again in 2004, overriding the muffled expressions of concern from a handful of remaining GOP moderates.

Perhaps most astonishing of all was how narrowly Republican tax-cutters drew the winner's circle. We have already noted the GOP's deft use of the Alternative Minimum Tax to finance its top-end tax cuts with a massive, creeping, hidden *increase* in taxes on those making between $100,000 and $200,000. Yet even this effort looked tame in comparison to the 2001 legislation's truly bizarre "reforms" of the estate tax. As Yale scholars Michael Graetz and Ian Shapiro have observed, the bill's sponsors rejected a compromise that would have eliminated the estate tax, permanently, for 95 percent of the already small slice of American households that were expected to pay it.[33] Instead, the GOP went for a home run. It sought to abolish the estate tax entirely, reducing it to zero—but only for a year. After that one year, the estate tax would return to the original, pre-2001 level. This odd structure—one year in which the heirs of huge fortunes wouldn't have to pay a penny to Uncle Sam—created rather strange incentives, to say the least.

Republican leaders evidently hoped this stratagem would provide an opportunity to kill the estate tax for good. Once the estate tax was eliminated, they reasoned, it would be nearly impossible for politicians to bring it back. Given the severe imbalances in organizational might on tax issues, this was hardly a crazy gamble. The AFL-CIO had only a single lobbyist working *quarter-time* to fight tax cuts for the wealthy when the 2001 bill was under debate—and when, of course, Capitol Hill was swarming with lobbyists seeking favorable treatment. But it's important to recognize whom the gamble benefited. For those with truly huge estates—such as the Walton family, which stood to save tens of billions from the repeal of the estate tax—this was a reasonable risk. They needed the home run, since any compromise that left the estate tax in place for the largest estates would have done nothing to shelter most of their wealth. For the "ordinary wealthy," if that phrase makes sense, it was a rotten deal. Again, however, the design of these economic smart bombs, with their precisely targeted payloads of cash, spoke volumes about the priorities of GOP leaders.

Making America Safe for CEOs

Tax cuts weren't the only way in which Republicans improved the fortunes of the winner-take-all economy's winners. The party also became relentlessly hostile to the idea that corporate managers—the biggest of the big winners—might require oversight. The concept of encouraging countervailing powers, so that there would be someone with the organizational resources needed to check and monitor managers' actions (including decisions related to their own pay), was dismissed with scorn.

One possible check was unions, but by now Republicans were confident they could keep them on the sidelines.[34] After winning control of Congress, they wasted little time in back-benching another possible check, private litigation. That trial lawyers were one of the major sources of campaign funds for Democrats made the initiative an irresistible twofer. In 1995, a bipartisan coalition passed the Private Securities Litigation Reform Act (PSLRA) over President Clinton's veto, putting new hurdles in the way of shareholders seeking legal remedies against corporations and underwriters peddling false information.[35] Republican Congressman Chris Cox was a major architect of the bill. A decade later, President Bush would appoint Cox as head of the SEC, where, under his leadership, fines for corporate violations fell sharply and career staffers saw their autonomy greatly reduced.[36] In 1998, a similar coalition passed important amendments to the PSLRA, requiring all class-action lawsuits for securities fraud to be brought in federal court, making litigation more difficult.

Even more striking was the GOP's resistance to efforts to increase the independence of boards of directors and shareholders' capacity to effectively check managers. As his first choice to head the SEC, President George W. Bush selected Harvey Pitt, a lawyer who had gone from a position as SEC general counsel in the 1970s to make a lucrative career defending those accused of financial malfeasance. After his 2001 appointment, Pitt promised a "kinder, gentler" agency, but his close ties to the accounting industry and his ham-fisted efforts to protect it became an immediate political liability when the bursting of the tech bubble was accompanied by a series of astonishing scandals.

Enron's 2001 collapse was the most spectacular, but it was just one of many corporate falls from grace. The names in the headlines changed—Tyco, Adelphia, HealthSouth, WorldCom—but the story, again and again, was the same: In a system riddled with conflicts of interest and self-dealing, executives looted their companies, enabled by pliant accountants and banks that happily took their fees, while docile or disinterested boards looked the other way. Companies were brought to ruin, employees lost their jobs, and workers saw their pensions disappear—not just by the hundreds but by the thousands. Millions of middle-class Americans who had invested through mutual funds or pension plans also paid dearly.[37] A few executives were found guilty of criminal wrongdoing, but many, many more could view the carnage they inflicted from extremely comfortable retirements.

The evidence that lax rules too often left foxes guarding the henhouse was overwhelming. Even in the absence of organized pressure, this extraordinary string of collapses and scandals pushed a reluctant Congress to consider reforming American structures of corporate governance. Eventually the public uproar produced meaningful legislation, the Sarbanes-Oxley Act of 2002. Yet this effort to rein in corporate excess was the exception that proved the rule. It largely confirmed the extraordinary skew of Washington policymaking toward economic insiders. Without an organized, persistent capacity to pressure officials, outrage alone was unlikely to produce fundamental change.

True, the massive public outcry made opposition to reform difficult. Democrats, sensing a rare chance to go on the offensive at a time when the GOP was riding high, tried to push the issue. Moreover, their slim majority in the Senate after June 2001 (when GOP Senator Jim Jeffords of Vermont became an independent who caucused with the Democrats) gave them some leverage. Yet most analysts suggest that the Sarbanes-Oxley Act would never have happened had not the collapse of the telecommunications giant WorldCom occurred just as the 2002 elections approached.[38] Until that moment, even a stunning series of scandals had failed to dent the confidence of Republican leaders. Adopting the Scarlett O'Hara defense, they planned to drag their feet and simply wait for public furor to subside. These plans died with WorldCom—and Sarbanes-Oxley was born.

The once unlikely enactment of meaningful corporate reform showed that politicians could come to fear regular voters on high-stakes economic matters, but only when conditions were just about perfectly aligned for the electorate to exact retribution. Even then, the GOP learned, the consequences could be contained. With the critics of corporate excess lacking any real capacity for organized combat, GOP leaders were able to resist more serious reforms that the experience of other countries suggested might have put the greatest checks on managerial power.[39]

As fiercely fought as Sarbanes-Oxley had been, it was hardly a giant slayer. The bill focused on weak claimants—the discredited accountants and stock analysts who had given their seal of approval to shady corporate dealings—rather than weak claims. It did nothing to alter the basic problem of compliant compensation boards driving up camouflaged CEO pay. Indeed, when Harvey Pitt's successor at the SEC, William Donaldson, tried in 2003 to use the authority granted by Sarbanes-Oxley to modestly change the nomination rules for boards so as to increase shareholder control, the business community unleashed a torrent of attacks that tied the SEC in knots for more than a year (the SEC received over thirteen thousand comment letters on the proposal). The stalemate was good for "lazy, inefficient, grossly overpaid and wrongheaded CEOs," wrote one disgusted SEC commissioner shortly before his term ended and the newly reelected President Bush appointed a more business-friendly replacement. "The worst instincts of the CEO community have triumphed."[40]

"I Call You My Base"

During the 1990s, the GOP fully embraced Gramm's "crimson with the blood of investors" doctrine. On Wall Street and beyond, business could count on Republicans to be the party that, in the famous words of conservative patron William F. Buckley Jr., "stands athwart history yelling Stop." Except, that is, when the party was standing athwart history yelling Full

Speed Ahead. As the winner-take-all economy raced relentlessly forward in the first decade of the new century, Republicans promoted that development at every turn. Whether the lever was huge tax cuts, further financial deregulation, or lax oversight, the GOP was there to give a helpful push.

And the willingness to provide that aid was hidden right out in the open. Less than a month before his tumultuous victory in November 2000, George W. Bush had made a guest appearance at the Al Smith charity event in New York. At the $800-a-plate dinner, where Bush and Al Gore took turns offering self-deprecating jokes before a diamond-studded crowd of the economy's biggest winners, the soon-to-be victor signaled what was to come with a wink: "This is an impressive crowd—the haves and the have-mores. Some people call you the elites; I call you my base."[41]

Chapter 9

Democrats Climb Aboard

In May 2000, a few months before Al Gore and George W. Bush shared the stage at the Al Smith dinner in New York, Democrats held their own big-money event. They knew that Gore—buoyed by Clinton's high-charged economy but burdened by his tarnished personal reputation—faced an extremely well-financed Republican challenger. The month before, the GOP had held a black-tie event that shattered previous single-event fund-raising records, bringing in over $21 million. Terry McAuliffe, the tireless head of the DNC, responded by waving the party's populist flag. The Democrats would fill Washington's MCI Center with fourteen thousand guests wearing jeans and dining from plastic plates on barbecue flown in from the best rib joints in Little Rock and Memphis. At the event, McAuliffe evoked laughter and catcalls when he read the GOP's upscale fund-raiser menu: "Karnut and colusuri rices with wheatberry, whatever all that is . . . In Syracuse, New York, where I grew up, Millie McAuliffe never made this kind of food."

In his memoir, *What a Party!*, McAuliffe gleefully recounts how the Democrats' populist symbolism not only upstaged the GOP, but managed to raise a new record of $26 million. What he spares us is the underlying math. If, as he says, thirteen thousand of the guests paid only $50, it means they contributed less than a million to the party's haul (truthfully, there probably wouldn't have been much left after paying for the ribs' airfare). The rest came from the more select group McAuliffe introduces a few pages earlier, where he recounts how he and Gore sat in a room full of big donors, including prominent lobbyists, as each of them committed to raising $500,000 a piece for the event. The barbecue, jeans, and middle-class audience were just a photo op.[1]

By the end of the 1990s, the true culinary metaphor for the Democrats' new posture on the economy was not barbecue, but the English one journalist Robert Kuttner has employed: a horse-and-rabbit stew. This fictitious dish is nicely balanced, consisting of one horse and one rabbit. The rabbit, in this case, would be the few remaining elements of social investment that the Clinton administration had been able to get through a mostly gridlocked Congress. The horse was the almost complete adoption of Wall Street's economic agenda: a heavy dose of budgetary austerity, combined with a ringing endorsement of the radical restructuring of the financial sector that would soon send the American economy over a cliff.

What happened to the Democrats? Over the course of the 1990s, the party first accommodated and eventually embraced the winner-take-all economy. Its populist tradition more and more appeared like a costume—something to be donned from time to time when campaigning—rather than a basis for governing. The Democrats not only lost their ability to articulate the case for policies that would provide meaningful checks on concentrated economic power. As many of the party's elected officials tilted increasingly to the moderate right on economic matters, they also lost their capacity to deliver legislative victories on lunch-pail issues. And on critical struggles related to the spectacular expansion of Wall Street, powerful Democrats chose to fully support the new economic order.

Positively Wall Street

We began the last chapter with Phil Gramm, who epitomized, spearheaded, and profited from the Republican Party's increasingly vigorous championing of the winner-take-all economy. We can introduce this chapter with a parallel story of a figure whose rise to prominence tracked the arc of the evolving Democratic Party, and whose actions in Washington encapsulate the Democrats' equally significant, if distinctive, contribution to the new balance of economic power. There are many candidates for this part—Joe Lieberman, Dianne Feinstein, Robert Rubin, Bill Clinton himself—but since the epicenter of the new economy was Gramm's "holy place" of Wall Street, it seems appropriate to focus on the senior senator from New York, Charles Schumer.

On issues unrelated to finance, Schumer is a strong liberal voice in the Democratic Party. In the fight over Obama's health plan, for instance, he emerged as a forceful advocate for creating a new public insurance option to compete with private plans. In 2007, as he moved into an increasingly prominent role in the party leadership, he penned a book called *Positively American: Winning Back the Middle-Class Majority One Family at a Time*. The narrative device of Schumer's book centered on a fictitious family, the Baileys. Schumer saw the Baileys, living on Long Island and making $75,000 a year, as representative of the critical, middle-class constituency the Democratic Party needed to attract. At a party celebrating the book launch, Schumer said the book was written "with passion and out of conviction" and with "a yearning to set this country and this party on a better path . . . We lose the path sometimes. The government has to become much more connected to the people."[2]

There were certainly a lot of connected people in the elegant Fifth Avenue apartment across from the Metropolitan Museum where Schumer spoke. It was owned by his hosts, financier Steven Rattner and Maureen White, former finance chair of the Democratic National Committee. Both of them were prominent fund-raisers for the nascent presidential campaign of then-Senator Hillary Clinton of New York. She was there as well, along with New York Mayor Michael Bloomberg, who had made his billions providing sophisticated equipment that had helped turbocharge the vast new financial empires of Wall Street.

The gathering of luminaries was indicative not only of Schumer's growing political stature, but also of his long-standing and intimate ties to the nation's greatest concentration of staggering wealth. From the moment he entered Congress in 1981, Schumer had aligned himself closely with Wall

Street. He began by seeking a seat on the House Financial Services Committee. For an ambitious New York politician, it was a sensible move. Indeed, it is common practice for legislators to gravitate to specializations that match the concerns of powerful local economic interests. Of course, it also turned out to be an extraordinarily good time to hitch one's wagon to the financial industry. Like Wall Street, Schumer was slated for a rapid ascent.

Schumer quickly established himself as an aggressive and extremely adept fund-raiser. You may recall that we encountered him in chapter 7, where in his very first term in Congress he was one of just two House Democrats who rallied to the leadership's plea to transfer campaign cash to underfunded challengers in the run-up to the 1982 election. As he rose through the ranks in the House, he played a critical role in helping Democrats build strong ties to the financial industry. In the words of a detailed *New York Times* profile, "Mr. Schumer became a magnet for campaign donations from wealthy industry executives, including Jamie Dimon, now the chief executive of JP Morgan Chase; John J. Mack, the chief executive at Morgan Stanley; and Charles O. Prince III, the former chief executive of Citigroup. And he was not at all reluctant to ask them for more. Donors describe the Schumer pitch as unusually aggressive."[3]

Apparently so. Over the five election cycles from 1989–90 to 1997–98, Schumer raised $2.5 million in contributions from securities and investment firms—more than *triple* the haul of the runner-up in the House, Republican Dick Zimmer. In 1999, following a successful (and very well-funded) campaign, Schumer moved to the Senate, where he maintained his focus on issues crucial to Wall Street. He took a seat on the powerful Banking and Finance Committee, an excellent site to hone his prodigious fund-raising skills. From 1999–2000 through 2005–2006, only one member of Congress raised more money from securities and investment firms than Schumer's $3.7 million. That was John Kerry, whose presidential run doubtless boosted his totals just a wee bit.

Strikingly, while Kerry and Schumer ran first and second, numbers three, four, and five were all Democrats as well—Joe Lieberman, Hillary Clinton, and Chris Dodd. Schumer's success was part of a major development in the evolution of the Democratic Party's finances: a big push to gain support on Wall Street. The financial services industry has come to represent one of the Democrats' most reliable donor bases, especially during the crucial early stages of the campaign, when fund-raising prowess culls the list of viable contenders.[4]

The increasing reliance of Democrats on finance-industry donations, in turn, reflected Wall Street's growing economic and political clout.[5] In a list of the country's top corporate givers, twenty-five of sixty-five come from the financial services industry, according to the Center for Responsive Politics. Since 1989, individual employees of the financial services industry and finance-industry PACs have contributed $2 billion to federal campaigns. If one looks at the 100 biggest contributing firms since 1989, the financial sector totals more than the contributions of energy, health care, defense, and telecoms *combined*.[6] Deep-pocketed individuals associated with financial firms are also extremely well-represented among the big bundlers who now provide the majority of early financing for many presidential campaigns. Hedge funds have become increasingly prominent, and increasingly lean Democratic. In the past few years of Democratic congressional control, the financial services industry has contributed nearly a third of all the campaign money going to the chairs of the House and Senate committees charged with monitoring the bank bailout.[7]

Schumer was the perfect person to broker the strengthening relationship between Democrats and Wall Street. Following the party's disappointing showing in the 2004 elections, he became head of the Democratic Senatorial Campaign Committee (DSCC). Over the next two cycles, he helped orchestrate the Democrats' impressive comeback. Schumer turned out to be an exceptional recruiter, convincing prospective candidates that the time was right to take on the GOP. Yet his greatest talent was fund-raising. Over the course of his two cycles at the helm of the DSCC, it raised an unprecedented $240 million. Funds from Wall Street increased 50 percent, and in the 2007–2008 cycle the DSCC raised *four times* as much from Wall Street as its GOP counterpart did. Even as the DSCC vastly expanded its fund-raising, the share of DSCC funds coming from Wall Street tripled over the course of a decade.[8]

Observers of banking and finance, as well as lobbyists, have regularly identified Schumer as a "go-to" guy on Capitol Hill—not unlike Phil Gramm. Indeed, while their voting records on most issues could not have been further apart, Schumer often teamed with Gramm in advancing positions favorable to Wall Street. Schumer was a supporter of Gramm-Leach-Bliley, the bill that finally repealed the Glass-Steagall Act. In 2001, the two senators launched a successful bipartisan effort to sharply reduce the fees Wall Street paid the federal government to finance regulatory activity, cutting the financial sector's anticipated costs by $14 billion over the coming decade. They achieved this success at a time when the SEC and other agencies were scrambling (and, it soon became clear, failing) to keep up with the rapidly expanding speed, complexity, and volume of Wall Street activity. As apprehension over Wall Street's practices grew, Schumer was well positioned to limit or channel such efforts. In 2006, for instance, he supported the successful efforts of the credit-ratings agencies to limit SEC supervision of their activities.

Gramm and Schumer's roles in the changing regulation of finance nicely fit the respective roles of their two parties in fostering Wall Street's post-1990 bonanza. GOP's Gramm was more often the battering ram. Although he knew how to play defense as well, he was the guy who could lead conservative majorities to pass legislation sought by economic elites. Schumer, by contrast, was more often the master of drift. He was the one who made sure that his party—the one most likely to push for serious oversight of Wall Street—remained as friendly as possible to the interests of the captains of finance.

Nothing signals how this worked more clearly than Schumer's sustained efforts to protect the favorable tax treatment of private equity and hedge fund managers. Within the lofty heights of the winner-take-all economy, hedge fund managers hold the highest perches of all. In 2007, the top twenty-five hedge fund managers earned nearly $900 million on average.[9] Despite their awe-inspiring incomes, some of these financiers have been able to exploit features of tax law that predate the rise of hedge funds to pay only a 15 percent federal tax rate. Yes, 15 percent. "Carried interest" provisions allow fund managers to treat some of the spectacular *fees* investors pay them as capital gains—a favorable treatment supposedly reserved for those who are putting their own investments at risk. Warren Buffett used to say that it was outrageous that he and his secretary paid the same tax rate. Those benefitting from the "carried interest" loophole can do him one better. They pay a dramatically *lower* rate than their secretaries.

As egregious as this loophole is, the defense game of Wall Street supporters like Schumer kept it firmly in place. Adopting the Scarlett O'Hara defense, he insisted that he supported reform but wanted to get it right— something that, hopefully, would happen *tomorrow*. On grounds of "fairness," he maintained that any reform must also apply to executives at energy, venture capital, and real estate partnerships. Coincidentally, this happened to be precisely the position advanced by leading lobbyists for the financial industry. It was a poison pill that Schumer knew would stall the legislation—which it did. A reform that failed to meet Schumer's requirements passed the newly Democratic House in 2007, only to die in the Senate. As we write midway through the fourth year of Democratic control of Congress, the rules governing taxation of hedge funds look more vulnerable than ever but remain unchanged.

Schumer's policy role, combined with his success in fund-raising, has garnered scathing criticism from many close observers of Wall Street practices. John Bogle, founder of the Vanguard Group and a passionate advocate for ordinary shareholders, bluntly concludes that Schumer "is serving the parochial interest of a very small group of financial people, bankers, investment bankers, fund managers, private equity firms, rather than serving the general public . . . It has hurt the American investor first and the average American taxpayer."[10]

Yet one could also say Schumer has simply followed a time-honored American practice. As Tip O'Neill, who ran the House when Schumer began his Washington career famously said, "All politics is local." In a political system organized around geographic representation, public officials can be expected to protect local economic powerhouses. Recall that the share of finance in the economy had roughly doubled during Schumer's tenure in Washington. By 2007, more than a *third* of all wages in New York City were being earned on Wall Street—up from one-eighth in 1972.[11] For a New York official, one could argue that not protecting the interests of that industry would be political malpractice. But Schumer was hardly alone. Plenty of Democrats were embracing, rather than resisting, the winner-take-all economy.

Chronic Enablers

Schumer's story is dramatic, but it reflects a deeper shift in the Democratic Party. With the rewards at the top spiraling upward, Democratic politicians faced growing incentives to accommodate the winner-take-all economy. Many of the trends described in chapter 7 intensified after 1990. The organizational heft of business continued to grow. Perhaps reflecting a growing confidence about what organized expenditures could accomplish in Washington, spending on lobbying shot upward during George W. Bush's time in office. Democrats thus faced greater incentives than ever to be responsive to the new economy's big winners. Equally important, there was almost no organized force in American society pressuring them to do anything else.

The financial needs of ever more expensive campaigns added to the imperatives. Despite the efforts of organizational entrepreneurs like Tony Coelho, the 1980s DCCC head who kicked off the Democrats' big hunt for corporate cash, the party continued to trail badly in the money chase. In the 1991–92 cycle, the Democratic committees pulled in $140 million in hard and soft money, compared with $244 million for the GOP.[12] This financial weakness hurt the Democrats three times over. First, it put them at an electoral disadvantage. Second, it increased the need of the Democratic Party to adopt stances that would appeal to big donors. Finally, the party's shaky finances continued to create incentives for individual politicians to chart their own course—which again was likely to lead them to seek favor with those who could bankroll campaigns.

All of these tendencies grew even stronger after the electoral cataclysm of 1994. In a flash, Coelho's trump card—you need to deal with us because we're in charge—was gone. The GOP already possessed a formidable fund-raising edge, rooted in its organizational prowess and the natural affinity between the party's policy agenda and the interests of corporations and the wealthy. To this, the GOP could now add the blunt advantage of incumbency—an advantage it quickly exploited with Tom DeLay's aggressive K Street Project.

As a result, Democratic politicians found themselves cross-pressured on economic matters, and the tension increased over time. Issues that smacked of redistribution, or threatened to impinge on the autonomy of executives or their firms, placed Democrats in the awkward position of needing to reconcile conflicting party identities: Were they the party of the little guy and organized labor or a reliable partner of business? For Republicans, the economic wish lists of corporations and the wealthy were rarely viewed as threatening by the other major organized players within their party alliance. Democrats were not so lucky.

The Clinton Solution

As in so many areas, it was Bill Clinton who pointed the way for Democrats trying to resolve this conundrum. Clinton is sometimes portrayed as a stalking horse for the Democratic Leadership Council, which advocated a swing to pro-business stances within the party. Clinton, however, was always a master triangulator, able to strike a balance between mildly populist campaign rhetoric and a set of policy prescriptions that were largely unthreatening to the business community. Even his signature liberal initiative after his election in 1992, health-care reform, had been carefully crafted to appeal to business—although at the end of the day the Business Roundtable and the Chamber of Commerce came out against it, while the NFIB went into strident opposition.[13]

After his 1992 election, and especially after the 1994 midterm elections, Clinton the populist messenger mostly gave way to Clinton the moderate manager. The administration's 1993 decision to place the highest priority on deficit reduction and jettison its plans for social investments marked the critical moment in the Democrats' broader economic repositioning.[14] At the time, Clinton faced considerable pressure from strong economic voices like Robert Rubin (then head of Clinton's National Economic Council) and Fed Chair Alan Greenspan. In both 1992 and 1996, he also faced political threats from Ross Perot's surprisingly effective third-party effort. And in a foreshadowing of the circumstances that would face the next Democrat to occupy the White House, Clinton knew that even if he adopted a more progressive policy stance, it would assuredly be blocked in the Senate by his own party's moderates.

Forced to scrap his plans for significant social investments, Clinton's populist side recoiled. "Where are all the Democrats?" he asked his aides. "We're all Eisenhower Republicans ... We stand for lower deficits and free trade and the bond market. Isn't that great?"[15] Clinton eventually decided that, great or not, it was the best option he had—and in 1993 he proposed a budget plan that looked remarkably like the one his predecessor had signed off on in 1990.

In effect, Clinton replaced his social investment strategy with an "interest rate" strategy. Restored fiscal responsibility was to be the mechanism for generating economic growth. Eisenhower Republicans indeed. Over time, and especially as the economy recovered, Clinton would come to embrace what was termed "Rubinomics" with greater enthusiasm. Its pillars were tight budgets with strict constraints on domestic spending, combined with sustained support for the reconstruction and vast expansion of Wall Street that was under way—horse-and-rabbit stew.

The political rewards were limited. Democrats suffered a historic, calamitous defeat in the midterm elections immediately after Clinton's tough budget. By 1996, however, the economy had improved sufficiently to ensure Clinton's own reelection and bolster the party's position on economic management. Yet the attempt to rebrand the party as a sound economic steward came at a serious cost. Most obviously, by accepting very tight budget constraints, Democrats gave up the opportunity to offer significant direct support to the middle class. Social expenditures that would have improved education, health care, and energy independence, or restored public infrastructure, had to be sacrificed. The Democrats were now committed to the management of austerity.

Yet this was not the only cost. Ironically, the more Democrats committed themselves to austerity, the more they allowed Republicans to play Santa Claus. As one of the godfathers of the conservative renewal, Irving Kristol—the founder of the neoconservative journal the *Public Interest* and father of the contemporary conservative writer Bill Kristol—had anticipated, Republicans could exploit the Democrats' fiscal self-restraint. In May 1980, Kristol had rejected concerns that "supply-side" tax cuts would lead to budget deficits by stressing the higher political logic of tax cuts:

> *And what if the traditionalist-conservatives are right and a ... tax cut, without corresponding cuts in expenditures, also leaves us with a fiscal problem? The neo-conservative is willing to leave those problems to be coped with by liberal interregnums. He wants to shape the future, and will leave it up to his opponents to tidy up afterwards.*[16]

Although Republicans suddenly became apoplectic about deficits after they lost the White House in 2008, the record of the previous quarter-century suggests they took Kristol's advice to heart. Under Reagan and the second President Bush, deficits and debt skyrocketed. And for much the same reason: increased defense spending without adequate revenues to fund it, along with massive tax cuts for the well-off. Clinton and, later, Obama, were left to "tidy up afterwards." This partisan division of labor had long-term consequences for the two parties' economic reputations.

All Hat and No Cattle

Two gifted wordsmiths, Malcolm Gladwell and Michael Lewis, have shared a fascination with the gap in the world of sports between reputation and reality. Increasingly sophisticated statistics suggest that some "stars" have reputations that way outdistance their true value to their teams. Gladwell targeted the basketball player Allen Iverson. The former MVP looked great on the court, but wasn't.[17] In *Moneyball*, Lewis generalized this observation.[18] He identified a key characteristic of innovative organizations in professional sports: their capacity to see beyond conventional metrics of player evaluation in order to exploit hidden value. Lewis's hero was Oakland A's general manager, Billy Beane. Beane built a squad capable of competing with far richer teams like the Yankees, because he saw past superficial flash and inflated reputations. He understood the underlying characteristics—including boring ones like the ability to patiently accept a base on balls—that made particular players valuable to their teams.

For Gladwell and Lewis, sports provided an entertaining and revealing point of entry into a broader social phenomenon: We can often be blinded by flash. Even when smart people are closely observing something they care about, there can be a chasm separating reputation from true performance. Two talented political scientists, Larry Bartels of Princeton and Mark Smith of the University of Washington, have separately made this case with respect to the two political parties and economic performance.[19] It turns out that over the past few decades, with respect to economic policy, the Republican Party looks a lot like Allen Iverson—all hat and no cattle, as George W. Bush might say. Careful examinations show that on all the major indicators, the economy has performed notably better under Democratic presidents than under Republican ones. And yet, as Smith's research shows, Republicans, with their simple, consistent message of tax cuts, generally maintained a reputation as the more effective party on economic issues.

The fallout was most clear in the declining fortunes of Democrats with a critical component of the New Deal coalition: the white working class. The white working class is generally defined as white voters without a college degree, though sometimes analysts use the simpler definition of white voters who tell pollsters they're working class. Defined either way, this traditional backbone of the Democratic Party has shifted away from Democrats and toward Republicans. This is true within the South and outside it, and among both religious and nonreligious voters. Across the board, white working-class voters are about 20 percentage points less likely to say they're Democrats than they were a generation ago.

Even before Barack Obama infamously speculated about how such voters were so "bitter, they cling to guns or religion" during the 2008 campaign, this defection had become the subject of endless speculation and hand-wringing among Democrats—and a growing number of sophisticated analyses among political experts. These studies have zeroed in on a verdict at odds with the conventional diagnosis of cultural backlash. While evangelicals moved away from the Democrats on cultural grounds, that is not true among the white working class as a whole. Instead, Democrats lost ground among white working-class voters not in spite of economic issues, but because of them. As *New Yorker* writer George Packer ably sums up the findings: "Social issues like abortion, guns, religion, and even (outside the South) race had little to do with the shift. Instead . . . it was based on a judgment that—during years in which industrial jobs went overseas, unions practically vanished, and working-class incomes stagnated—the Democratic Party was no longer much help to [the working class]."[20]

The shifts in the Democratic Party didn't just decrease the momentum for economic activism. They also diminished the capacity of the party to reach out to voters on economic grounds. Internal conflicts have made it more difficult to take a clear, coherent posture toward fundamental economic issues, including ones that would signal concretely what the party could do for the middle class. Repeatedly, stalemate on high-profile issues soured voters on government and fueled cynicism about politics. Repeatedly, Democrats faced demands to tone down their populist appeals and shift to economic messages that might resonate with upscale voters and business interests. Deficit reduction, embraced initially by Mondale and then again by Clinton, represented just such an accommodation. This ambivalent posture, of course, is in stark contrast to the clear, consistent stance of the GOP regarding markets, low taxes, and deregulation. However limited the effectiveness of the Republicans' economic strategies have been, their straightforward anti-Washington message has resonated—especially since the message has jibed with the polarized gridlock that voters have seen play out before them.

Democrats and the Politics of Drift

In contemporary discussions of the parties, commentators oscillate between two poles: seeing the parties as both equally hopeless or seeing one as fundamentally wrong and the other as basically sound. In the former view, both parties wear black hats. In the latter, one wears black, the other white.

The story of Republicans and Democrats is not black and white, but black and gray. In promoting the winner-take-all economy, Republicans proved the zealots. When legislation directly promoted the upward redistribution of income—from the Reagan and Bush tax cuts to the key laws deregulating financial markets—Republicans could generally claim primary authorship. Democrats, by contrast, were more likely to be implicated in the part of winner-take-all politics that we have termed drift. As economic change undercut existing public policies designed to limit inequality and insecurity, Washington's dominant response was to do nothing. Since the Democratic Party was where we would expect some kind of response to come from, its failure to act is a central part of winner-take-all politics. If Republicans wore black hats, increasingly the Democrats wore gray ones.

The political attraction of drift to Democrats grew in close accordance with the weight of organized economic interests within the party. Businesses saw the wisdom of donating to Democratic incumbents not just for political access, but because it offered them low-profile political protection. And no form of protection was more low-profile than drift. After all, drift allows policy change to occur silently, through what political scientists have termed "nondecisions"—that is, without visible legislative choices. Drift is far less likely to attract the notice of voters, who pay only sporadic attention to politics and have limited information about policy. For cross-pressured politicians in a tight spot between voters and interest groups, drift is often the easiest and safest solution.

Drift wasn't only the path of least political resistance for Democrats. It was often the only path. The radicalizing Republican Party and the worsening institutional hurdles threw up daunting barriers to meaningful legislative change. The most formidable of these hurdles was the Senate filibuster. Given the overrepresentation of rural, typically Republican states in the Senate, getting to fifty-one (on budget matters) or sixty (on just about everything else) represented an enormous challenge. Thus, a profound if little appreciated asymmetry developed between the two parties. To win, the GOP often needed only stalemate. To renew the federal government's commitment to the middle class, Democrats needed to pass multiple pieces of substantial, ambitious legislation. Always, as we know, they would do so in the face of fierce Republican opposition. Perhaps less expected, but just as important, was the resistance they typically faced within their own party.

The Moderate Morass

The first source of potential resistance within the party came from "moderates"—a term that reflects the up-for-grabs status of these Democrats' votes, rather than any particular ideological position. For Democrats, securing the allegiance of their most reluctant members for meaningful reform became a recurring, massive structural problem. Nowhere was this problem more vexing than in the U.S. Senate.

In part, this reflects the way the Senate is composed, with its astonishing bias in favor of small states. When the Constitution was adopted, the ratio of the most populous to the least populous state was about 20–1. Today it is about 70–1. At some times, the divide between large and small states has conferred no particular advantage on one party or another, but over the last few decades it has given a substantial edge to Republicans.[21] It has also meant that racial and ethnic minorities, concentrated disproportionately in a few big states, are wildly underrepresented in the Senate.

Given the contemporary contours of American politics, a bias toward small states is, quite simply, a bias toward conservatism. After the 2004 elections, for example, Republicans held fifty-five of the one hundred senate seats, even though Democrats had won considerably more overall votes in those one hundred elections.[22] When George W. Bush was wooing Democrats for his tax cuts, his targets were often senators from rural states whose constituents had voted overwhelmingly for him. After the 1992 and 1996 elections, Clinton could rarely exert this kind of pressure—certainly not on members of the GOP and often not even on members of his own party.

Yet the issue is not just how votes in the Senate are allocated. A stance in the middle is a stance that generates leverage—and that leverage attracts the attention of savvy political actors. As we have seen, it is these senators, holding the potentially pivotal votes, who have the most sway. Alas for middle-class voters, they are also the ones whom affected interests most assiduously seek to cultivate.

Consider the case of Max Baucus, the powerful Democratic chair of the Senate Finance Committee. An unassuming Montana rancher, Baucus attracted little attention in Washington until he rose to be the senior Democrat on the powerful Finance Committee in 2000. Interest groups were not slow to notice. Between 1999 and 2005, according to a Public Citizen report, Baucus took in more interest-group money than any other senator with the exception of Republican Bill Frist, who was Senate majority leader for much of that time. Baucus received more money from business PACs than any other senator.[23]

Baucus's office also became a training camp for lobbyists—only three other senators had more former staffers working on K Street. When he became finance chair, their stock went up: According to *Congressional Quarterly*, "Former aides of Baucus, in particular, have been in demand on K Street by companies that hope to limit damage to their business interests."[24] While Baucus was playing a critical role in developing the 2003 Medicare Prescription Drug Bill, his former chief of staff and a legislative aide were part of the high-octane lobbying team from PhRMA (Pharmaceutical Research and Manufacturers of America). After the bill passed, his top staffer at Finance left to open his own lobbying outfit with a host of health and drug industry clients, including PhRMA.

In his critical role at Senate Finance, Baucus has provided support for business-friendly legislation. He supported the Bush tax cuts (with very modest revisions), and despite his expressed concerns about budget discipline, advocated their extension. He has backed the elimination of the estate tax. In the lead-up to the prescription drug bill, Baucus had no difficulty signing onto the GOP's plans, which is why he and fellow moderate John Breaux were the only Democrats invited to join the conference committee meetings where the legislation was crafted.

Being that last vote—the one that needs to be "rented," in Breaux's immortal telling—has other benefits as well. As we saw in the career of Breaux himself, or more recent cases like Evan Bayh or Joe Lieberman, it can elevate one to a status of statesman in the eyes of pundits who see being in the middle as intrinsically virtuous. Of course, it is also the best bargaining position, giving these legislators a steady stream of chips to cash in for other purposes. One can't but appreciate the appeal of a posture that simultaneously attracts media kudos and pork.

In an individual case it may be impossible to pin down what is making a particular moderate's vote hard to get. Is it genuine conviction? The constraint of a conservative local electorate? A desire for leverage or attention? The favors of lobbyists? What is clear is that Democrats in the gridlock-prone Senate repeatedly found themselves dealing with a small, shifting, but crucially placed swing group that made it exceptionally difficult to craft a legislative coalition.

Republicans for a Day

On critical economic issues, business interests could often count on a handful of moderate Democrats to complement the expected solid bloc of Republicans. In many cases, this was more than enough. Yet there was another group that expanded the conservative coalition, potentially making up for any losses from groups one and two: Republicans for a Day.

"Republicans for a Day" were Democrats, even "fighting liberal" Democrats like Chuck Schumer, who defected from the party on specific economic issues in deference to powerful local interests. Here the geographic foundation of Capitol Hill played a critical role. All representatives must

balance multiple constituencies. Yet in every state some economic inter-
ests play such a formidable local role that they demand special attention.
Each state economy has its 800-pound gorillas who command respect.
That state's Democrats, if they hope to survive, will provide it.

From Michigan (autos) to Delaware (corporate governance) to Oregon (timber) to Pennsylvania (coal), examples abound. Blanche Lincoln
of Arkansas included among her constituents much of Wal-Mart's Walton family (which boasts four of the ten largest fortunes in America, according to *Forbes*), making her support for estate tax repeal unsurprising.
Dianne Feinstein and Barbara Boxer, often seen as quite far apart among
Democrats on economic issues, were both strong defenders of Silicon
Valley's implacable hostility to restrictions on stock options. The financial
industries of banking, insurance, and real estate could generally count on
extensive support from Democrats in New York, Connecticut, and New
Jersey.

How much can a handful of lost votes mean? A lot. In a system already
prone to inertia, a few lost votes can mean the difference between action and inaction. Moreover, Republicans for a Day were generally most
influential on precisely those issues where they were most likely to defend powerful economic interests. They would frequently gravitate to the
committees (often eventually becoming chair) where their local interests
needed representation.

The importance of Republicans for a Day was amplified by the shifting
character of Republicans for a Lifetime. On economic issues, fewer and
fewer Republicans proved willing to depart from the party line. The demise of moderate Republicanism made it nearly impossible to substitute
a Republican vote for a Democratic one. Party polarization on economic
issues meant every Democratic vote was increasingly critical.

The GOP confronted no real parallel to this challenge. Serious economic reform often means going after concentrated economic interests.
And going after concentrated economic interests activates opposition in
the particular localities where those interests are powerful. This is what
makes the behavior of Republicans for a Day like Boxer or Schumer kick
in. The Republican economic agenda of redistributing resources through

deregulation and high-end tax cuts usually didn't require it to go after powerful local interests. It involved instead providing concentrated benefits to attentive constituencies, with the costs broadly diffused across the public.

In short, as with so many aspects of winner-take-all politics, the impact of local economic power on the parties was not symmetrical. Rather, it systematically weakened the prospects for Democratic populism. Revealingly, it was a Democratic leader, Speaker Tip O'Neill, who insisted that "all politics is local." Dick Armey, Republican majority leader, offered a quite different aphorism: "Never offend your base."[25]

Waiting for Sixty

The outsized power of moderate Democrats and Republicans for a Day is directly connected to the practices of the contemporary Senate. These include a toxic combination: intense polarization and the prolific use of the filibuster—a perfect recipe for winner-take-all politics.

The filibuster is now used so relentlessly that it has become common to treat it as a natural, quasi-constitutional feature of the political landscape. The idea that you need sixty votes to approve legislation is treated as equivalent to the idea that you need sixty-seven to override a veto. Yet the latter provision is written into the Constitution; the filibuster is not.

Indeed, until fairly recently, filibusters were rare occurrences. As the eminent legislative scholar David Mayhew has observed, for most of American history, filibusters were typically reserved for matters of vital interest to regional minorities—specifically (and most notoriously) southern defenders of Jim Crow. Filibusters were also used on occasion to signal the intensity of minority views, or to run out the clock at the end of a congressional session. Yet normally even hugely controversial pieces of legislation could pass by the narrowest of margins without provoking obstruction. Such was the case, for instance, with the fiercely contested tariff bills that were the late nineteenth and early twentieth century's biggest brawls over economic governance—the equivalent to our tax and budget bills today.

Mayhew's most striking example, however, is FDR's 1937 court-packing plan—a proposal to remove the Supreme Court's obstruction of his agenda by increasing its size and allowing him to appoint more malleable members. One can hardly imagine a more ambitious and controversial bill. The court-packing plan ultimately failed—but it did so because it could not gain a Senate majority. The accounts of contemporaries suggest that when its passage looked more likely, the head-counters were looking for a simple majority. Filibustering was not considered a significant part of the picture.

What we now take for granted as a feature of the "system"—that senators representing just a tenth of the U.S. population can potentially stop legislation from becoming law—is in fact quite new. The growing use of the filibuster dates to the 1970s. Only since the early 1990s has there been something approaching a de facto "rule of sixty." As Mayhew concludes, never before has the Senate possessed "any anti-majoritarian barrier as concrete, as decisive, or as consequential."[26] According to the research of UCLA political scientist Barbara Sinclair, only about 8 percent of major bills in the 1960s were filibustered. By the first decade of the next century, that number would be about 70 percent.[27]

What happened? The rise of the filibuster has spawned a cottage industry for congressional scholars, and we can offer only the briefest treatment here.[28] The first stage of the transformation, dating to the mid-1970s, involved two linked developments: the reduction of the vote total needed to end a filibuster from sixty-seven to sixty, and the introduction of a streamlined cloture process in which a simple vote indicating a willingness to continue debate (deny cloture) replaced "real" filibusters.

Ironically, the timing and content of these moves suggest they were designed largely to make filibusters *less* of a problem. The rule changes came at a time—the mid-1970s, amid liberal ascendance—when Congress was passing big laws at a rapid clip. Stopping all congressional business for endless debate on a single bill seemed too costly to allow. It was made doubly costly by the emerging realities of campaign politics. The opportunities of modern transportation and the imperatives of modern fundraising were conspiring to abbreviate the legislative workweek. Politicians were eager to do their work and get out of town; real filibusters would get in the way. Cloture would make the legislative gears turn smoothly.

Obviously, it didn't turn out that way. Over time, the reforms combined to make filibusters a much more, rather than less, important part of the political landscape. True, with the new cloture arrangement, filibusters were less costly to the legislative process. That also meant, however, that they became less costly to wage. Norms that had frowned on the use of the filibuster began to erode. Over the course of the 1980s, as turnover in the Senate produced more and more members who saw the filibuster as part of the routine, that erosion continued. The filibuster ceased to appear extraordinary.

So far, this has little to do with the core political story of this book. It is a relatively self-contained if cautionary tale of unintended consequences. In the early 1990s, however, all this changed. As the parties became more intensely divided, the incentives of the minority party to obstruct grew as well.[29] The turning point—here, as in the rise of the small-business lobby—was the debate over the Clinton health plan. The astute journalist Mark Schmitt, a staffer for Democratic Senator Bill Bradley at the time, recalls: "Bob Dole, then the majority leader, made the phrase 'You need 60 votes to do anything around here' his mantra." What Dole should have said is, "You need 60 votes to do anything around here *now*." Many longtime senators, Schmitt remembers, had never seen some of the parliamentary maneuvers Republicans pulled "out of the dusty toolbox" of obstruction. Indeed, he witnessed Ted Kennedy "asking staffers for advice about how to break one of these tactics, which he had never seen in 34 years in the Senate."[30]

Regular resort to the filibuster may have been unprecedented, but it worked. It worked really well. You didn't just block reform with a filibuster; you bloodied your opponent. Tying Washington up in knots made the majority look ineffectual and fueled popular disdain for politics, which was hugely beneficial to the minority. As Sinclair puts it, the Senate Republicans who blocked Clinton "not only didn't pay a price, but they ended up gaining control . . . It is hard to make yourself popular, but to make the other guys look incompetent is not that difficult, and it worked for the Republicans in the first Clinton Congress, and the Republicans would argue the Democrats used these techniques as well."[31]

For a political system already designed to encourage stalemate, the implications of this development are profound. Some budget matters aside, every significant piece of legislation must now garner sixty votes in the Senate. Obviously, getting to sixty is a lot more difficult than getting to fifty—especially when "reaching across the aisle" means reaching toward a party that is moving farther and farther away. For Democratic leaders, however, Republicans were just the beginning of their problems. Under the no-win rules of winner-take-all politics, passing reform required more votes than in the past *and* votes from the other party were harder to come by *and* even your cross-pressured supporters often had their own incentives to defect. A better combination for enforcing drift would be hard to find. With the continuing radicalization of the GOP, the revolutionary expansion of the filibuster, the imperious rule of moderate barons, and the regular appearance of Republicans for a Day, it was no wonder that when Clinton looked in the mirror he saw an Eisenhower Republican.

Enabling Tax Cuts

Democrats have faced an ever-steeper climb to overcome gridlock. At the same time, they have felt less pressure to take up the challenge. That's not to say they never mustered the energy. Unfortunately, they were not always expending that energy on behalf of the middle class. In all the critical policy ventures enabling the winner-take-all economy, Democrats played a supportive part. Sometimes they did so actively and enthusiastically, sometimes just by failing to hold their ranks. But either way they critically contributed to the steady shift of government's attention away from the middle class.

Tax policy presents the most surprising and revealing example—not least because it's so clear that Republicans and Democrats differ here. Republicans have pushed intensively for tax cuts highly skewed to the top. The more progressive the tax, the more energetically Republicans have tried to cut it. When Democrats have had majorities, such cuts have not been a priority. When they have advocated tax cuts, they have been modest and focused on the middle class. Moreover, Democrats have been willing to support high-end tax increases (Clinton) or allow high-end tax cuts to expire (Congress after 2006 and President Obama after 2008). The differences between the two parties on this core issue have been stark.

And yet, many Democrats have been willing, in practice, to provide critical support for the GOP's aggressive tax-cutting. This was not just a matter of providing bipartisan cover. In crucial cases, Democratic support made the initiatives possible. It is often forgotten that at the time George W. Bush's extraordinarily skewed tax cuts passed, the GOP needed the votes of at least two Democrats, even when they could evade a filibuster by working through reconciliation. With Georgia's Zell Miller already firmly supportive, they needed only one. Not a problem. A tightly organized White House and House GOP successfully framed the issue as "would you like a tax cut?" Once tax cuts were on the agenda, many Democrats were willing to join the effort. With powerful interests vigorously pushing the bill, Democrats like Baucus, Breaux, Landrieu, and Lincoln, whose sterling reputations for moderation hinged on their self-proclaimed vigilance in protecting budget propriety, were quick to sign on. Strikingly, even blue state Democrats like Dianne Feinstein were willing to do the same.

These weren't modest defections—exceptions to be discounted against the backdrop of generally progressive voting records. The 2001 law was a once-in-a-decade event, a chance to shape the fundamental priorities of government. A senator's vote on such a bill says more about his or her commitment to the middle class than one hundred votes on the minimum wage.

The behavior of moderate Democrats on the estate tax is particularly revealing. A surprising number of Democrats not only signed onto the 2001 bill, with its strange 2010 phaseout. They have also been willing to discuss, and on occasion vote for, permanent repeals or "compromises" that would cost hundreds of billions of dollars in federal revenue over the coming decade—revenue losses that would either show up as debt, taxes on the less affluent, or cuts in programs. Along with the GOP, these Democrats have defended such positions by stressing the trumped-up threat of the estate tax to small businesses and family farms, even though the overwhelming benefits of their proposed reforms would have flowed to the exceptionally wealthy.

Standing Up for Better Pay—for CEOs

Democrats also played a starring role in the number-one drama regarding executive pay in the 1990s: stock options. Over the decade, stock options rose from less than a quarter of executive compensation to half—before the stock market downturn of 2000 brought the good times to a tempo-rary pause.[32] Options were loudly touted by managers as a vehicle for link-ing pay to performance. The practice was a little different, to say the least: Options were generally designed to induce high payouts and lower their visibility. Crucially, these flaws stemmed from the particular manner in which most American firms structured options. Firms in other countries use stock options, too, but with restrictions (such as payouts depending on a company outperforming others within the same industry) that link pay much more closely to performance. In principle, nothing stopped the adoption of similar rules in the United States. In practice, CEOs and their defenders fought sensible regulations tooth and nail. For them, the pay-without-performance aspects of huge executive pay packages were a fea-ture, not a bug.

To its credit, the Financial Accounting Standards Board (FASB)—the private-sector organization that, with SEC sanction, oversees the ac-counting practices of firms—recognized the problem early on. For execu-tives, one of the great attractions of stock options was that they made it possible to hide the cost of massive pay packages, exploiting an account-ing fiction that treated these lucrative payments as costless at the time of issue. In 1993, FASB announced plans to require the expensing of stock options. At the time options were issued, companies would be required to estimate the likely costs of this form of compensation. Adopting the practice of expensing would have dramatically increased the cost of issuing stock options and likely diminished their rapid growth.[33]

It never happened. Managers, especially in the rapidly growing tech industry, mobilized. SEC Chair Arthur Levitt reported that during the first few months of his tenure in 1993, he spent an astonishing one-third of his time on this single issue, "being threatened and cajoled by legions of businesspeople who wanted to kill the proposal." Led by Senator Joe Lieberman, Democrat of Connecticut (backed by California Democrats Barbara Boxer and Dianne Feinstein, whose Silicon Valley constituents were at the center of the options boom), elected officials moved quickly to block the proposed reform. By overwhelming margins, the Senate passed a resolution expressing its disapproval. Facing clear indications that FASB's proposed action could lead elected officials to strip it of its authority, even the SEC's sympathetic head, Arthur Levitt, advised the embattled board to retreat. He later called it the biggest mistake of his tenure at the agency. Besieged on all sides, FASB backed off.[34]

We need to be clear about what happened here. This is a striking example of drift, with the market racing off in a new direction and government failing to catch up. But this drift was not a matter of sloth or ignorance. Regulators saw a chance to moderate the explosion of CEO pay, not through burdensome interference but through the simple enforcement of honest, transparent accounting. Their efforts to do so were blocked through sustained and forceful interventions—with Democrats leading the way. The absence of legislative action does not mean the absence of politics. In this case as in so many others, Washington's failure to respond to new economic realities resulted from systematic, organized political action by and in support of the wealthy.

Backstopping Deregulation

When it comes to fostering a winner-take-all economy, Democrats have generally played second fiddle to the Republicans. But there is one place where they can legitimately make a case for equal billing: support for Wall Street's remarkable transformation. True, Phil Gramm was generally out in front. Yet with the financial industry realizing that most of what it wanted to do merely required that government stay on the sidelines, Democrats were not far behind.

Leading Democrats supported many of the deregulatory initiatives of the 1990s—for a variety of motives. Some genuinely believed freer markets would naturally police themselves, the long historical record to the contrary notwithstanding. Others embraced the political logic of cultivating Wall Street and were either unaware of or untroubled by the countervailing risks—risks not just to their standing as the party of ordinary workers, but also to the economy itself. Publicly, many Democrats insisted they were merely trying to "level the playing field." Once deregulation had built up steam, parts of the financial industry that still faced regulation needed the same favorable treatment as their competitors. At the same time, perversely, the increased competition encouraged all the participants to pile on more (and more lightly regulated) risk. As the conservative jurist Richard Posner has argued, deregulation had "a built-in momentum."[35] Of course, new regulations would have leveled the field as well, but in a policy environment awash in lobbying money there was no chance of achieving majority support for that.

After the financial meltdown of 2008, many chastened Democrats suggested they were simply carried along by the intellectual tide in favor of unbound markets. But market triumphalism held sway not because of the lack of a case on the other side or the absence of expressed concerns, but because the pushback within the party was so much weaker than it once had been. With labor atrophied, mass-membership federations crumbling, and voters disorganized, the incentives for resisting the deregulatory wave were meager compared with the financial rewards. Revealingly, for all the talk of unfettered markets, Democrats proved more than willing to embrace dubious loopholes and subsidies, and to assist market insiders in hiding what they were doing, when lobbyists pushed hard enough.

Indeed, those alarmed by the increasingly casino-like features of

American capitalism found powerful Democrats distressingly unsympathetic. Schumer and other like-minded Democrats had strong allies at the other end of Pennsylvania Avenue. In the Clinton administration, Treasury Secretary Robert Rubin and his deputy (and, later, successor) Lawrence Summers headed a formidable cadre of Wall Street support. Rubin, of course, had come straight out of Wall Street, having spent the previous twenty-six years in the top echelons of Goldman Sachs. Summers was Rubin's protégé and successor as treasury secretary, a fiercely brilliant economist who shared Rubin's enthusiasm for financial deregulation if not his Wall Street pedigree.

The brief clash over derivatives provided a powerful example of what the two sides of Pennsylvania Avenue could do. By the late 1990s, concern over the massively expanding use of these new financial instruments was growing. Derivatives combined impressively varied forms of mischief—vastly expanded use of leverage, incredible opacity, and an ever-tightening web of invisible threads among firms—into a single perilous package. In one of his most famous warnings about the new Wall Street, Warren Buffett referred to derivatives as "weapons of mass destruction." In 1998, Brooksley Born, Clinton's chair of the Commodity Futures Trading Commission (CFTC), invited comment on whether certain swaps and derivatives needed to be regulated. Alarmed, Rubin and Summers, along with Fed Chairman Alan Greenspan, undercut Born at every turn and eventually forced her to retreat. Rubin followed up by seeing if he could reduce the CFTC's jurisdiction, even as Gramm would initiate legislation to remove the threat once and for all.

Perhaps the most telling illustration of Democrats' role in enabling Wall Street was the merger of the banking giant Citicorp and the financial conglomerate Travelers to form Citigroup in 1998. You will recall that this was such a blatant violation of the Glass-Steagall Act that Citicorp's John Reed was asked about it at the merger's announcement, where he replied that his partner in the deal, Sandy Weill, might need to talk to "his friend," President Clinton. Reed and Weill apparently were confident. They had arranged their deal under a loophole that gave them a two-year window during which the Federal Reserve would review the merger.

Within that period, Phil Gramm's namesake legislation Gramm-Leach-Bliley removed the offending regulatory barrier. Though Weill would later insist that "we didn't rely on somebody else to build what we built," he was proud to display the pen Clinton used to sign the landmark bill in his Citigroup office.[36]

Shortly thereafter, Robert Rubin, who had been a tireless advocate of Glass-Steagall's repeal, resigned as secretary of the treasury. He became a senior adviser at the newly formed financial giant. At Citigroup, Rubin would be instrumental in pushing the envelope of ever-greater risk. He would resign a decade later, after a series of quarterly losses totaling more than $65 billion had transformed his firm, the poster child of deregulation, into a ward of the state. Rubin personally had done somewhat better, having received in excess of $126 million in cash and stock over his time at the company.[37]

Mark Hanna Democrats

During the heyday of the winner-take-all economy, the Democrats' capacity to improve the financial balance sheet of the middle class steadily deteriorated. The party's own balance sheets, however, just kept looking better and better. The continued effort to reorient party practices to winner-take-all realities was accompanied by a slow march toward financial parity with the GOP's national organizations.

By 1992, Democrats had reduced the GOP national party committees' financial advantage to less than 2–1. From there—even as the party struggled against stiff headwinds from DeLay's K Street Project and George W. Bush's fund-raising prowess—the Democrats steadily cut into the Republican edge. Bill Clinton, of course, was a formidable source of cash. In 2004, Democrats, following Howard Dean, began to tap the extraordinary possibilities of online fund-raising. That in turn led to an astonishing development: For the first time in memory, the DNC actually raised slightly more money than the RNC. The combined GOP committees still had a nontrivial lead, but as the Bush presidency drew to a close, their financial edge was on the order of 25 percent, rather than the 3–1 or 6–1 advantages they had grown accustomed to.

The DNC's financial success stemmed in significant part from the Internet, which greatly increased the organization's fund-raising capacity among small and medium donors—the sorts of donors the RNC had so effectively targeted in the late 1970s and 1980s with direct mail. But the Democratic Party's spectacular budgetary improvement also reflected a much more aggressive pursuit of large donors. There was, of course, Chuck Schumer's tremendous fund-raising record, which focused on Wall Street and led the Democratic Senatorial Campaign Committee to far outpace its Republican counterpart. But it was on the House side where Democrats' intense new focus on fund-raising represented the biggest departure.

Ever since the devastating loss of 1994, Democrats had sought a path back to control of the House of Representatives. The Republicans' advantage never rivaled the big majorities Democrats had typically held before 1994. Yet their seats were well protected, and the prize of majority status persistently eluded the Democrats' reach. When Democrats finally took back the House in 2006, the field general was Rahm Emanuel. Nancy Pelosi knew what she was getting when she picked the second-term congressman from Illinois to head the Democratic Congressional Campaign Committee (DCCC). Unlike most members of Congress, Emanuel had been a skilled political operative before he became an elected official. More specifically, he had cut his political teeth as a campaign finance specialist, first for Chicago Mayor Richard Daley and then for an aspiring presidential candidate, William Jefferson Clinton. A sympathetic biographer of the DCCC's successful 2006 campaign describes what Emanuel brought to the table:

> *Emanuel spent more of his time courting cash than doing anything else. No matter how attractive a candidate or appealing his message, it meant little if he could not advertise on television, print brochures, or pay campaign workers to knock on doors . . . In the 2006 campaign, Emanuel and his staff were judging candidates almost*

exclusively by how much money they raised. If a candidate proved a good fund-raiser, the DCCC would provide support, advertising, strategic advice, and whatever other help was needed. If not, the committee would shut him out ... Most of Emanuel's fund-raising time was spent meeting with wealthy lawyers or financiers, telling them this was the year to give, even as Nancy Pelosi and other Democrats were also raising enormous sums.[38]

In between his stint as a top aide in the Clinton administration and his election to Congress, Emanuel had spent a few years making a large amount of money in the financial sector.[39] This, too, fed into his education. By the time he reached Capitol Hill, his understanding of politics had crystallized. In a summary that would have warmed the heart of Mark Hanna, the great political fixer of the Gilded Age, Emanuel reportedly told staffers: "The first third of your campaign is money, money, money. The second third is money, money, and press. And the last third is votes, press, and money."[40]

For those of you keeping score at home, that's money 6, votes 1.

Chapter 10

Battle Royale

By the fall of 2008, as the presidential election campaign reached peak intensity, the United States faced a full-fledged financial calamity rooted in the winner-take-all economy. A financial system built to induce high-stakes gambles fell like a house of cards when the housing bubble burst. As credit seized up, the stock market collapsed. Home foreclosures skyrocketed, consumers closed their wallets, and unemployment began a rapid rise. Belatedly, policymakers responded with desperate measures to forestall total collapse, but the economy remained dangling precariously on the edge.

The downturn interrupted a roaring economic expansion—for those at the top. 2007, the last year of the "Bush boom," marked a milestone of sorts: It closed with the richest 1 percent of families within a few tenths of a percentage point of matching the share of national income that the top 1 percent had enjoyed on the eve of the Great Depression. But despite falling just short of the 1928 mark, the rich had little grounds for complaint. Over the 2002–2007 expansion, their pretax incomes had grown by more than 10 percent a year on average (after adjusting for inflation), leaving them with nearly a quarter of all U.S. family income in 2007—$1.34 million per family, on average.[1] In stark contrast, the typical family's income, at just over $52,000, was below what it had been at the end of the last expansion in 2000. And in 2008, it fell to just over $50,000, lower than at any point since 1997.[2]

The damage to the economy was paralleled by the damage to leading officials' reputations and the ideas they championed. Religious commitment to market infallibility, once a badge of honor among opinion leaders, was now widely perceived as a big part of the problem. Former Fed chief Alan Greenspan, long an unchallenged economic guru, was widely derided for having first pumped up the housing bubble and then having sat on his hands while regulatory failures mounted. Throughout, Greenspan had doggedly argued that markets knew best, and that regulators had no business second-guessing the decisions of investors and firms. Belatedly, Greenspan's historic connection to the radical libertarianism of Ayn Rand began to look less like an amusing idiosyncrasy and more like a serious liability for the principal architect of American economic policy.

Greenspan's fall from grace was not an isolated case. After his triumphant run at Treasury, Robert Rubin had moved to a position as a lavishly compensated wise man at Citigroup. Only after the crash did it become clear that he had aggressively advocated the leverage-expanding strategies that brought the company to ruin and left it a ward of the federal government. Phil Gramm's perch at the Swiss bank UBS was equally tenuous. An aggressive participant in the new world of financial manipulation, UBS suffered massive losses that required a huge bailout from the Swiss government. While regulators combed through the ashes, it was disclosed that one of UBS's profitable business lines during the bubble was the facilitation of widespread tax evasion among wealthy Americans (the case broke when a UBS executive turned state's witness, admitting that he had engaged in shady practices that included smuggling a client's diamonds into the country in a tube of toothpaste).[3]

No one's reputation, however, took as hard a hit as George W. Bush's. While the worst economic disaster in seventy years unfolded, the president seemed a hapless observer. Though privately capable of describing what was happening in his own inimitable way ("If money isn't loosened up, this sucker could come down"), Bush was awkward and ineffective in public.[4] Fearing he lacked the *gravitas* called for, the administration's message makers increasingly chose to leave him offstage. In the rapidly worsening crisis, Bush's two-bladed Swiss army knife (tax cuts for the wealthy and deregulation) was useless.

As our two-party system almost guarantees, the GOP's struggles redounded to the Democrats. The meltdown fed an already brewing backlash against Republicans. The 2006 and 2008 elections saw the Democratic Party's most successful back-to-back results since the 1930s, with the new majorities in the House and Senate far exceeding the pinnacles reached by Reagan's or Bush's GOP. Though conspicuously smaller than the Democratic congressional margins overseen by FDR and LBJ, these new majorities included far fewer conservative Southern Democrats than they, Jimmy Carter, or even Bill Clinton had faced. And, of course, accompanying these majorities would be a charismatic new president promising change. Observing the transformed landscape, the congressional scholar Barbara Sinclair concluded that "for Democrats the stars are better aligned for a cooperative relationship and legislative success than at any time since 1965."[5]

The stars seemed aligned for more. Periods of political renewal have historically rested on three coinciding circumstances: a strong sense of crisis that involves popular repudiation of the preceding regime, the presence of sizable Democratic majorities in Congress, and the arrival of a president willing and able to articulate the case for major change. On the frigid Washington morning of Barack Obama's inauguration, all of these elements seemed to be in place.

It would not take long, however, before the politics of renewal ran headlong into the entrenched realities of winner-take-all politics. No one for whom renewal mattered most—not President Obama, not congressional Democrats, and certainly not the American middle class who had been losing out so badly—would emerge from the collision unscathed.

Seeking Renewal

The rise of a young African American to the presidency, defeating two larger-than-life opponents along the way, was itself an extraordinary story. Having first vanquished a Hillary Clinton candidacy that had appeared unstoppable, Obama went on to soundly defeat John McCain, becoming the first nonincumbent to win a popular vote majority since 1988. And he did all this while remaining unflappable at a time of crisis. By Inauguration Day, Obama's optimistic call for change suggested to an anxious public that a reform moment had arrived.

Despite his relative political inexperience (two years in the Senate, seven in the Illinois State Senate), Obama gave strong indication that he understood the basic challenges he faced. Of course, great politicians are skilled producers of crafted ambiguity. Who knows what their views really are? Yet Obama—during the campaign and after—showed an unusual penchant for presenting detailed and nuanced speeches on complex and volatile matters from race to the Middle East. And just such a speech was his campaign address of March 27, 2008, entitled "Renewing the American Economy" and held at the Cooper Union in New York.

In the midst of a growing economic crisis and a heated Democratic primary, before an audience that included former Fed chief Paul Volcker, New York mayor Bloomberg, former SEC head William Donaldson, and dozens of leading Wall Street figures, Obama proceeded to offer a penetrating analysis of the country's predicament. He began by stressing that since the time of Hamilton and Jefferson, Americans have struggled to maintain balance between "self-interest and community, markets and democracy, the concentration of wealth and power and the necessity of transparency and opportunity for each and every citizen." Government, he insisted, was necessary to provide "the rules of the road," and to ensure that market power was not unchecked. Obama noted that the core challenges of today were hardly unprecedented: "The concentrations of economic power and the failures of our political system to protect the American economy and American consumers from its worst excesses have been a staple of our past: most famously in the 1920s, when such excesses ultimately plunged the country into the Great Depression."

Most critically, Obama stressed that the problem was at root a political one. In front of a collection of the nation's biggest economic winners, the young presidential candidate ticked off some of the basic failings of winner-take-all politics that we have described in this book:

We've lost some of that sense of shared prosperity. Now, this loss has not happened by accident. It's because of decisions made in boardrooms, on trading floors and in Washington. Under Republican and Democratic administrations, we've failed to guard against practices that all too often rewarded financial manipulation instead of productivity and sound business practice. We let the special interests put their thumbs on the economic scales . . .

The American economy does not stand still and neither should the rules that govern it . . . Unfortunately, instead of establishing a twenty-first century regulatory framework, we simply dismantled the old one, aided by a legal but corrupt bargain in which campaign money all too often shaped policy and watered down oversight. In doing so we encouraged a winner-take-all, anything goes environment that helped foster devastating dislocations in our economy.[6]

By the time candidate Obama became President Obama ten months later, these challenges were only more clear and the new president, it seemed, only more committed to tackling them. The ambitious initiatives he announced—a huge economic stimulus plan, a major revision of federal spending priorities, near-universal health care, a massive overhaul of financial regulation, and ambitious climate change legislation—were meant to mend some of the most serious distortions of the winner-take-all economy. To achieve them, the president would need every element of the fragile politics of renewal, not least the large Democratic majorities in Congress that greeted him.

Democrats on Top

Like Charlie Brown trying to kick the football held by Lucy, Democrats had grown accustomed to having victory snatched from their grasp. But in 2006 and 2008, the football wasn't pulled away. Along with George W. Bush's plummeting poll numbers, the major expansion of the party's organizational capacity discussed in the last chapter buoyed the Democrats' congressional standing. When the opportunity for a "wave election" emerged in 2006, Democrats did a considerably better job of seizing the moment than they had in 1982. They won six seats in the Senate, recapturing control of the chamber by the narrowest possible margin. Results in the House were equally impressive. Despite very narrow majorities, the GOP's House fortress, protected by gerrymandering, incumbency, and superior finances, had held firm since 1994. In 2006, however, it fell. Democrats succeeded in winning thirty seats, making Nancy Pelosi the new Speaker of the House and the highest-ranking woman in American political history.

In congressional politics, back-to-back partisan routs are exceptionally rare: Each victory pushes the ascendant party deeper into enemy territory, making a backslide much more likely than further advances. Yet the combination of economic crisis and Bush fatigue helped Democrats follow up their extremely strong showing in 2006 with an equally decisive victory in 2008. Having already improved their 2006 advantage by gaining three seats through special elections, they picked up another twenty-one seats in the House. When the courtroom dust had finally settled in Minnesota, where the comedian and author Al Franken barely bested Republican incumbent Norm Coleman, Democrats had added a staggering eight in the Senate. And when Pennsylvania's Arlen Specter fled an increasingly incendiary GOP base to become a Democrat, the partisan shift grew to nine. No doubt shocking even themselves, Democrats had reached the magical Senate number of sixty.

It was not just congressional Democrats who had shown newfound organizational prowess. The president himself had ascended to office using Hillary's playbook—Edmund's, that is, not Clinton's. During the long slog to victory, Obama's campaign manager David Plouffe had taken the Internet-based organizing campaigns of Dean and Kerry to a whole new level. Obama's fund-raising, fueled by the Internet, broke all records. For the first time in modern history a Democratic presidential candidate had a large financial advantage over a Republican one—enough so that even after far outspending McCain during the 2008 campaign, Obama could bequeath a large surplus, rather than the traditional burden of debt, to the DNC.

Yet Obama's organizational prowess was not limited to fund-raising. Befitting the first community organizer to win the presidency, Obama's campaign built an army of support using Internet tools. The first visible payoff was the campaign's critical outmaneuvering of Hillary Clinton in state caucuses—a forum that requires the large-scale mobilization of intense supporters. The Clinton campaign never recovered. By Election Day, "Obama for America" could count on two million active volunteers, a donor base of four million contributors, and a self-selected e-mail list of thirteen million supporters. In the words of journalist Charles Homans, "With the click of a mouse, Plouffe could reach a group of true believers the size of the population of Illinois."[7]

After the election, this extraordinary mobilizing tool morphed into a distinct entity, Organizing for America, housed within the DNC. Presidents had tried before to transform campaign armies into tools of governance, with limited success. But the size and sophistication of the president's organization, along with the new mobilizing possibilities imbued in the Internet, made it inevitable that analysts would speculate about the leverage it would give the Obama administration in the looming politics of organized combat.[8]

Girding for Combat

From the beginning, Obama took an altogether different approach from that of the last Democrat in the White House, Bill Clinton. At war with parts of the Democratic Party and eager to sustain his outsider image,

Clinton had stocked key positions with Arkansans and longtime supporters (most notoriously elevating his childhood pal Mack McLarty to the
crucial position of chief of staff). Obama's approach could not have been
more different. The first man in almost half a century to move directly
from the Senate to the Oval Office, he saw effective engagement with
Congress as critical. In a polarized system where organized interests were
well entrenched and defense was a lot easier to play than offense, knowing
how to build legislative alliances and craft legislation that could *pass* were
identified as the essential skills.

The prominent presence in his administration of his defeated opponents, Hillary Clinton and Joe Biden—both ex-senators as well—
encouraged analysts to draw parallels to Lincoln's "team of rivals" so
vividly recounted in Doris Kearns Goodwin's recent history.[9] Yet if a single appointment embodied the strategic vision of Obama's presidency, it
was the president's announcement just days after the election that Rahm
Emanuel would be his chief of staff. That he would pick someone who
knew Congress so well for this critical post—"Rahm is family" said Nancy
Pelosi—spoke volumes.[10] So did the fact that the ambitious Emanuel,
widely viewed as on the fast track to be Speaker of the House, accepted
what some might have viewed as a demotion. Both the president and his
new top aide clearly saw a historic opportunity to reform American governance, and both saw Congress as the key.

Emanuel was just the beginning. The president moved from there to
assemble what the journalist Matt Bai accurately calls "the most Congress-
centric administration in modern history."[11] Emanuel's top deputy was
to be Jim Messina, formerly chief of staff for Senate Finance chair Max
Baucus. The key post of legislative director went to Phil Schiliro, former
aide to the crucial chair of the House Energy and Commerce Committee,
Henry Waxman. Schiliro in turn selected Lisa Konwinski as his deputy;
she had previously worked for the important moderate Democrat Kent
Conrad. Peter Orszag was brought over from the Congressional Budget
Office to fill the critical policy job as the head of the Office of Management and Budget. The list goes on and on. As Emanuel himself recounted
to Bai: "That was a strategy . . . We had a deep bench of people with a lot

of relationships that run into both the House and Senate extensively. And so we wanted to use that to our maximum advantage."

The "congressionalist" structure reflected an appreciation for the politics of organized combat, an understanding that producing real changes in governance meant confronting the reality of deeply entrenched interests operating on favorable legislative terrain.[12] The composition of Obama's economic team reflected a different sort of concession to the reality of organized combat—a recognition that the delicate sensitivities of the winner-take-all economy demand their own accommodation. The key positions went to two veterans of the Clinton administration, Tim Geithner and Larry Summers. Of the two, Summers had the greater political experience, having served as treasury secretary (where, as we saw in chapter 9, he pushed for financial deregulation). But neither could be seen as a congressional favorite. Rather, they were respected figures within the mainstream of Democratic economic thinking with strong ties to Wall Street.

Of the two, Geithner's Wall Street ties were the stronger. He had been offered the top spot at Citigroup (though "sorely tempted," he declined).[13] As head of the Federal Reserve Bank of New York in 2008, he had engineered the $182 billion bailout of the giant insurer AIG. The terms of the bailout, which Geithner's New York Fed had insisted be kept secret, were so generous to major Wall Street firms like Goldman Sachs that Geithner was forced to defend the rescue before Congress alongside his predecessor as treasury secretary, Henry Paulson. But Geithner and Summers had credibility and a reputation for effectiveness and the coveted ability to "calm the market." Their appointment may have done little to reinforce the populism that Obama had regularly deployed on the campaign trail. But it did reassure Wall Street, economic policy mandarins, and the crucial Democratic moderates who would have to be brought along that the president could work with a resourceful and well-connected Wall Street as well as confront it. The need to offer such assurances reflected a paradox that the young administration would confront repeatedly: how to heal a fragile economy without simply reasserting the dominance of the forces that had brought that economy to the brink of ruin. The new administration was not just seeking to repair a ship at sea; it was trying to redesign the ship as well.

The Obama team was assembled to advance an agenda crowded with staggering challenges, both a profound immediate crisis and an accumulation of public needs resulting from decades of debilitating drift. On issue after issue—from financial market regulation to climate change legislation to health-care reform—the administration's policy ambitions posed substantial threats to the biggest beneficiaries of the winner-take-all economy. And so, it should come as no surprise that as the new president assembled his troops for organized combat, he was not the only one gearing up for battle.

"Sight Unseen"

Like his immediate predecessor, the new president began by emphasizing his desire to end the partisan divide of modern Washington. Unlike his predecessor, Obama followed up with some concrete, if largely symbolic, steps—retaining Robert Gates as secretary of defense, appointing Republican Ray LaHood as secretary of transportation, and offering New Hampshire Senator Judd Gregg the position of commerce secretary (Gregg declined). Even GOP leaders acknowledged the administration's unusually intensive efforts to open channels of communication in the early days. The administration's opening proposals on its crucial economic stimulus bill included a less symbolic gesture: a very large tax-cut component designed in part to garner GOP support.

It quickly became clear, however, that one of the greatest obstacles that Democrats would face was intense, unwavering, and highly unified Republican opposition. Given the yawning ideological gap between the two parties, this was no surprise. Yet the Republicans' near-monolithic opposition went beyond simple policy differences. For the GOP, the political logic behind a purely oppositional stance was not only exceptionally powerful, but had a proven track record. It was a strategy famously urged by conservative strategist William Kristol in 1993, when Kristol had

forcefully advised Republicans to oppose any health-care reform compromises with President Clinton "sight unseen." If Democrats failed to
register legislative achievements, Kristol had argued, they, not the GOP,
would get the blame. In the House, Newt Gingrich had reached the same
conclusion: Anything that tied Washington in knots, anything that highlighted petty bickering, was likely to benefit the minority, anti-Washington
party.[14] Voters were more likely to punish the majority for stalemate than
the minority for obstruction. In light of the GOP's weakened status in
2009 and Obama's ambitious agenda, replicating Gingrich's stance was a
political no-brainer.

And yet the question remains: Why didn't a pattern of greater compromise or cooperation develop with moderate Republicans in Congress?
Each politician, after all, faces a unique local situation, and what helps a
political party is not always helpful to the individual politicians who make
it up. Traditionally, successful bipartisanship has hinged on this disconnect. We have seen repeatedly how appeals to cross-pressured members
of the opposite party can pad a majority, as the Bush administration ac-
complished, for instance, on some of its big tax cuts.

For the Obama administration the most obvious target was "the Maine
caucus" Olympia Snowe and Susan Collins, the senior and junior senators from the state that Obama had carried by an impressive 18 points
in the 2008 election. But Democrats quickly found that peeling off Collins or Snowe, or any other Senate Republican, was extremely difficult.
On bill after bill, GOP opposition was almost perfectly lockstep. Some of
the credit for the battered party's impressive display of unity must go to
Minority Leader Mitch McConnell, who effectively argued that Republicans who broke ranks would legitimate Democratic initiatives with the
public. As one Republican Senator put it in early 2010, "McConnell has
pointed out that if we don't hang together, we're going to hang separately,
not just on the financial regulatory bill but on every other bill coming
down the pike."[15] And then there was the threat from the Republican base
whose impressive organization we discussed in chapter 8. Arlen Specter's
fate—pushed from the party by a right-wing primary challenge—was a
dramatic reminder of the risks of excessive moderation.

Still Going . . . Right

The fundamental problem, however was that there just weren't many Republican moderates for Obama to court. We have argued—in this book and, at greater length, in our 2005 book, *Off Center*—that the GOP's evolution in Congress since the 1970s has been one long move to the right.[16] Like a retreating glacier, the GOP's moderate edges continually vanish first, leaving a hardened core of increasingly unflinching conservatives. Again and again, Democrats smashed painfully into an unyielding wall of solid opposition.

How do we know the GOP has moved so far to the right? One way is to look at how its legislators vote. Political scientists have carefully analyzed roll calls over many years to develop systematic measures of the relative rankings of legislators from left to right. And what these measures show, as noted in chapter 8, is that while both Democrats and Republicans have become more unified and distinct, the biggest story has been the Republican Party's long-term transit to the right. This process was not completed under Reagan, or under Gingrich. It now turns out that it wasn't even completed under George W. Bush.

Indeed, as measured by roll-call votes, the already dramatic rate of rightward movement in the GOP has *actually accelerated in the past two election cycles.*[17] At one level this may seem paradoxical—shouldn't a losing party moderate its message?—but at another, it makes sense: The most moderate elements of the party are generally those in districts or states requiring a more nuanced stance, and these are precisely the districts and states where Republicans were most likely to lose as the party's fortunes declined.[18]

Just as conservative Southern Democrats bore the brunt of the Gingrich revolution, the past two election cycles have been very hard on Republican moderates. Of the twenty-five most moderate GOP members of the House before the 2006 election, only ten remained in office after the 2008 election.[19] Taken as a group, the ninety-four GOP representatives who served in 2006 but were no longer in the House after 2008 were considerably more moderate than their colleagues who remained. The gap between those who lost or retired and the intensely conservative entering GOP class of 2006 was even larger.[20] Remember: Before 2006, the GOP House caucus was already *extremely* conservative. It has gotten much more so since.

At the height of the 2008 economic crisis, the increased conservatism of the House GOP was on full display. In an echo of 1990 worthy of Shakespeare, a right-wing revolt once again signaled the demise of a Republican monarch. This time, though, the victim was not the tepid compromiser George H. W. Bush, but the conservative movement's greatest leader only a few years before, George W. Implored by a desperate Bush administration to pass the Troubled Asset Relief Program (TARP) and avert an economic meltdown, the House GOP split sharply on generational lines. Eighty-two percent of House members planning to retire that year voted in favor of the administration's proposal. Not a single first-term Republican did so. All told, more than two-thirds of the House GOP voted no, and the bill failed. The Dow responded by dropping 7 percent and posting its biggest single-day point loss (777.68) in history. When a spooked Congress voted four days later on a revised package, thirty-three Democrats and twenty-four Republicans switched from no to yes— enough to assure passage but still less than half of the House Republican caucus.[21]

The same hardening of conservatism played out in the Senate as well. The 2006 midterm results were a somewhat mixed bag, as the defeat of such Republican moderates as Lincoln Chafee in Rhode Island were partly balanced by defeats of hard-core conservatives like Rick Santorum. Still, the caucus as a whole shifted rightward. In 2008, that shift became more of a lurch. The eight Republicans who were replaced by Democrats in 2008 included the third (Smith), fourth (Coleman), ninth (Stevens), tenth (Warner), and eleventh (Domenici) most moderate GOP senators. The fifth (Specter) changed parties early in 2009.[22] In one fell swoop, the Senate's club of GOP moderates was cut in half, leaving the GOP's two most moderate members, Susan Collins and Olympia Snowe, looking increasingly lonely.

The rightward shift of the GOP has been so dramatic that by 2004, one of the men whom we credited with the Republican revival, former RNC chief William Brock, was deploring the "dangerous" tilt toward "a political system that looks, and feels, like a political barbell: one where all the weight is at the ends of the spectrum, leaving those in the center with little voice or opportunity for impact."[23] Brock's lament understandably papered over the most striking feature of the tilt: The barbell was becoming much heavier on the Republican end.[24] This was especially true in the House. As their ranks grew between 2005 and 2009, House Democrats moved slightly *rightward* rather than leftward. But the two parties continued to polarize, because House Republicans moved rightward even faster. In this environment, reaching a hand across the aisle looked more and more like an exercise in futility—a long pole probably wouldn't suffice.

Exhibit A for the rightward shift of Republicans has to be South Carolina Senator Jim DeMint. Within the shrunken GOP caucus, DeMint anchors the right wing. Yet in the early days of the Obama administration, he emerged as a prominent, if shrill, voice on economic issues. In a January 2009 speech to the Heritage Foundation, DeMint outlined a Republican alternative to the administration's economic stimulus plan.[25] Introducing his own version of historical perspective, he denounced the Obama proposal as "the worst piece of economic legislation Congress has considered in a hundred years." He then identified the infamous bill he had in mind—the 1909 passage of the Sixteenth Amendment, which had cleared the way for a federal income tax.

DeMint's identification of 1909 as the year everything began to go wrong provided a pretty good clue for where he was heading. Indeed, DeMint's "American Option" doubled down on the Bush tax cuts of 2001 and 2003, which had been introduced at an economic conjuncture that could not have been more different. DeMint's plan would have made permanent *all* of the Bush tax cuts for the rich. The liberal Center for American Progress estimated the cost at $3.1 *trillion* over a decade—more than triple the cost of Obama's stimulus plan. And unlike the Obama plan, the huge hole in the budget produced by DeMint's plan would be permanent rather than temporary.[26]

The Party of No

With his potshots at insufficiently pure Republicans and his ominous if perplexing warnings that Obama's Washington resembled "Germany . . . before World War II," DeMint is an easy target.[27] Yet when it came to the floor for a vote, DeMint's American Option received the support of all but four GOP senators. And when push came to shove, no Republicans in the House supported the stimulus plan—none, even though the plan was backed by Bush-appointed Fed Chief Ben Bernanke and Chamber of Commerce President Tom Donohue. Only three—Collins, Snowe, and Republican-for-just-a-few-more-days Specter—did so in the Senate. In a fateful sign of things to come, Republicans seemed to be coalescing around a one-word strategy: "no."

Outside of government, some prominent Republicans were troubled enough to voice dismay. Bruce Bartlett, one of the architects of Jack Kemp's original supply-side tax-cut proposals and a policy adviser in the Reagan and George H. W. Bush administrations, declared that the Republican fiscal philosophy had become "distorted into something that is, frankly, nuts—the ideas that there is no economic problem that cannot be cured with more and bigger tax cuts, that all tax cuts are equally beneficial, and that all tax cuts raise revenue."[28] Decrying the nearly unanimous Republican opposition to the stimulus, Bartlett had harsh words for his party. The GOP, he said, "no longer bears any resemblance to the party of Ronald Reagan" and is "dominated by extremists unable to see how badly their party was alienating moderates and independents."[29]

Yet a year later, that near-party-line vote on the stimulus plan would look like the high tide of bipartisanship. Promising massive immediate benefits to citizens at a time of desperate need, the stimulus bill was among the *most likely* initiatives to gain support across the aisle. On issues that required sacrifice, or less certain rewards, such as health care, Republican opposition was monolithic. Senate Finance Committee Chairman Max Baucus devoted months to negotiating with any Republican who claimed, however implausibly, a willingness to discuss compromise on health care. After many months of negotiations, staunch economic conservatives like

Charles Grassley and Mike Enzi walked away from the conference table. Having slowed the bill's progress for months, they joined a relentless attack designed to erode public confidence in the health-care bill and the legislative process itself. Grassley would echo 2008 GOP vice-presidential candidate Sarah Palin's frenzied talking points about federal death panels. Enzi would brag about his stalling tactics, telling a Wyoming Chamber of Commerce luncheon that "if I hadn't been part of the debate, you would already have universal health care."[30]

At the end, exactly zero Senate Republicans supported the health-care plan.[31] Olympia Snowe, the single Republican who remained in play when Baucus's negotiations broke down, ultimately demurred. After almost a year of protracted discussion—a result largely of diligent Republican efforts to obstruct action at every possible turn—Snowe invoked the Scarlett O'Hara Defense. She could not support the bill because the discussion was being needlessly rushed. When the health-care bill appeared to implode a month later after Democrats lost the late Ted Kennedy's seat in Massachusetts, the fruits of a Republican strategy of obstruction and delay were on full display.

Ultimately the Democrats were able to resort to the legislative tactic of reconciliation (which permitted Democrats to avoid a filibuster and move forward without GOP votes) to secure a triumph. This was an option that would be unavailable for most of their legislative agenda. And while it allowed the administration to claim a notable victory, it did so at a high price. The prolonged stalemate had cost reformers a precious year and encouraged a dangerous souring of the public mood.

Why had Democrats spent so long in futile search for bipartisanship? They had the largest majorities in Congress in three decades. Republicans, for their part, had the lowest party approval ratings in memory. On issue after issue, polls showed dramatically higher support for Democrats. True, voters expressed a love of bipartisanship, but surely Democrats were in the driver's seat and could craft terms for a reasonable compromise? That we all know this question is hopelessly naive says a lot about what has happened in Washington over the past few decades—and points us to an increasingly critical bulwark of winner-take-all politics.

Frozen Coffee

A generation ago, the question would not have been naive at all. Consider a document recently unearthed by an enterprising undergraduate at Yale, David Broockman.[32] While combing through the LBJ Archives in Austin, Texas, for a thesis on the politics of Medicare, Broockman found a letter written just after LBJ's sweeping 1964 reelection. The letter was from Mike Manatos, Johnson's Senate liaison, to Larry O'Brien, who had directed Johnson's reelection effort. Manatos was engaged in that time-honored and crucial preparation for legislative battle: counting votes. Regarding Medicare, he announced that the math looked good. Start with the previous year's razor-thin defeat, add three absent supporters, plus a net gain of three seats from the election and voilà: "If all our supporters are present and voting we would win by a vote of 55 to 45."

Remember, the Medicare bill was regarded as hugely important. Long sought by Democrats and equally passionately opposed by most Republicans, it was the health-care reform of its day. Indeed, many conservatives still worship Ronald Reagan's Medicare-will-end-freedom speech, which articulated the same fears of the now overwhelmingly popular program that current conservatives apply to health-care reform. Yet on one critical dimension, the political world has changed fundamentally.

Today, an aide writing a similar memo to Obama's chief of staff, Rahm Emanuel, would have to change only a single word: "If all our supporters are present and voting we would *lose* by a vote of 55 to 45." Slowly, almost without notice, and certainly without any larger national conversation, Washington replaced a normal requirement of fifty-one votes to pass bills in the Senate with a requirement of sixty. In a system already prone to gridlock, the bar for new legislation has gotten dramatically higher. The new "rule of sixty" greatly increases the level of consensus required for action, precisely at the moment when the prospects for consensus have never been lower. What was once a high jump is now a pole vault—though it often seems that majorities are attempting it without the aid of a pole.

Of course, the Senate has always served as a brake on legislation. The famous story (alas, probably apocryphal) involves Jefferson admonishing Washington for agreeing to the establishment of a second chamber. "Why," responded Washington, "did you pour that coffee into your saucer?" "To cool it," Jefferson replied. "Even so," said Washington, "we pour legislation into the senatorial saucer to cool it."

Nicely put, but less satisfying in the modern context. Even as our society has become more dynamic, the Senate has become much more sclerotic. Grafted onto the worsening malapportionment of the Senate, the de facto requirement that all legislation obtain sixty votes means that senators representing even small slices of the population or distinctly minority opinions can tie the institution up in knots. With increasingly unified parties squaring off—a development the founders, who disliked the idea of regularized party competition, never anticipated—even a beleaguered and discredited caucus, if it holds together, will be extremely powerful. And in the contemporary context, where blame for failure is likely to fall on the majority, that caucus has enormous incentives to stick together. In a highly polarized political system, the "rule of sixty" is a recipe for frozen coffee.

Imagine, for a moment, if the United States, like almost all other democracies, had a parliamentary system. If House passage were sufficient for legislation, Obama would have had a first year to rival the great reform waves of the twentieth century. Reasonably robust financial reregulation, climate legislation, and health-care reform—all would have passed. A stimulus package more appropriate in scale and structure to the nation's immense economic challenges would have been enacted. The House presumably could have passed the Employee Free Choice Act as well (it did so easily in 2007), but in this case the Democratic leadership decided to hold back until there was some indication the Senate would follow suit.

Instead, the American system produced excruciating efforts to thread the needle. Reforms have sometimes come, but the hill has been dramatically steeper and the required concessions to powerful economic interests markedly larger. Advocates of reform needed to woo improbable Republicans—Republicans who were not only much further apart from Democrats on economic policy matters than they used to be, but also faced new political incentives to avoid compromise. Alternatively, at least during the critical few months when the Senate Democrats had a caucus of sixty, they needed to find a formula acceptable to *every* member of their caucus.

With the toxic combination of a sixty-vote rule and intense polarization, the contemporary Senate began to resemble the famously dysfunctional Polish parliament of the seventeenth and eighteenth centuries, the Sejm, which operated in the shadow of the *liberum veto*—a requirement of unanimous consent. This arrangement created enormous opportunities for powerful actors (including those in other countries) to buy off a single nobleman. With no capacity for action, the Polish state was subjected to repeated incursions, and ultimately dismemberment, by its powerful neighbors. Confronting their own version of the *liberum veto*, the administration and congressional leaders knew that they would need to work relentlessly to round up every last vote. With few or no Republicans in play, they needed *all* the Democrats. Democrats with varied local circumstances. Democrats with different views. Democrats with large egos or simmering resentments. Democrats seeking special favors. Democrats susceptible to intense lobbying.

It was an invitation to the politics of organized combat.

Organization Still Matters

If the electoral landscape had changed dramatically in 2006 and 2008, the organizational landscape had not. Middle-class Americans may have gotten a stronger champion in the White House, but on K Street the winner-take-all economy still had plenty of powerful defenders.

Even as the Bush administration went into decline, lobbyists had continued to increase their capacity in Washington, with reported expenditures spiraling upward. In response to the GOP's eroding position, however, powerful sectors of the economy altered their patterns of giving. The pharmaceutical industry, for instance, had made two-thirds of its contributions to the GOP in the first half of the decade. After 2006, however, it gave slightly more to Democrats than to Republicans. The "FIRE" sector we've met in previous chapters (the broadest definition of finance, including insurance and real estate) had a distinct GOP bias from the mid-1990s through the mid-2000s, but gave Democrats a slight edge in the 2007–2008 electoral cycle and a larger one in the early days of 2009.[33]

The adjustments in portfolios were not limited to campaign contributions. During the heyday of Republican rule, when Tom "the Hammer" DeLay was the House GOP's enforcer, he had called lobbyists into his office and strong-armed them to hire Republicans and fire Democrats. These tactics had an effect, but the majority of lobbying firms appear to have sustained a more flexible structure. Revealingly, they built distinct "red" and "blue" teams, each staffed by professionals with strong links to a specific party.[34] As the political winds shifted, one or the other team might be more valuable—and, when experienced Washington hands retired or lost office, firms could sign promising free agents of either party.

Just as had happened in the mid-1990s, the transfer of power on Capitol Hill after the 2006 election led lobbyists to reach out to the new "in" party. Firms scrambled to attract staffers and retiring legislators who could help them press their case. To take just a few examples that could be endlessly multiplied, the lobbying shop BGR, which had once been an all-Republican affair, first signed up Michael Meehan, who had previously worked for Democratic presidential nominee John Kerry.[35] It then moved to hire David DiMartino, whose résumé included an impressive trifecta: stints as deputy chief of staff to Senator Ben Nelson, national spokesman for the Kerry presidential campaign, and deputy communications director for the Democratic Senatorial Campaign Committee.

In the spring of 2008, JPMorgan Chase hired Democrat Peter Scher as executive vice president in charge of global government affairs (he replaced former congressman and U.S. Senate candidate Rick Lazio, whose Republican affiliation was now an underperforming asset). Scher's credentials included previous service as the Clinton administration's special trade negotiator in the Office of the U.S. Trade Representative and as chief of staff at the Commerce Department, where he worked with a future commerce secretary (and chairman of Al Gore's 2000 presidential campaign), William M. Daley. At JPMorgan, Scher and Daley would be reunited, since each of them now had seats on the bank's executive committee.

Yet there is a strong case that neither of these influential posts, nor the valuable connections associated with them, was Scher's most important credential. Rather, it was an earlier position: chief of staff to Max Baucus. After the 2006 election, few entries on a Washington résumé opened as many doors as ones signaling a connection to the senior senator from Montana. As the preconditions for a reform window began to align, experienced political hands were quick to appreciate Baucus's pivotal role. His Senate Finance Committee would handle much of the action. Aside from the floor of the Senate itself, Finance was the place where reform was most likely to hit a roadblock.

That it was access to Baucus that created cachet on K Street is highly revealing. When the GOP reigned, former DeLay aides had been in demand, because it was the intensely conservative House GOP leadership that had its foot on the gas. Now access to the powerful Senate moderate was imperative, for his committee potentially had its foot on the brake. Most of the initiatives that could reverse the tilt in Washington toward the well-off and well-connected ran through Baucus's committee. And so the well-off and well-connected ran *to* the Montana senator.

An Economic Upswing—for Lobbyists

As the politics of organized combat moved into full swing, the Obama administration and K Street were like captains of two playground squads jockeying to get the best players for their side. It was not a fair fight. Organized interests could not only offer vastly bigger paychecks; they had first-mover advantages as well. By the time Emanuel began to assemble his team, many members of the Baucus entourage (as well as those of other prominent moderates like Blanche Lincoln from Arkansas) had already migrated to K Street.[36] Beyond Scher, two former Baucus chiefs of staff, as well as a former legislative assistant and two other former staffers, were working for lobbying firms with a large health-care portfolio. *Four* former chiefs of staff for Baucus worked as lobbyists for organizations with an interest in climate legislation, along with eight other former Baucus staffers. The prominent lobbying firm of Mehlman Vogel Castagnetti, whose clients included the American Petroleum Institute, could boast former staff chiefs for both Baucus *and* Lincoln.

These brief descriptions capture only the tip of the iceberg. For most Americans, 2009 was a bleak economic year, but just as Wall Street was rediscovering its mojo, so did K Street. Lobbyists reported expenditures just shy of $3.5 billion, a new record.[37] Of course, these reported expenditures grossly underestimated the true outlays geared to swaying Congress, since many grassroots and Astroturf mobilizations, as well as massive media buys, were not included. Altogether it was, in the words of James Thurber, director of American University's Center for Congressional and Presidential Studies, "the most active time that I have ever seen in the advocacy business—from 1973 on."[38]

Consider the organized mobilization related to the two biggest legislative battles of 2009, over the critical issues of financial regulation and health care. Each was central to the security and standing of the middle class—financial regulation because it could tame the risk-taking activities that had enriched Wall Street at Main Street's peril; health care because it could provide middle- and working-class Americans with greater security in their health insurance and begin to rein in skyrocketing health costs.

As always, Wall Street was not shy. Although some banks directly receiving TARP money refrained from certain highly visible practices that might generate obvious headlines ("Bank X Contributes Taxpayer Money to Senator Y"), finance was as active as any sector of the economy in 2009. A Public Citizen report noted that banks, insurers, realtors, and investment firms had hired some 940 lobbyists who had formerly worked for the federal government. Included among the finance lobbyists were at least seventy former members of Congress. Visa, Goldman Sachs, the Private Equity Council, and Prudential Financial all had thirty or more former federal officials on their lobbying teams.[39]

The organizational activity on financial issues was extraordinarily one-sided. The collapse of Wall Street did produce unprecedented organization on behalf of tougher regulation. A coalition of labor, consumer, and civil rights groups joined to form Americans for Financial Reform, which put together a seven-member staff, fourteen field offices, and a $2 million budget. All of which sounds pretty impressive—until one reviews the weapons for organized combat fielded by financial interests. Commercial banks alone spent more than $50 million on lobbying just in 2009. Financial institutions ramped up campaign giving as well.[40] All told, the financial industry gave more campaign contributions over the course of 2009 than any other sector, with a total of $78.2 million in contributions to federal candidates and party committees.

And by early 2010, Wall Street was increasingly open in showing its displeasure with the Obama administration, and tilting its contributions accordingly. The *Wall Street Journal* cited a major Democratic fund-raiser on Wall Street, who said that some people who raised money for Mr. Obama were disappointed: "They put themselves on the line internally with their companies for Obama, and now they look stupid." JPMorgan Chase's Jamie Dimon set the tone by holding a well-publicized meeting with House Minority Leader John Boehner. Over drinks, Boehner pressed his case that the House GOP—with its unanimous opposition to the Democrats' financial reform bill—was a more reliable ally for Wall Street.[41]

The organizational effort on health care was just as massive. Altogether, over half a billion dollars was spent on health-care lobbying in 2009, according to the very conservative estimates contained in official figures. With staggering sums of money at stake, powerful interests like insurance and drug companies engaged in the same complex strategy adopted by Wall Street: make sure that reform was either consistent with their economic needs or did not happen at all. While the insurance industry's trade association, AHIP (America's Health Insurance Plans), publicly expressed its support of health-care reform, it pushed hard to trim reformers' sails. Meanwhile, its members bought an insurance policy of their own, quietly channelling tens of millions of dollars through the Chamber of Commerce to fund advertisements critical of the emerging health-care bills.[42] The Chamber, the biggest of lobbying heavyweights, was fast becoming the most powerful outside group resisting the Obama agenda, and defending the winner-take-all political system that business had helped construct.

Get Off My Lawn

The architect of the Chamber's onslaught was Thomas Donohue, a hard-charging, acerbic leader whose style reflected his previous position as head of the American Trucking Association. During his thirteen years at the helm, Donohue had shifted the Chamber's focus back toward America's largest firms. In just his first four years, he had more than doubled the Chamber's annual fund-raising to more than $100 million (revenues would triple over the first twelve years of his tenure). He also greatly increased its core organizational capacity, raising $35 million for general operating expenses in 2000, compared with just $3 million four years earlier. With these new resources, he hired a greatly expanded team of policy experts and a long bench of lobbyists with close ties to the GOP.[43]

Donohue did not shy away from confrontation—once publicly expressing the hope that someone would punch John Sweeney, then-president of the AFL-CIO, "in the mouth." Upon taking charge at the Chamber, he promised to rouse the organization, which he described as a "sleeping giant." In addition to his fund-raising success, he developed strategic innovations that allowed companies to quietly channel resources through the Chamber for political activities that would not leave embarrassing fingerprints. Not surprisingly, given their shared interests, the Chamber developed an excellent working relationship with the Bush administration.

The Obama administration presented a very different challenge. Having supported the administration's stimulus package—while pushing for business-friendly tax cuts and generally supporting the efforts of moderate Democrats and Republicans to trim the package—the Chamber blanched at the other main elements of the President's agenda. Much like business leaders of the mid-1970s, the Chamber saw a broad and threatening effort to shift the balance of governance. "You've got an administration pushing the federal government into a bigger and bigger footprint," said Bruce Josten, the Chamber's top lobbyist. "CEOs start to get concerned when they see that."[44] Donohue preferred things the way they were. He relished the fight. "This is a *great* place," he told a reporter as the conflict heated up. "If you walk on our lawn, we're going to turn on the sprinklers."[45]

As 2009 wore on, the Chamber emerged as the biggest and most aggressive opponent of the administration's reform initiatives. It unleashed a massive wave of ads in opposition to the Democrats' proposed financial services agency, which aimed to protect consumers from unscrupulous lending practices and other abuses. The commercials falsely claimed that "even the small butcher" could be subjected to regulation. The Chamber increased its lobbying expenditures by 60 percent from the previous year—spending a staggering total of $144.5 million in officially reported outlays. The money was directed at killing all the major reform elements of the President's agenda: health-care reform, financial regulation, climate change legislation, and the president's budget, with its phaseout of the Bush tax cuts for the rich. As Congress tried to push forward in the fall of 2009, the Chamber spent a total of $79.2 million in a single quarter. No single organization has ever come close to spending so much on lobbying in so little time.

In January 2010, as President Obama prepared his State of the Union address, Donohue rose to offer his "State of American Business" address. In his remarks, he vowed that the Chamber would extend its focus beyond Capitol Hill to the upcoming elections, promising "to organize and carry out the largest, most aggressive voter education and issue advocacy effort in our nearly hundred-year history." As the White House and congressional Democrats tried to move forward, the Chamber was there on the outside turning on the sprinklers. On the inside, critics were gearing up to defend their own patches of protected turf.

"You're No Genius"

In 1981, Hollywood released a pretty good neo-noir movie, *Body Heat*. The film starred William Hurt as a not-too-bright lawyer whose lover persuades him to murder her husband. Hurt turns to a low-life client—played, as all movie low-lifes apparently were at the time, by Mickey Rourke—for help. Rourke responds by repeating some advice Hurt's character had once given him: "Any time you try a decent crime there is fifty ways to fuck up. If you think of twenty-five of them you're a genius. And you're no genius."

In the early days of the Obama administration, it often seemed that those seeking to challenge winner-take-all politics and produce meaningful economic reform faced similar odds. The large and flexible arsenal of the administration's opponents wasn't the only advantage they enjoyed. Another was that they were defending highly favorable institutional terrain. Every major initiative had to pass through multiple stages, each of which presented a different challenge. To triumph, opponents typically needed success at only one of these stages, and there were many routes to success. In the Obama administration's first, critical year, all the varied instruments in the winner-take-all tool kit of successful obstruction were ready.

In some cases, the overwhelming strength of opponents, combined with the legislative math of the Senate, was enough to take reform off the table from the beginning. Such was the fate of plans to offer meaningful industrial relations reform. 2009 was a horrible year for unions. The economic crisis produced not only an astonishing 10 percent drop in private-sector union membership in a single year, but a milestone of sorts: For the first time, more union members worked in public sector jobs than private sector ones.

The Obama campaign had promised to move forward with the Employee Free Choice Act, legislation designed to arrest the slide in unions' reach that had exacerbated both economic inequality and winner-take-all politics. Now, despite a strongly Democratic congress, labor simply lacked the muscle to advance its biggest priority. After launching an aggressive counteroffensive focused on red-state Democrats, the Chamber's Donohue could afford a little trash talk: "Some people are walking around [talking] about a compromise. There ain't gonna be a compromise! There's not the votes for that thing."[46] Though the labor bill died a quiet, backroom death, its demise spoke volumes. One of the few initiatives that might have had broader political significance by shifting the balance of organized power in Washington never got started.

The same was largely true for issues related to executive compensation and corporate governance—crucial elements of the winner-take-all economy that were overshadowed by the immediacy of the crisis on Wall Street. Just as during the fight over Sarbanes-Oxley in 2002, the most basic sources of managerial power that allowed huge payouts to executives even as their companies floundered were off the table. Instead, executive pay reforms were largely symbolic and fleeting, focused on companies that had taken bailout money and not yet repaid it. They made headlines but barely a dent in the winner-take-all economy.

In other cases, powerful groups played a double game, seeking to squeeze the debate in ways that would reduce the range of possible options to just two: preserving the status quo or passing a version of reform that accommodated organized interests and failed to seriously attempt to fix the problem. Many of these battles were over matters that were complex and technical but hugely consequential, that is, precisely the kind of fights in which lobbyists and interest groups excel. At the end of the day, pundits would focus on which politician or party had won or lost, announcing the final score to the folks at home. They would typically ignore the all-important details of policy, and therefore miss the ways that effective lobbying could assure that powerful interests won either way.

Defenders of the status quo worked every angle. In the House, where reformers invariably had the strongest hand, organized groups nonetheless worked to limit the damage. As the journalist Noam Scheiber described the strategy of the financial industry, lobbyists there were "playing with, well, house money."[47] If they removed something objectionable in the House, it was unlikely to reappear in the Senate, while if they lost, they would get additional chances to take care of the problem later. Such was the case with climate change legislation, where an ambitious House agenda rapidly lost momentum in the Senate. There, the ever-present threat of a filibuster and the much stronger position of oil, coal, and energy-intensive agribusiness interests virtually ensured that any surviving legislation would be radically stripped down. The bipartisan trio seeking to design a bill in the Senate engaged in extensive bargaining with the same powerful interests that had shaped the Bush administration's energy bill. The one wavering GOP participant, Senator Lindsey Graham, insisted that his participation was intended to produce a "business-friendly" bill.

Recognizing this, the administration often made huge concessions from the very beginning. In an especially fateful decision, President Obama sharply reduced the size of his proposed stimulus package from the roughly $1.2 trillion price tag his own economic advisers said was necessary. Although the media hardly noticed (nightly news broadcasts raised the issue in only three of fifty-nine news stories surveyed by Media Matters for America) many prominent economists—including Mark Zandi, who had advised the McCain campaign—viewed the package as too small.[48]

The decision reflected political realities: Congressional leaders had already signaled that the bigger plan had no chance of passage in the sixty-vote Senate.[49] Even so, to gain the vital support of Collins, Snowe, and Specter, as well as wavering Democratic moderates, the Senate leadership was forced to make additional stimulus-sapping concessions—increasing the share of tax cuts and lowering the price tag from an already too-small $900 billion to something closer to $800 billion by cutting some of the provisions most likely to have an immediate impact on employment, such as money for school construction and desperately needed fiscal relief for the states. The final compromise, at $787 billion, was actually smaller than either the original House bill ($828 billion) or Senate bill ($838 billion) had been—and even the smaller number was artificially inflated by the inclusion of a regularly scheduled $70 billion "patch" to prevent more families from being hit by the Alternative Minimum Tax.

All these changes further diminished the plan's effectiveness. In turn, the compromise inflicted a double blow—to the economy and to the

political fortunes of Democrats. Less stimulus meant higher unemployment. Higher unemployment contributed to the gradual erosion of popular support for the new administration. And greater discontent created an
environment ripe for conservative organization and Republican gains.

Yet nothing mobilized the opposition more than the administration's
signature issue, health-care reform. Tellingly, the administration focused
much of its energy from the outset on cutting deals with powerful industry groups—drug companies, hospitals, and the insurance industry
in particular—in hopes of co-opting them. The administration offered a
big carrot: The basic design of the legislation promised huge new publicly subsidized markets for health-care insurers and providers. With
this conceded, the contest turned to the critical issue of whether cost-
containment arrangements might be incorporated that would, over time,
control the ever-heavier health-care costs that were crushing government, businesses, and families. It was these provisions that continued to
galvanize industry groups, who worked tenaciously to remove them from
reform proposals, water them down, or block reform altogether.

Indeed, the Senate was where ambitious reforms went to die. In the
world's greatest deliberative body, Democratic holdouts and the "Maine
wing" of the Republican caucus held an exceptionally strong bargaining
position. In a few cases—Lincoln of Arkansas, Landrieu of Louisiana,
Nelson of Nebraska—these were senators from red states who had electoral incentives to be wary. Yet on health care, perhaps the hardest vote
belonged to Joe Lieberman of Connecticut, where electoral incentives
(but not the demands of the state's most powerful organized interest, insurance companies) clearly pointed in the other direction.

Lieberman's opposition to the public option, an idea popular within his
state except among insurance industry execs, set the tone for the whole
debate. Popular provisions that would have allowed more generous benefits at lower cost, like a public health insurance option to compete with
private plans or an expansion of Medicare, were jettisoned. Amendments
that industry groups favored, like a requirement on Americans to have
insurance coverage, or a hands-off attitude toward drug company profits,
were more likely to succeed, public concerns notwithstanding. On health

care, as on so many other issues, the path to winning over wavering senators ran almost entirely through organized interests rather than voters. It
was a path that often required a compromise with, rather than a frontal
challenge to, the winner-take-all economy and winner-take-all politics.

Only on the critical matter of financial regulation was the political dynamic somewhat different. As with every other issue, Democrats would
struggle to find Republican support in the Senate—a goal that the lead
Senate Democrat Christopher Dodd had set at the outset but which became more pressing after Scott Brown's election reduced the Democratic
Senate majority to fifty-nine. Despite extensive concessions to banking
interests along the way, discussions followed a now-familiar routine.
Dodd spent months seeking to reach agreement with Richard Shelby,
the senior Republican on his committee, before throwing up his hands to
start again with Republican Senator Bob Corker. Yet Corker too eventually demurred, as all forty-one Republicans publicly announced their opposition to the bill headed toward the Senate floor.

The difference was that Democrats felt that here was a struggle that
might resonate with voters. Like the political dynamic in 2002 that had
led Republicans to reluctantly embrace the Sarbanes-Oxley bill, each
party had to worry about voter retribution if their support for the winner-
take-all economy was too blatant, too close to election day. And by 2010
Wall Street was even more reviled than the corporate hustlers of a decade
before had been. Given this context, it was striking that GOP leaders felt
free to engage in a brazen double game combining populist rhetoric and
elitist action. Even as they aggressively marketed their capacity for ob-
structionism to Wall Street leaders, they implemented GOP spinmeister
Frank Luntz's advice by assuring voters that they were only trying to stop
legislation because it promised to institutionalize bailouts for those same
Wall Street leaders. When this strategy failed, Republicans retreated, and
Democrats gained the handful of votes they needed to get a bill through
the Senate. Yet it was a bill filled with concessions, with two *New York
Times* reporters describing Wall Street executives as "privately relieved
that the bill does not do more to fundamentally change how the industry
does business."[50]

Obstruction, Reaction, and Confusion

The most formidable tactic of obstruction was the simplest: delay. Time was not on the administration's side. FDR, LBJ, and Reagan had all achieved their signature policy breakthroughs early in their presidency. Erosion of presidential standing was expected for a new president as the "honeymoon" faded into memory. Against the backdrop of stubbornly high unemployment, it was certain.

The passage of time battered not just the president's approval ratings, but the attractiveness of reform itself. Month after month of argument without agreement, coupled with relentless negative ads and anti-Washington rhetoric from GOP leaders, softened public support while deflating the administration's supporters. Regaining their footing, Republican leaders zeroed in, just as Gingrich and his troops had, on popular distaste for the spectacle of Washington deal-making. As John Thune, a member of the GOP Senate leadership, summed up the strategy, "throwing grenades is easier than catching them."[51] In the deepest of ironies, the defenders of winner-take-all struck a chord with a public disillusioned with winner-take-all politics.

The most agitated citizens were the constellation of activists, organizations, and voters whose leaders billed their conservative uprising the "Tea Party movement." The movement burst onto the scene in the summer of 2009, filling congressional town hall meetings on health care with incensed protesters and then filling Washington's National Mall with tens of thousands of activists condemning the nation's descent into "socialism" (sixty thousand to seventy thousand, according to an unofficial estimate from the D.C. Fire Department, though movement organizers claimed more than a million).[52]

The Tea Party rally in Washington was organized in part by Freedom Works, a conservative lobbying organization headed by Newt Gingrich's former number two in the House, Dick Armey. Freedom Works was not the only conservative organization that sought to harness Tea Party energy. Fueled by donations from rich conservatives—such as billionaires David and Charles Koch, whose father, Fred Koch, helped create the conservative John Birch Society—a loose federation of groups helped translate fury against Obama into a formidable organizational force. Besides Freedom Works, the list of conservative groups associated with the movement included Americans for Limited Government, launched by Republican Senator Tom Coburn; the 912 Project, Glenn Beck's conservative activist network; and Americans for Prosperity, chaired by David Koch. Plenty of long-standing conservative organizations, like Grover Norquist's Americans for Tax Reform, climbed on board as well.

Though the Tea Party protests were directed at policies pressed by Obama and congressional Democrats, the immediate pressure was felt mostly within the Republican Party. As conservative as Republicans had become, Tea Party leaders vowed they would face primary challenges from their right if they did not lower taxes, cut spending, and get government's hands off the economy. But the movement could be more pragmatic as well. Key Tea Party organizers supported Scott Brown's successful candidacy in Massachusetts, backing a relatively moderate Republican in the bluest of blue states after Brown had made clear that he would be the potentially decisive vote against the health-care bill.

Pundits seized on the Massachusetts outcome as indicative of public angst and anger, and there was plenty of both. But the truth was less neat: One in seven voters expressed strong support for the Tea Party in early 2010, and another one in five some sympathy. Activists within the Tea Party represented a small group—around 5 percent, based on the share of Americans who said they had attended a Tea Party event or meeting, according to a February 2010 poll.[53] These were not, for the most part, voters battered by the economic downturn. Roughly three in four had gone to or completed college, compared with 54 percent of all respondents to the 2010 survey; and two in three had household incomes of $50,000 or greater, compared with 42 percent of all respondents. Above all, however, the Tea Party activists were Republican and on the right: nearly nine in ten had voted for a Republican candidate in the last House election, and 77 percent described themselves as "conservative."

The Tea Party movement was a sign of the ideological intensity and organizational strength on the conservative edge of the political spectrum. That intensity and strength were more lacking on the other side. Organizing for America largely failed to make the transition from an Obama campaign tool into a grassroots force for shaping governance. Liberal advocacy organizations kept the fire burning on specific issues— notably Health Care for America Now! on health care, and Americans for Financial Reform on financial market regulation—but, like Organizing for America, they found it difficult to mobilize even those voters most involved in the 2008 campaign. In part, these difficulties reflected the "congressionalist" path of reform that the president had felt compelled to follow. Watching the sausage be made in Washington simply did not inspire passionate grassroots support. Nor was it simple for organizers to bring leverage to bear on crucial but complex policy provisions—as opposed to support for or opposition to a candidate or entire piece of legislation. Watching would-be reformers slowly trudge through the quicksand of winner-take-all politics, driven to cut deals as they went, left the most active elements of the Democratic Party dispirited and despondent.

The larger electoral environment, however, was one of anxiety and confusion. The Tea Party wasn't the only feature of the political drama that many voters were unsure about. Most also had a strikingly limited sense of what was going on in D.C., beyond knowing they were disgusted by the mess and dispirited by the painfully slow recovery of the economy. In January, just after the health-care bill had surmounted a series of GOP filibusters, a poll by the respected Pew Research Center asked voters how many Republicans had supported the health-care bill in the Senate.[54] The correct answer was none, of course—an answer that only about one in three voters offered, about the same as said it had gotten between five and twenty GOP votes. Nearly four in ten said they had no idea. This was the same share who said they didn't know how many votes it took to end a filibuster. Just 26 percent got that question right, which might sound good—until one realizes that the question was multiple choice and almost exactly the same proportion said it took just fifty-one votes.

The confusion about process was matched by confusion about policy. Poll after poll on the health-care bill, for example, showed that a majority of Americans were against the bill. What was often missed was that a nontrivial share of those opposed—roughly one in four of the opponents—said they were against the bill because it didn't go far enough.[55] Even more important, those opposed to the bill said they actually liked most of its key elements. The major features of the House and Senate bills had a net positive rating (the share of supporters minus the share of opponents) of around twenty-two points. Alas for congressional Democrats who had voted for these bills, public awareness of these provisions barely cleared the 50 percent mark.[56] In other words, almost half of voters, on average, didn't even know about them.

If understanding was low, anger was high—and, just as William Kristol had predicted when Bill Clinton was president, the anger was increasingly directed at the party that was supposed to be in charge despite relentless GOP obstruction. By early 2010, Democrats still enjoyed a slight edge over Republicans in surveys, but the more pertinent result was that voters said they were fed up with both parties, with the state of the economy, and with Washington. Like the farmer in Steinbeck's great novel, the question on their minds appeared more and more to be "Who can we shoot?" The history of recent electoral politics suggests that in a midterm where the most intense anger is on the side of the minority party, it is Democrats who are most likely to be the target.

Buzz Saw

Almost exactly a year after Obama's inauguration, he appeared before reporters as he struggled to come to terms with the "buzz saw" that had hit his legislative agenda. A few days before, he and other reformers had stood by as a year's work—a year that, in political time, was irreplaceable—appeared to go down in flames. The voters of Massachusetts had just handed Ted Kennedy's seat to the GOP, eliminating the Democrats' sixty-seat supermajority and putting not just the administration's health-care bill but the entire reform agenda in jeopardy.

As it turned out, the administration and its congressional allies would right themselves and win notable victories in the months to follow. Yet with Brown's election the already steep climb up Capitol Hill had gotten a lot steeper. Even if the new administration were not carrying the burden of near-double-digit unemployment, it was almost certain to lose a large number of seats in the midterm elections. And with those losses the hill would get steeper still. One can practically hear the sound of a reform window closing in November.

In our highly individualist political culture, the response of pundits will be immediate: a relentless focus on identifying whose decisions were to blame, with an emphasis on whatever hobbyhorse the particular pundit is in the habit of riding. The administration should have been more moderate, or more bipartisan, or more aggressive. The complaints will echo the round of recriminations that followed the Clinton administration's defeats—where once again, Monday-morning quarterbacks were confident that if only their (after-the-fact) advice had been followed, all would have been well.

Remembering that politics is organized combat suggests a different view—a view closer to the advice of the low-life in *Body Heat* than the confident pronouncements of pundits.

Surely, the administration and its allies made mistakes. And given how close the outcome on every issue was, the cost of these mistakes was sometimes high. Yet blaming poor decision-making or individual fecklessness is too easy an out, too convenient a way to ignore deeper truths. For decades, winner-take-all politics has posed extraordinary and increasing obstacles to concerted government action on behalf of the middle class—even under the most favorable of political circumstances.

Mickey Rourke's analysis comes closer to capturing the harsh mathematics of winner-take-all politics, and points toward a more balanced assessment of President Obama's early record, and a tougher assessment of the American political system. In a context of polarized parties—one of which categorically rejects the idea that government should provide a meaningful check on the marketplace—disenchanted, disengaged, and disorganized voters, the Senate with its malapportionment and filibuster, and, everywhere, tenacious and well-resourced lobbyists, the number of ways for reformers to screw up is beyond counting. That those pushing for reform won historic, if incomplete, policy victories on behalf of the middle class is to their lasting credit. The 2008 election made a genuine difference. But the partial and politically costly nature of those victories revealed it would take more than an election to pry up the poisonous roots of winner-take-all.

Conclusion

Beating Winner-Take-All

Our country faces massive challenges, accumulated over decades of inattention to middle-class concerns combined with energetic action on behalf of the economically powerful. Yet profound obstacles loom in the path of any sustained campaign to renew American democracy and the conditions for broadly shared prosperity. The thirty-year war that we have chronicled in this book has given rise to high political hurdles that stand solidly in the way of those seeking renewal today. The catch-22 of winner-take-all politics is that the only viable and defensible route to fixing our broken political system runs through our broken political system.

That, of course, is guidance in itself. So much of today's economic commentary fixates on global economic forces beyond democratic control. In this perspective, countries can erect flood walls against broader economic tides only at great cost and with limited success. We are told that increased trade and capital flows have benefited highly skilled elite workers while penalizing the mass of the less skilled who must now compete with billions of low-wage workers. The core message is supremely fatalistic. In this new economic world, commentators confidently declare, the most that affluent nations can hope to do is bring more workers into the skilled category through investments in human capital while minimizing the fallout for those left behind.

The truth revealed in *Winner-Take-All Politics* is almost exactly the opposite. Our investigation of the clues at the scene has shown that far from a simple skill divide based on educational achievement, the real economic schism separates the overwhelming majority of Americans, including most highly educated ones, from the tiny slice that has reaped the lion's share of economic growth. Recall the startling facts revealed by the DNA evidence on American incomes: From 1979 until 2006, the top 1 percent received 36 percent of all the income growth generated in the American economy, while the highest-income 1/10th of 1 percent—one out of every 1,000 households—received nearly 20 percent, even after taking into account all federal taxes and all government and employer-provided benefits. Only a vanishingly small share of Americans have received the "golden ticket" that lets them travel into the rarefied stratosphere of the winner-take-all economy.

Unlike the kids who failed to find the ticket wrapped in a candy bar in *Charlie and the Chocolate Factory,* however, those who've missed out on the upward journey have not had the consolation of knowing that their lesser fortunes were the result of pure blind chance.[1] Nor have they even had the pleasure of enjoying their ticketless economic lot undisturbed. They have instead watched as the game has become more tilted against them, their economic standing growing less secure, their chance of climbing the economic ladder stagnating. There have been winners in the winner-take-all economy. There have been losers as well—many, many more losers.

To explain *this* split—how the United States morphed from the Broadland of shared prosperity that defined the immediate decades after World War II into our present Richistan of hyperconcentrated rewards at the top—technological change and globalization prove to be of surprisingly limited relevance. They matter, to be sure. But what matters more is how these forces have been channeled by major changes in what government has done and not done over the course of the thirty-year war. Where the conventional wisdom confidently declares, "It's the economy," we find, again and again, "It's the politics." And because it is domestic politics, not global economic trends, that matter most, the future is within our control. This is the very good news that this book delivers. As hard as winner-take-all politics will be to change, the economic developments that precipitated our present crisis represent political choices, not technological imperatives.

The Continuing Sway of Organized Combat

Winner-Take-All Politics also reveals *where* in our politics the central problems lie: in the fierce realities of organized combat. The foremost obstacle to sustainable reform is the enormous imbalance in organizational resources between the chief economic beneficiaries of the status quo and those who seek to strengthen middle-class democracy. Powerful groups defending the winner-take-all economy—business coalitions, Wall Street lobbyists, medical industry players—are fully cognizant of the massive stakes involved, and they are battle-ready after years of training. Vigilant and highly skilled at blocking or diverting challenges, these organized forces possess big advantages over the disorganized. On rare occasions, a vibrant politics of renewal emerges. If the momentum or attentiveness of reformers flags, however, opponents are fully capable of snatching victory from the jaws of defeat.

Here health-care reform is the exception that proves the rule. The passage of comprehensive reform in 2010 was a remarkable achievement. And yet, meaningful legislation required enormous concessions to organized interests. Before the process even started, key industry players, from doctors to hospitals to drug companies, saw their main concerns addressed. To mollify these groups, reforms that would have allowed critically needed cost-containment while offering more secure and affordable coverage to the middle class—from the public option to effective bargaining over drug costs—were dropped. We say this not to criticize the Obama administration or its allies. Had these huge compromises not been made, health-care reform would not have passed. Our point is that the scale of the necessary concessions reveals the continuing sway of organized combat.

And health care remains the most favorable case, a century-long Democratic goal that featured substantial, sustained reform advocacy. The closer we move to the core of the winner-take-all economy, the greater the imbalances in organizational might between critics and defenders become. Nowhere is this more evident than in financial reform. Here the economic stakes for Middle America could hardly be greater. Within months of triggering the greatest economic crisis in three-quarters of a century, an obscenely profitable financial sector had reinstated many of its standard lavish practices, once again backed by explicit and implicit taxpayer subsidies. Recessions, it turned out, were for suckers, not bankers.

Yet while public furor at Wall Street boils over, organized activity to channel that justifiable fury into policy reform barely simmers. The issues involved remain mind-numbingly complex. Banks are organized; their customers are not. House Minority Leader John Boehner may have felt moved at an American Bankers Association meeting in March to issue a populist rallying cry to the Wall Street elite to stand up to "little punk staffers" on Capitol Hill who were fashioning regulatory fixes.[2] But the financial industry needed no encouragement. Indeed, it had the lobbying field almost entirely to itself, its resources simply dwarfing the modest organizational capacities of its opponents. The entire $2 million budget of Americans for Financial Reform, the largest financial reform group, was a small fraction of the typical annual bonus for a single moderately high-level player on Wall Street.

The financial catastrophe made reform a real possibility, yet the struggle to prevent a replay of 2008 wears on. At every turn, the chief architects of the crisis stand ready to defend their freedom to extract fortunes when times are good while burdening taxpayers when they are not. Bankers have many friends in both parties, well placed to force a choice between limited reform and no reform at all. Genuine fear of voter anger has given restricted reform an opening. As with the fight against economic insiders that led to the Sarbanes-Oxley legislation almost a decade ago, however, winning the battle might be consistent with losing the war.

And lest we forget, other bastions of the winner-take-all economy are even better protected. The sway of high-level executives, subjected to genuine countervailing power in many affluent democracies, remains unchallenged. Serious efforts to strengthen those who might provide meaningful checks and balances, such as truly independent boards of directors or empowered shareholders, remain largely beyond the pale. Meanwhile, modest efforts to give unions a steadier foothold—something that workers want, and the norm in other mixed economies—have proved unrealistic even under unified Democratic control of government.

Against this backdrop of extraordinary imbalances in organized power, the Supreme Court's 2010 *Citizens United* decision sounds remarkably tone-deaf. The Court's majority concluded that unrestricted floods of corporate money simply maximized "speech" and constituted no challenge to a democracy founded on equal access to the public sphere. But the *Citizens United* majority was kicking on an open door. As our tour of winner-take-all politics has demonstrated, those with the greatest economic resources already have ample opportunity to deploy their formidable advantages in politics.

A Tale of Two Parties

The growth of these advantages since the late 1970s has reshaped American politics—and America's two great parties. The decline of the organizational underpinnings of middle-class democracy forced Democrats and Republicans alike to adapt or decline, producing the second major set of obstacles to reform.

The changes are most glaring on the Republican side. Reagan's party was more conservative than Nixon's; Gingrich's, more conservative than Reagan's; George W. Bush's, more conservative than Gingrich's. The transformation of the GOP, along with its manifest failures as a governing party, finally caught up with it in the 2006 and 2008 elections. Yet, strikingly, this only made the party more conservative still. Neither electoral rebuke nor the economic catastrophe fueled by financial deregulation nor the Democrats' passage of health-care reform has done anything to shake the party's commitment to the restoration of the Gilded Age. Instead, the party's loudest voices proclaim that George W. Bush's failure was not abandoning the moderation of his father, but belatedly trying to compromise with Washington insiders. Indeed, one GOP congressman, Louie Gohmert, responded to the passage of health-care reform by carrying the argument that Washington had lost touch with Americans to the next illogical step: proposing the repeal of the Seventeenth Amendment's requirement that Senators be directly elected.[3]

Even as the country faces grave challenges, Republicans have provided scant support for any serious reform legislation. Even as the costs of policy drift mount, they have launched filibusters at an unprecedented rate and resorted to every other available form of obstruction. Pundits have a hard time resisting the siren call of bipartisanship (regardless of what the substantive impact of compromise would be). Self-described "centrists" in D.C. media circles triangulate between the two parties even as one heads further right. "Can't we all get along?" they ask. The GOP has offered the answer in the fiery denunciation of health-care reform by House Republican Leader John Boehner: "Hell no, you can't."[4]

This is not a matter of falling personal civility. It's a matter of fundamental political strategy. The incentives to obstruct have grown. Not only has the GOP rank and file in Congress become genuinely more conservative; its leaders have openly acknowledged they see few benefits to compromise. As Senate Minority Leader Mitch McConnell described the GOP's rejectionist strategy on health care, "It was absolutely critical that everybody be together because if the proponents of the bill were able to say it was bipartisan, it tended to convey to the public that this is O.K., they must have figured it out."[5] Like Gingrich before them, today's GOP leaders see only gain in bringing Washington to an acrimonious standstill.

Of course, the few remaining GOP moderates might have their doubts. Yet the intensification of the Republican base, signaled by the emergence of the Tea Party movement and stoked by an influential conservative entertainment wing—personified by Fox News' Glenn Beck and Sean Hannity and perennial right-wing talk jock Rush Limbaugh—has continued to prevent any sustained move to the center.

In a country marked by searing discontent, the immediate political wave might well be on the side of the Party of No. High unemployment and the typical riptide of midterm elections means the "out party" can anticipate an almost inevitable rebound. Meanwhile, Republican obstruction perversely generates many of the most reviled features of Washington—conflict, gridlock, desperate backroom deals—that the out party can run against.

Republicans have triumphed by trashing Washington before, after all. Distressingly little evidence suggests that relentless obstruction carries negative electoral consequences. Few Americans are aware of the magnitude of the filibuster's impact. Even fewer know that the scale of its use is unprecedented. And fewer still understand the complex policy provisions that will determine whether reform in area after area truly succeeds.

In an environment in which broad organizations that might help ordinary citizens sort out these complexities are weak or altogether absent, the politics of organized combat and the politics of electoral competition can occupy surprisingly separate domains. As Democrats struggled to craft a legislative response to the extraordinary financial crisis, opponents of reform could play a double game. On the one hand, GOP leaders appealed openly to bankers for financial support by touting their opposition to financial reform. On the other, conservative organizations and leading GOP strategists crafted "populist" commercials and sound bites for voters that described the Democrats' reform legislation as just another bailout that put taxpayers on the hook for corporate irresponsibility. It's the political equivalent of having one's cake and eating it too: Stand up for Wall Street in the corridors of power while donning the mantle of Wall Street's populist scourge. That the GOP would see political upside in such a naked strategy provides some of the most chilling evidence about the limits of electoral accountability in American politics.

Whether Republicans will get to eat their cake remains to be seen, of course. The scale of the financial crisis and the growing clarity of the misdeeds that catalyzed it have focused public anger to a degree rare in the struggles over the winner-take-all economy. As in the wake of Enron's and WorldCom's collapse in the early 2000s, reformers have unusual momentum and opportunity to rewrite financial rules. But the ferocity of the GOP opposition and sustained pressure of Wall Street channeled reform, virtually guaranteeing that, beneath the appealing label of "account-ability," the fine print would sustain many of the special favors that allowed Wall Street to tilt the American economy—and American politics—in its risk-seeking direction.

Democrats have always had a much more Janus-faced posture with respect to the winner-take-all economy. And so it should come as no sur-prise that since 2008 they have both orchestrated the most serious politi-cal challenge to that order in three decades and, while doing so, revealed more than a little of their continuing ambivalence. Because the multiple sources of cross-pressure described in previous chapters remain largely in place, the commitment to rebuilding middle-class democracy within the party is, to put it charitably, uneven. Especially in the Senate—with its antiquated apportionment favoring conservatives and its modern inven-tion of supermajority rule—the most conservative Democrats, frequently aided in particular areas by more liberal Democrats turned Republicans for a Day, have often held sway.

Once again, health-care reform's tortuous journey provides a case study. The leverage of the most conservative Democrats was used to di-minish or eliminate some of the most important reformist impulses of Democratic leaders (many of which, like the public option and more seri-ous requirements on employers to provide or finance insurance, prom-ised substantial budgetary savings). In other areas the results have been worse. On tax policy, the stimulus plan, climate change, and labor law reform—just to name some of the most prominent fights with the great-est long-term stakes—pivotal Senate Democrats generated costly delays, scaled back the more serious reform efforts of the House, or blocked those efforts entirely.

This tension—between economic liberals seeking to harness govern-ment authority on behalf of the middle class, and economic conservatives with stronger connections to powerful economic interests—has long hamstrung D.C. Democrats. Today, it means the fate of renewal rests not just on the fortunes of Democrats as a whole but on the balance between these internal factions. And that balance, in turn, reflects not merely the electoral success of Democrats but the unusual structure of American political institutions as they've evolved in recent decades—the final set of obstacles to the restoration of middle-class democracy.

Reclaiming Democratic Governance

The thirty-year war represents the least pleasant phase of a recurrent pattern of American democracy. Eras of drift punctuated by periods of renewal are what you get when you combine a dynamic market economy, an increasingly complex and fast-moving society, and a political system prone to stasis and to the protection of entrenched interests.

Of course, many argue that this stalemate is precisely what the Founders intended. Yet the Founders were looking over *both* shoulders as they designed the Constitution. On the one side they saw, and heroically rejected, the tyranny of an absolute monarch. On the other side, they saw the squabbling, veto-ridden factions empowered by the Articles of Confederation. The Founders sought to steer a course between the twin dangers of tyranny and incapacity. They worked at a particular time and place. They had extremely limited democratic practice to draw on. They faced daunting constraints, ranging from the clout of slaveholders to the very real risk of seeing their work rejected by state governments. And, like all of us, they could not see the future. That the core features of the Constitution have endured for so long is testament to their achievement.

It is no criticism of this achievement to observe that not everything worked out as planned. Profound developments in American society have made the drift of governance both more pervasive and more consequential. Among other failures of foresight, the Founders largely failed to anticipate the rise of an astonishingly dynamic capitalism, with its capacity to fundamentally reshape not just markets but society itself—often for the better, but not automatically so. By the time reformers in the Progressive Era struggled with challenges not so different from the ones we face today, the Founders' vision of a relatively stable economy based on very wide distribution of the crucial resource of the day, land, was a rapidly fading memory.

By the early twentieth century, the rural property holders' political economy of the Founders' vision had less and less connection to the world in which Americans actually lived. That is why, in the decades that followed, the United States—like every other prosperous democracy—slowly but steadily expanded the capacity of government to channel and, when necessary, counterbalance a vibrant capitalism. Effective governance could help provide citizens with basic economic security, a healthier environment, legal protections from predation in pursuit of profit, and the needed social investments—from decent roads to good schools—that would lay the foundation for further opportunity. All of this could improve citizens' lives, while simultaneously diminishing the threat that a new economic aristocracy would replace the hereditary aristocracy that the Founders had risked their lives to defeat.

Since the Progressive Era, the need for collective governance has continued to grow. Yet over the past three decades, the capacity for collective governance has declined. Those who have defended the gridlock created by minority obstruction have portrayed the filibuster and other extra-constitutional hurdles as reflecting core principles of American democracy.[6] The Founders' vision was very different. Although their constitutional design rested heavily on checks and balances, supermajority requirements were reserved for particular circumstances: the passage of a treaty or constitutional amendment, the override of a presidential veto. The Founders were acutely aware of the dangerous consequences of minority obstruction (indeed, their very presence in Philadelphia was spurred by the manifest failures of the supermajoritarian Articles of Confederation). Conservatives keen to enlist the *Federalist Papers* might consult Hamilton's words on the subject in Federalist #22:

> *What at first sight may seem a remedy, is, in reality, a poison. To give a minority a negative upon the majority (which is always the case where more than a majority is requisite to a decision), is, in its tendency, to subject the sense of the greater number to that of the lesser... If a pertinacious minority can control the opinion of a majority, respecting the best mode of conducting it, the majority,*

in order that something may be done, must conform to the views of
the minority; and thus the sense of the smaller number will over-
rule that of the greater, and give a tone to the national proceed-
ings. Hence, tedious delays; continual negotiation and intrigue;
contemptible compromises of the public good. And yet, in such a
system, it is even happy when such compromises can take place: for
upon some occasions things will not admit of accommodation; and
then the measures of government must be injuriously suspended, or
fatally defeated. It is often, by the impracticability of obtaining the
concurrence of the necessary number of votes, kept in a state of inac-
tion. Its situation must always savor of weakness, sometimes border
upon anarchy.[7]

Of course, among the leading Founders, Hamilton was the most anxious to create a robust capacity for governance. Madison, however, agreed.
In Federalist #58, he acknowledged that supermajority rules might create
an "obstacle generally to hasty and partial measures," but went on to insist
that "these considerations are outweighed by the inconveniences in the
opposite scale. In all cases where justice or the general good might require
new laws to be passed, or active measures to be pursued, the fundamental
principle of free government would be reversed. It would be no longer
the majority that would rule: the power would be transferred to the minority."[8]

In ways the Founders could not have anticipated, Madison's "fundamental principle of free government" is in jeopardy. The United States has
developed a combination of features that imperil our government's capacity to deal with formidable collective challenges—and, indeed, if climate
change is as threatening as most scientists believe, imperil the planet on
which we live. An ever-more dynamic market economy and entrenched
economic interests coexist with a polity marked by polarized parties and
an enhanced capacity of the minority party to block new policy initiatives.

We need to look no further than the sunny West to see that combining
intense polarization, powerful entrenched interests, and supermajority

requirements allows a radicalized minority to obstruct without being held accountable—a poisonous cocktail fatal to governance. Today California is "beset by economic disaster and political paralysis," reports a typical recent lament—a meltdown exacerbated by the recession but rooted in supermajority budget and revenue rules that, amid rising polarization, create virtually insurmountable hurdles to consistent, sensible policy.[9] At the national level things are not yet so extreme, if only because not all critical legislative choices, such as budgeting, are fully vulnerable to minority obstruction. But California's crisis outlines a plausible future if the roots of winner-take-all politics are left intact.

From Drift to Renewal

The veteran journalist James Fallows puts our predicament well: "The most charitable statement of the problem is that the American government is a victim of its own success. It has survived in more or less recognizable form over more than two centuries—long enough to become mismatched to the real circumstances of the nation." The result is "a failure to adapt: increasing difficulty in focusing on issues beyond the immediate news cycle, and an increasing gap between the real challenges and opportunities of the time and our attention, resources, and best efforts." For Fallows, the "only sane choice is to muddle through."[10] The obstacles to a politics of renewal are simply too high.

Certainly, there is no magic bullet, no single cure. Yet the outlines of sensible reform are not hard to find. The true challenge, as we have argued throughout this book, is the politics. As in the past, the politics of renewal must have a long arc. It must be capable of action in the sphere of electoral spectacle and in the arena of organized combat. In too many cases, reformers with few organized allies on their side confront entrenched, resource-rich opponents. In such circumstances, even tangible successes may erode over time, as the organized reassert their dominance once public attention and the energies of reformers shift.[11] As in *Butch Cassidy and the Sundance Kid,* in which the Hole-in-the-Wall Gang of Redford and Newman spectacularly lost out to their much more resourceful and coordinated opponents, those who take on the entrenched defenders of the status quo will need more than luck, bravado, and derring-do. They will need more than wise and charismatic leadership. They will need organization.

The long period of postwar prosperity we termed "middle-class democracy" rested on mutually reinforcing economic and political conditions. The same must be true in reviving it. Indeed, over the long run, widely shared prosperity is unattainable without sustained action to rebalance our politics as well as our economics. Stronger representation for employees in the workplace is as much about broadening the distribution of political power as broadening the distribution of economic rewards. Making government more responsive to the middle class would not be just a political achievement; it would reshape the economy.

Until we see clearly how the economy is constructed by government inaction as well as action, many of the most effective reforms will evade our sight. Maintaining regulation-free zones in which traders and investors design and unleash weapons of mass financial destruction (credit-default swaps, exotic subprime loans, mortgage-backed securities) is as much a political choice as passing tax cuts that enrich those who have already amassed the most. A vibrant, dynamic capitalism requires the guidance that only a vibrant, dynamic democracy can provide.

In 2006 and 2008, palpable evidence that American governance had failed to provide such guidance helped give Democrats large majorities in Congress, control of the White House, and a rare opportunity to launch the politics of renewal. From that opportunity they have fashioned substantial initiatives: a stimulus package that helped rescue the economy from the abyss, a budget that introduced significant shifts in priorities and modestly increased the progressivity of taxation, an overhaul of student loans that expanded educational opportunity while attacking a blatant set of giveaways (guaranteed profits alongside government assumption of risk for private lenders), and, of course, a health-care reform bill that addressed some, but hardly all, of the extraordinarily deep failings of the status quo.

This is a genuinely impressive record. And yet it is one that largely nibbles at the edges of the winner-take-all economy. Historical precedent gives little reason for expecting President Obama's domestic agenda to become more ambitious over time. If the harder tasks have remained unmet, this is precisely because they are harder tasks—more fiercely protected by beneficiaries of the status quo, less conducive to the galvanization of popular pressure for reform. The almost inevitable electoral losses to come for the party in power, coupled with the continuing weight of economic difficulties, will make reform harder still. The budget deficit, overwhelmingly a product of the era of winner-take-all politics, looms as both a genuine challenge and an extremely convenient excuse for powerful interests to call a halt to renewal.

The long-term budget challenge is principally a result of runaway health-care costs, coupled with a tax system whose ability to fairly raise sufficient revenue to run broadly supported government activities— never strong to begin with—has been steadily crippled. But judging by Jim DeMint's "American Option," and the more forward-looking "Roadmap for America's Future" offered by Representative Paul Ryan, Republican of Wisconsin, the GOP prescription will continue to be politically unrealistic slashing of popular and vital programs like Social Security and Medicare.[12] With the news media portraying the conflict as a balanced struggle for fiscal sanity between two equally irresponsible parties, and with hundreds of millions being spent to sway public and elite opinion by deficit hawks like billionaire (and Nixon's commerce secretary) Pete Peterson, Democrats may be left holding the bag of fiscal responsibility. In this volatile environment, the failure of the health-care legislation to do more to slow costs could prove as fateful for the politics of the deficit as it was revealing of the power of organized interests. And Democrats could well find themselves, once again, playing out the script of Irving Kristol and adopting a "tidy up" stance prohibitive of serious social investments that would provide greater long-term political and economic benefits.

Truly reversing the stark trend toward economic hyperconcentration at the top will take more than concerted and sustained government action to improve the economic standing of the middle class. Political reform geared at diminishing the advantages of the privileged will also be essential. The aims should be threefold: to reduce the capacity of entrenched elites to block needed reform; to facilitate broader participation among those whose voices are currently drowned out; and to encourage the development of groups that can provide a continuing, organized capacity to mobilize middle-class voters and monitor government and politics on their behalf.

Of these three pillars, the last is the most important—and the most difficult to construct. We actually know how to increase voter turnout, with relatively straightforward reforms that have, not surprisingly, failed to gain traction within elite Washington. We actually know how to reform the filibuster and other extra-constitutional forms of obstruction (a determined majority could trim the filibuster at the beginning of the next session of Congress, as it did in 1975). Here, as elsewhere, the problem is not figuring out what would help, but creating the forces necessary to bring these changes about. Recall the words attributed to FDR: "You've convinced me. Now make me do it." Reform will rest on the creation of organized, sustained pressure on legislators to make American politics more responsive and open to citizen engagement.

We have seen that the organizations that traditionally bolstered middle-class democracy have declined. Nowhere is this clearer or more fateful than with regard to American labor. An expanded role for unions would make a big difference, and as the experience of our neighbor to the north demonstrates, it is not as economically implausible as some might insist. Yet recent political experience signals that the reinvigoration of unions is unlikely to be the primary catalyst during the early stages of a renewed middle-class politics. Business opposition is too unified and intense; the cross-pressures on many Democrats, too severe. The Chamber's Tom Donohue is right: there aren't the votes for that. For unions to play an expanded role in advocating for the middle class, some of these obstacles will need to be reduced first.

Elsewhere, however, there are greater grounds for optimism. Just as technological changes—from the rise of television to innovations like direct mail—helped transform the organizational landscape of the 1970s, today the revolution in information technology is having transformative and, in many respects, more constructive effects. The Internet has vastly lowered the costs of disseminating information and networking individuals who have shared interests and concerns but previously had little opportunity to be in contact with each other.

Although not as visible as its effects on the economy, this information revolution is reshaping politics as well. The most obvious effect is on campaign finance. Back in 2004, even as President Bush and the GOP raised huge amounts from wealthy donors, John Kerry was able to use Internet fund-raising to match Bush dollar for dollar in the presidential campaign. Even more astonishing, in 2008 Barack Obama had a large financial advantage over Republican John McCain. Of course, both Kerry and Obama raised huge amounts from wealthy donors and relied on "bundlers" who could assemble networks of big-money contributors. Still, the capacity to raise giant sums from small donors through the Web is a major, and still evolving, development.

Yet a long bridge separates electoral contests from organizational combat. Just as businesses spend far more on lobbying than on campaigns, organizations seeking to empower middle-class democracy must be able to sustain momentum in Washington after elections are over. The critical issue is whether new technologies can help revolutionize governance as well as electoral finance, increasing the capacity to monitor public officials, assemble the information needed to help shape policy, and inform and motivate citizens to weigh in as needed.

The experience of Obama's Organizing for America (OFA), the vast e-mail network created by his political strategists during the 2008 campaign, suggests how difficult this task remains. Despite having the largest outreach list of its type ever, with a reported 13 million members, OFA found it challenging to keep even its most active members focused on and motivated by complex policy debates. Nor did a White House girded for organized combat always see interest in mobilizing the activists who had placed Obama in office. As one former congressional staffer complained to a writer for the *Nation*:

The White House, it seems to me, Rahm [Emanuel] and whomever else, [they don't] give a crap about this email list and don't think it's a very useful thing. They want to do stuff the delicate way—the horse-trading, backroom talks, one-to-one lobbying. So they see it as more effective to get [deputy chief of staff] Jim Messina on the phone with all these folks; the way to deal with this is to get on the phone. [They say] 'unleashing a massive grassroots army is only going to backfire on us.' [13]

If this is Emanuel's view, he has a point. The decisive votes in the Senate continue to rest with the moderate barons and potential Republicans-for-a-day, and this is likely to be even more true in the next few years. Once again, the catch-22 of winner-take-all politics looms large: beating back the forces of organized combat may require, as in the health-care debate, that organized combat takes precedence.

And yet, in the long run, the politics of renewal cannot become deeply grounded without mass engagement as well as elite leadership. And as hard as it may be to direct public attention and enthusiasm toward procedural and institutional reforms, fixing the playing field of American politics remains the essential task. It is a task that will require the quiet heroism of sustained renewal. Political reformers will need to mobilize for the long haul, appreciating that it is not electoral competitions alone that are decisive, but also the creation of organized capacity to cement a meaningful middle-class democracy by turning electoral victories into substantive and sustainable triumphs.

If there is hope for more than simply "muddling through," it lies in the story of renewal that we traced in chapter 3. From the early 1900s until the New Deal, America's leaders were engaged almost continuously with the problem of reform. Not all leaders, of course, and the efforts did not always yield visible or quick effect. But in an era in which the tail of the economy so often wagged the dog of politics, farsighted men and women acted on Walter Lippmann's wise if daunting counsel that democracy had to lift itself up by its own bootstraps.

And it did. The key conditions for the politics of renewal would not emerge until the crisis of the 1930s. But when they did, and the politics and policy of middle-class democracy were constructed, reformers were able to build on a foundation laid down by sustained organized action over the preceding decades. In those fateful years of foundation-laying, a reform movement grew up state by state and debate by debate, bringing with it changes whose full import would only become clear with time. Progressive reformers, not just in the White House but in state capitols and the newly democratized Senate—men like Robert La Follette of Wisconsin and Robert Wagner of New York—kept the pot of reform simmering. The milestones accumulated unevenly over time: the direct election of senators, the creation of the income tax, the broadening of the franchise to women, the introduction of the nation's first public programs of economic security. But they accumulated, and beneath the big victories lay a deeper wave of change, pushed along by a thirty-year struggle.

A quarter century before Franklin Delano Roosevelt described political equality as "meaningless in the face of economic inequality," his distant cousin Teddy Roosevelt declared that "the supreme political task of our day . . . is to drive the special interests out of our public life."[14] They were not speaking metaphorically. Political equality is an abstraction, but the threat it faces from the concentration of economic and political power is not. For all the contradictions of the Progressive movement, reformers of a century ago shared the conviction held by the Founders that democracy was the rule of the many, not the all-powerful one or the fortunate few. It will have to be so again.

Acknowledgments

So many generous colleagues and friends have helped us with this book that we would have to write another to enumerate all our debts. We could never have navigated the vast and complex landscape this book tries to cross without their able guidance. They bear no blame for the missteps we surely took, nor any unwanted responsibility for where we ended up. But they deserve much credit for pointing out paths to deeper understanding that we could not have found on our own.

Our first debt is to the experts at universities around the country and abroad who have listened to early versions of these arguments and given us valuable suggestions. We owe special thanks to Fred Block for organizing a wonderful conference in Tomales Bay, California, where we were grilled (in a friendly, California way) by a generous group of scholars who shared our desire to better understand American inequality, including Andrea Campbell, Neil Fligstein, Larry Jacobs, David Karol, Lane Kenworthy, Bob Kuttner, and Suzanne Mettler. They sharpened our thinking and steered us away from many mistakes. They also provided an opportunity to spend time with some of our favorite people in one of the most beautiful places in the world.

Although not at this conference, Larry Bartels, Thomas Edsall, Paul Krugman, Nolan McCarty, Keith Poole, Howard Rosenthal, Philipp Rehm, and Martin Gilens all contributed important insights to this book—through their own pioneering work and (in the cases of Bartels, Gilens,

McCarty, and Rehm) through their helpful reactions to ours. We owe a great debt as well to Theda Skocpol and the members of the American Political Science Association Task Force on Inequality and American Democracy—which has inspired a growing body of scholarship that has informed our thinking.

This book would have been impossible to write without relying on the intensive investigations of hundreds of scholars and journalists (a profession more vital and diverse today than ever) who have explored this vast subject matter. We hope the endnotes give a small indication of our huge debt to those efforts. Writing a book like this is, in some ways, a deeply personal and private matter. Yet we realized every day that our private efforts rested on the contributions of a huge, sometimes invisible community.

Our visible community included a stellar team of research assistants at Berkeley and Yale. Devin Caughey, Lee Drutman, Chloe Thurston, and Sophie Raseman were not just intrepid trackers chasing down our elusive suspects. They contributed in important ways to the shaping of our arguments and our understanding of these issues. Elizabeth Kelly, a brilliant Yale Law School student, provided great help with the historical material in chapter 3, and organized an intensive fact-checking process that involved her super-capable ally, Josh Rosmarin. Tory Bilski kept the New Haven part of the operation moving forward with her usual efficiency and grace—whether the problem was logistical or grammatical.

Our deep thanks as well to the team of professionals that helped turn our initial musings into a book. Sydelle Kramer, our agent, has been a steady guide throughout the long process, with a remarkable capacity to iron out problems and offer insight. We have learned that it is always best to do what she advises—including publishing this book with Simon & Schuster. At the press, we have worked with a stellar and committed group. Dedi Feldman saw potential in this project early on and helped bring it to life; we hope she will be pleased with the end result. Roger Labrie has been an indefatigable editor, offering just the right mix of sympathy and prodding necessary to whip the book into better shape. Our copyeditor and production editor—Jeanette Gingold and Jonathan

Evans—were there at the end to make the book read better and move us toward the finish. We are the grateful beneficiaries of their skill and professionalism. This has been a team project from start to finish.

Our wives, Oona and Tracey—who have supported us both intellectually and personally at every step and who have shown great patience and empathy as we missed more than one deadline in the urge to dig just a little deeper—deserve far, far more than a written acknowledgment. But that is all we can give here, and we do so with loving appreciation.

Notes

Introduction: The Thirty-Year War

1   Graham Bowley and Zachary Kouwe, "Rivals Await Blankfein's Bonus at Goldman Sachs," *New York Times*, February 3, 2010. Stephen Grocer and Aaron Lucchetti, "Traders Beat Wall Street CEOs in Pay," *Wall Street Journal*, April 6, 2010.

2   Louise Story and Eric Dash, "Banks Prepare for Big Bonuses, and Public Wrath," *New York Times*, January 9, 2010; "Goldman Sachs 2009 pay up as profit soars: Bank posts $4.79 billion 4Q profit; 2009 bonuses, pay up 47 percent," MSNBC .com, January 21, 2010, http://www.msnbc.msn.com/id/34972351/.

3   Bloomberg, "John Paulson Tops Alpha Hedge Fund Pay List," *Telegraph*, April 16, 2008.

4   Story and Dash, "Banks Prepare for Big Bonuses."

5   John Arlidge, "I'm Doing 'God's Work.' Meet Mr. Goldman Sachs," *Sunday Times*, November 8, 2009.

6   Christian E. Weller and Jessica Lynch, *Household Wealth in Freefall: Americans' Private Safety Net in Tatters* (Washington, D.C.: Center for American Progress, April 2009), 7.

7   Peter S. Goodman, "U.S. Job Seekers Exceed Openings by Record Ratio," *New York Times*, September 26, 2009.

8   Calculated from the Congressional Budget Office (CBO), *Historical Effective Tax Rates, 1979–2006* (Washington, D.C.: CBO, April 2009), available at www.cbo.gov/ ftpdocs/100xx/doc10068/effective_tax_rates_2006.pdf (data available at www.cbo .gov/publications/collections/tax/2009/average_after-tax_income.xls); and CBO, "Historical Effective Tax Rates, 1979 to 2005: Supplement with Additional Data on Sources of Income and High-Income Households, Dec. 23, 2008), available at www.cbo.gov/ftpdocs/98xx/doc9884/12-23-EffectiveTaxRates_Letter.pdf (data available at www.cbo.gov/doc.cfm?index=9884&type=2). As discussed in chapter 1, the CBO uses both Census Bureau income data (which is good at capturing middle-class incomes) and income-tax data (which is good at capturing the incomes of the rich). Its measure of income is comprehensive (wages, salaries, self-employment income, rents, taxable and nontaxable interest, dividends, realized capital gains, cash transfer payments, and cash retirement benefits, as well as all in-kind benefits, such as Medicare, Medicaid, employer-paid health insurance premiums, food stamps, school lunches and breakfasts, housing assistance, and

energy assistance). Federal taxes are subtracted from income and account for not just income and payroll taxes paid directly by individuals and households, but also taxes paid by businesses (corporate income taxes and the employer's share of Social Security, Medicare, and federal unemployment insurance payroll taxes). The CBO assumes that the employer's share of payroll taxes is passed on to employees in the form of lower wages, and that corporate income taxes are borne by owners of capital in proportion to their income from interest, dividends, capital gains, and rents.

9   Jodie T. Allen and Michael Dimock, "A Nation of 'Haves' and 'Have-Nots,'" Pew Research Center for the People and for the Press, September 13, 2007, http://pewresearch.org/pubs/593/haves-have-nots.

10   Using individual income tax returns, Jon Bakija and Bradley T. Heim find that "executives, managers, supervisors, and financial professionals account for about 60 percent of the top 0.1 percent of income earners in recent years, and can account for 70 percent of the increase in the share of national income going to the top 0.1 percent of the income distribution between 1979 and 2005." Bakija and Heim, "Jobs and Income Growth of Top Earners and the Causes of Changing Income Inequality: Evidence from U.S. Tax Return Data" (working paper, Williams College, Office of Tax Analysis, March 17, 2009).

Chapter 1. The Winner-Take-All Economy

1   What's more, the statistics for the United States are available all the way back to the establishment of the income tax in 1913. The latest numbers released by Piketty and Saez are for 2007, thus covering a far longer period than any similar evidence. All of the data described here are available in Excel format through Emmanuel Saez's website, http://elsa.berkeley.edu/~saez/TabFig2007.xls.

2   Robert Frank, *Richistan: A Journey Through the American Wealth Boom and the Lives of the New Rich* (New York: Crown Publishers, 2007).

3   Jon Bakija and Bradley T. Heim, "Jobs and Income Growth of Top Earners and the Causes of Changing Income Inequality: Evidence from U.S. Tax Return Data," working paper, Williams College, Office of Tax Analysis (March 17, 2009).

4   For example, according to work done in 2009 by the economist Richard Burkhauser and his colleagues, this pattern also shows up in the so-called internal data for the Current Population Survey—the original responses to the survey, which are not as severely truncated at high income levels as the official results provided to outside researchers. Richard V. Burkhauser, Shuaizhang Feng, Stephen P. Jenkins, and Jeff Larrimore, "Recent Trends in Top Income Shares in the USA: Reconciling Estimates from March CPS and IRS Tax Return Data," Institute for the Study of Labor Discussion Paper No. 4426 (September 2009).

5   For a more systematic exploration of the role of partisanship, see Lane Kenworthy, "How Much Do Presidents Influence Income Inequality?" (October 7, 2009), forthcoming, http://www.u.arizona.edu/~lkenwor/challenge2010.pdf. Ken-

worthy concludes: "If we turn to data that include the top 1%, we find only a weak association between president's party and changes in inequality since the 1970s."

6   A treasure trove of Congressional Budget Office data is available at http://www .cbo.gov/publications/collections/taxdistribution.cfm.

7   Jared Bernstein and Karen Kornbluh, "Running Faster to Stay in Place: The Growth of Family Work Hours and Incomes," New America Foundation Work and Family Program research paper (June 2005), 5.

8   The data (from the Organization for Economic Cooperation and Development) are available at http://stats.oecd.org. The EU15 is comprised of Austria, Belgium, Denmark, Finland, France, Germany, Greece, Ireland, Italy, Luxembourg, the Netherlands, Portugal, Spain, Sweden, and the United Kingdom. The measure used is GDP (expenditure approach) per head, adjusted for inflation and purchasing power.

9   The OECD data on "total labour force % of population" are not available for 2005 and 2006 for the United States.

10   This discussion is again based on OECD data—in this case, on "average annual hours actually worked per worker." Output per hour worked was calculated for the U.S. and EU15 (excluding Germany, for which data are not available) using the Conference Board Total Economy Database, January 2010, available at http:// www.conferenceboard.org/economics.database.cfm.

11   Paul Krugman, "The Big Zero," *New York Times*, December 27, 2009.

12   Ron Scherer, "Number of Long-Term Unemployed Hits Highest Rate Since 1948," *Christian Science Monitor*, January 8, 2010.

13   U.S. Census Bureau, "Census Bureau Reports on Residential Vacancies and Home Ownership," Washington, D.C.: U.S. Department of the Commerce, April 27, 2009, available at http://www.census.gov/hhes/www/housing/hvs/qtr109/files/ q109press.pdf.

14   Robert Greenstein, Sharon Parrott, and Arloc Sherman, "Poverty and Share of Americans Without Health Insurance Were Higher in 2007—And Median Income for Working-Age Households Was Lower—Than at the Bottom of Last Recession," Center on Budget and Policy Priorities, Washington, D.C., August 26, 2008, available at http://www.cbpp.org/cms/?fa=view&id=621.

15   Emmanuel Saez, "Striking It Richer: The Evolution of Top Incomes in the United States (Update with 2007 Estimates)," University of California, Berkeley, August 5, 2009, available at http://elsa.berkeley.edu/~saez/saez-UStopincomes-2007.pdf.

16   Good summaries of recent mobility studies are contained in Katharine Bradbury and Jane Katz, "Trends in U.S. Family Income Mobility, 1967–2004," Federal Reserve Bank of Boston Working Paper No. 09–7 (August 20, 2009); Thomas L. Hungerford, "Income Inequality, Income Mobility, and Economic Policy: U.S. Trends in the 1980s and 1990s," Congressional Research Service Report for Congress (April 4, 2008); and Isabel Sawhill and John E. Morton, "Economic Mobility: Is the

American Dream Alive and Well?" Economic Mobility Initiative: An Initiative of the Pew Charitable Trusts (February 2008).

17   Wojciech Kopczuk, Emmanuel Saez, and Jae Song, "Uncovering the American Dream: Inequality and Mobility in Social Security Earnings Data Since 1937," National Bureau of Economic Research (NBER) Working Paper No. 13345 (August 2007), 14, 40.

18   Miles Corak, "Chasing the Same Dream, Climbing Different Ladders: Economic Mobility in the United States and Canada," Economic Mobility Initiative: An Initiative of the Pew Charitable Trusts (January 2009), 7.

19   See table 3.13: Change in Private Sector Employer-Provided Pension Coverage, 1979–2006 in Lawrence Mishel, Jared Bernstein, and Heidi Shierholz, *The State of Working America 2008/2009* (Cornell: Cornell University Press, 2008).

20   Jack VanDerhei, Sarah Holden, and Luis Alonso, "401(k) Plan Asset Allocation, Account Balances, and Loan Activity in 2008," Employee Benefit Research Institute No. 335 (October 2009): 16.

21   Alicia H. Munnell, Anthony Webb, and Francesca Golub-Sass, "The National Retirement Risk Index: After the Crash," Center for Retirement Research at Boston College Brief No. 9–22 (October 2009).

22   David Himmelstein, Deborah Thorne, Elizabeth Warren, and Steffie Woolhandler, "Medical Bankruptcy in the United States, 2007: Results of a National Study," *American Journal of Medicine* 122: 8 (2007): 741–746.

23   Organization for Economic Cooperation and Development, OECD Health Data 2009—Frequently Requested Data (November 2009), http://www.irdes.fr/EcoSante/DownLoad/OECDHealthData_FrequentlyRequestedData.xls.

24   Jacob S. Hacker, "The New Push for American Health Security," in *Health at Risk: America's Ailing Health System—and How to Heal It*, Jacob S. Hacker, ed. (New York: Columbia University Press, 2008), 120; Ellen Nolte and C. Martin McKee, "Measuring the Health of Nations: Updating an Earlier Analysis," *Health Affairs* 27, no. 1 (2008): 58–71.

25   Katherine Swartz, "Uninsured in America: New Realities, New Risks," in *Health at Risk: America's Ailing Health System—and How to Heal It*, Jacob S. Hacker, ed. (New York: Columbia University Press, 2008), 32–65.

26   The main survey that asks people about their spending (the Consumer Expenditure Survey) comes up with less than wholly reliable results, especially in the 1990s. In particular, it appears to miss a huge share of overall consumer spending: The survey misses almost half of aggregate spending on nondurable goods in 2000. More important, the share that is missing has been growing rapidly over time. (For example, the survey suggests implausibly that consumer spending *fell* sharply during the boom of the 1990s.) Orazio Attanasio, Erich Battistin, and Hidehiko Ichimura, "What Really Happened to Consumption Inequality in the U.S.?" NBER Working Paper No. 10338 (March 2004); Ian Dew-Becker and R. J. Gordon, "Un-

resolved Issues in the Rise of American Inequality," *Brookings Papers on Economic Activity* 38, no. 2 (Fall 2007).

27 Christian Broda and John Romalis, "Inequality and Prices: Does China Benefit the Poor in America?" (March 26, 2008). For a sense of how much hype there has been around this argument, see Steven D. Levitt, "Shattering the Conventional Wisdom on Growing Inequality," *Freakonomics* blog, May 19, 2008, http://freakonomics .blogs.nytimes.com/2008/05/19/shattering-the-conventional-wisdom-on-growing-inequality/.

28 E. N. Wolff, "Recent Trends in Household Wealth in the United States: Rising Debt and the Middle-Class Squeeze," Levy Institute Working Paper No. 502 (June 2007), 15. See also Conchita D'Ambrosio and Edward N. Wolff, "The Distribution of Wealth and the Polarization of Income in the United States from 1983 to 2004: Inequality and Polarization," paper prepared for the workshop "Income Polarization: Measurement, Determinants and Implications," Israel (May 26–28, 2008).

29 Matthew Miller and Duncan Greenberg, eds., "Special Report: The *Forbes* 400," *Forbes*, September 17, 2008; Nina Munik, "Money Trails: Don't Blink. You'll Miss the 258th-Richest American," *New York Times*, September 25, 2005.

30 Wolff, "Recent Trends in Household Wealth"; D'Ambrosio and Wolff, "The Distribution of Wealth."

31 N. Gregory Mankiw, "The Wealth Trajectory: Rewards for the Few," *New York Times*, April 20, 2008.

32 Ben S. Bernanke, "The Level and Distribution of Economic Well-Being," speech before the Greater Omaha Chamber of Commerce, February 6, 2007, http://www .federalreserve.gov/newsevents/speech/Bernanke20070206a.htm.

33 Michael Abramowitz and Lori Montgomery, "Bush Addresses Income Inequality," *Washington Post*, February 1, 2007.

34 David H. Autor, Richard J. Murname, and Frank Levy, "The Skill Content of Recent Technological Change: An Empirical Exploration," *Quarterly Journal of Economics* 118 (November 2003): 1279–1334; David H. Autor, Lawrence F. Katz, and Melissa S. Kearney, "Trends in U.S. Wage Inequality: Reassessing the Revisionists," NBER Working Paper No. 11627 (2005); David H. Autor, Lawrence F. Katz, and Melissa S. Kearney, "The Polarization of the U.S. Labor Market," *American Economic Review Papers and Proceedings* 96 (May 2006): 189–94; Claudia Goldin and Lawrence F. Katz, "Narrowing, Widening, Polarizing: The Changing Nature of U.S. Wage Inequality," paper presented at Brookings Panel on Economic Activity, Washington, D.C. (September 7, 2007).

35 Claudia Goldin and Lawrence F. Katz, *The Race Between Education and Technology* (Cambridge, MA: Belknap Press, 2008).

36 National Center for Educational Statistics, "Economic Outcomes—Table 20–1. Median Annual Earnings of Full-Time, Full-Year Wage and Salary Workers Ages 25–34, by Educational Attainment, Sex, and Race/Ethnicity: Selected Years, 1980–

2006," U.S. Department of Education, Institute of Education Sciences, http://nces
.ed.gov/programs/coe/2008/section2/table.asp?tableID=894.

37   Liana Fox and Elise Gould, "Employer-Provided Health Coverage Declining for
College Grads in Entry-Level Jobs," *Economic Snapshots*, Economic Policy Institute (July 18, 2007), http://www.epi.org/economic_snapshots/entry/webfeatures_
snapshots_20070718/.

38   Leslie McCall, "Expanding Levels of Within-Group Wage Inequality in U.S. Labor
Markets," *Demography* 37, no. 4 (2000): 415–30; Thomas Lemieux, "Increasing Re-
sidual Wage Inequality: Composition Effects, Noisy Data, or Rising Demand for
Skill?" *American Economic Review* 96, no. 3 (June 2006): 461–498.

39   Richard B. Freeman, *America Works: Critical Thoughts on the Exceptional U.S.
Labor Market* (New York: Russell Sage Foundation, 2007), 44.

40   Ibid., 46.

41   Andrew Leigh, "How Closely Do Income Shares Track Other Measures of Inequality?" *Economic Journal* 117 (November 2007): 589–603. The data are available at
http://people.anu.edu.au/andrew.leigh/pdf/TopIncomesPanel.xls.

42   On the U.S. and Canada, see Emmanuel Saez and Michael R. Veall, "The Evolution of High Incomes in Northern America: Lessons from Canadian Evidence,"
American Economic Review 95, no. 3 (June 2005): 831–849; Sami Mahroum,
"Highly Skilled Globetrotters: The International Migration of Human Capital," Organization for Economic Co-operation and Development, http://www.oecd.org/
dataoecd/35/6/2100652.pdf.

Chapter 2. How the Winner-Take-All Economy Was Made

1   Henry Paulson, Remarks Prepared for Delivery by Treasury Secretary Henry M.
Paulson at Columbia University, August 1, 2006, http://www.treasury.gov/press/
releases/hp41.htm.

2   Paul Krugman, *The Conscience of a Liberal* (New York: Norton, 2007), Ch. 7.

3   N. Gregory Mankiw, "The Wealth Trajectory: Rewards for the Few," *New York
Times*, April 20, 2008.

4   J. Bradford DeLong, "The Primacy of Politics for Income Distribution?" Grasping
Reality with All Six Feet, blog entry, August 20, 2006, http://delong.typepad.com/
sdj/2006/08/the_primacy_of_.html.

5   Ian Dew-Becker and R. J. Gordon, "Selected Issues in the Rise of American Inequality," *Brookings Papers on Economic Activity* 38, no. 2 (Fall 2007): 176–81.

6   Sherwin Rosen, "The Economics of Superstars," *American Economic Review*, 71,
no. 5 (1981): 845–58; Robert H. Frank and Philip J. Cook, *The Winner-Take-All
Society: Why the Few at the Top Get So Much More Than the Rest of Us* (New York:
Penguin Books, 1995).

7   Alan Murray, "Paul Volcker: Think More Boldly," *Wall Street Journal*, December
14, 2009.

8   Thomas Piketty and Emmanuel Saez, "How Progressive Is the U.S. Federal Tax System? A Historical and International Perspective," *Journal of Economic Perspectives* 21, no. 1 (Winter 2007): 3–24; Thomas Piketty and Emmanuel Saez, Excel file containing stand-alone results reported in *Journal of Economic Perspectives* article, http://elsa.berkeley.edu/~saez/jep-results-standalone.xls.

9   Calculated from Piketty and Saez, "How Progressive Is the U.S. Federal Tax System?" 15. The 4.5 percent figure is simply what the after-tax income share would have been if the ratio of after-tax to pre-tax shares for the top 0.1 percent had remained at its 1970 level.

10 Benjamin I. Page and Lawrence R. Jacobs, *Class War: What Americans Really Think About Economic Inequality* (Chicago: University of Chicago Press, 2009), 85–87.

11 Max B. Sawicky, "Do-It-Yourself Tax Cuts: The Crisis in U.S. Tax Enforcement," Economic Policy Institute Briefing Paper 160 (2005).

12 See David Cay Johnston, *Perfectly Legal: The Covert Campaign to Rig Our Tax System to Benefit the Super Rich—and Cheat Everybody Else* (New York: Penguin Group, 2005).

13 Jenny Anderson and Julie Creswell, "Top Hedge Fund Managers Earn Over $240 Million," *New York Times*, April 24, 2007.

14 Vincent A. Mahler and David K. Jesuit, "Fiscal Redistribution in the Developed Countries: New Insights from the Luxembourg Income Study," *Socio-Economic Review* 4, no. 3 (2006): 483–511; Luxembourg Income Study Project, Fiscal Redistribution Dataset, Version 2, compiled by David K. Jesuit and Vincent A. Mahler (February 2008), www.lisproject.org/publications/fiscalredistdata/fiscred.htm.

15 Thomas L. Hungerford, "Income Inequality, Income Mobility, and Economic Policy," *CRS Report for Congress*, April 4, 2008. We are grateful to Dr. Hungerford for providing the underlying data on redistribution, drawn from the Panel Study of Income Dynamics, used in these calculations. We should emphasize, again, that as striking as these statistics are, they greatly understate the degree to which public policy contributed to rising inequality. First, they are based on income surveys that miss trends at the very top. Second, and for the same reason, they have little to say about shifts in taxation affecting those at the very top—which, as just shown, are substantial. And third, they are narrowly focused on the role of government taxes and benefits in altering the inequality of market incomes, thus missing entirely the role of public policy in shaping market incomes in the first place.

16 For more on drift, see Jacob S. Hacker, "Privatizing Risk Without Privatizing the Welfare State: The Hidden Politics of Social Policy Retrenchment in the United States," *American Political Science Review* 98, no. 2 (2004): 243–260.

17 David S. Lee, "Wage Inequality in the United States During the 1980s: Rising Dispersion or Falling Minimum Wage?" *Quarterly Journal of Economics* 114, no. 3 (1999): 977–1023; David Card and John E. DiNardo, "Skill-Biased Technological Change and Rising Wage Inequality: Some Problems and Puzzles," *Journal*

of Labor Economics 20, no. 4 (2002): 733–83. Even Wal-Mart's CEO has publicly stated that the minimum wage is "out of date with the times. We can see firsthand at Wal-Mart how many of our customers are struggling to get by. Our customers simply don't have the money to buy basic necessities between pay checks." Quoted in Richard B. Freeman, *America Works: Critical Thoughts on the Exceptional U.S. Labor Market* (New York: Russell Sage Foundation, 2007), 50.

18   On Alaska's favored-state status, see Gary Richardson, "The Truth About Redistribution: Republicans Receive, Democrats Disburse," *Economists' Voice* 6, issue 10, article 3 (2009).

19   Karl Polanyi, *The Great Transformation: The Political and Economic Origins of Our Time* (Boston: Beacon Press, 1944).

20   Jelle Visser, "Union Membership Statistics in 24 Countries," *Monthly Labor Review*, January 2006; Kris Maher, "Union Membership Drops," *Wall Street Journal*, January 23, 2010.

21   David Card, "Effect of Unions on Wage Inequality in the U.S. Labor Market," *Industrial & Labor Relations Review* 54, no. 2 (January 2001): 296–315; Freeman, *America Works*, 50.

22   For evidence that unions affect the degree to which governments reduce inequality primarily through their link with social-democratic parties, see David Bradley et al., "Distribution and Redistribution in Postindustrial Democracies," *World Politics* 55, no. 2 (January 2003): 193–228.

23   Visser, "Union Membership Statistics."

24   Freeman, *America Works*, 82–84.

25   Alex Bryson and Richard B. Freeman, "Worker Needs and Voice in the U.S. and the U.K.," NBER Working Paper No. 12310 (June 2006).

26   In the early 1970s, AFL-CIO head George Meany obtusely opined that "the organized fellow is the fellow that counts. . . . Why should we worry about organizing groups of people who do not appear to want to be organized? . . . I used to worry . . . about the size of the membership . . . I stopped worrying because to me it doesn't make any difference." Freeman, *America Works*, 77.

27   For the story, see David Vogel, *Fluctuating Fortunes: The Political Power of Business in America* (New York: Basic Books, 1988), 150–59.

28   Frank S. Levy and Peter Temin, "Inequality and Institutions in 20th Century America," NBER Working Paper No. 13106 (May 2007), 33.

29   John Logan, "The Union Avoidance Industry in the United States," *British Journal of Industrial Relations* 44, no. 4 (December 2006): 654.

30   Robert J. Flanagan, "Has Management Strangled U.S. Unions?" *Journal of Labor Research* 26, no. 1 (December 2005): 48–49.

31   Henry S. Farber and Bruce Western, "Ronald Reagan and the Politics of Declining Union Organization," *British Journal of Industrial Relations* 40 (2002): 385–401.

32   See Kate Bronfenbrenner, "No Holds Barred: The Intensification of Employer Opposition to Organizing," Economic Policy Institute Briefing Paper No. 235 (May 30, 2009), 13.

33   Ibid., 9.

34   Jacob S. Hacker, *The Divided Welfare State: The Battle over Public and Private Social Benefits in the United States* (New York: Cambridge University Press, 2002); Jacob S. Hacker, *The Great Risk Shift: The New Economic Insecurity and the Decline of the American Dream*, (New York: Oxford University Press, 2006).

35   W. Craig Riddell, "Unionization in Canada and the United States: A Tale of Two Countries," in *Small Differences That Matter: Labor Markets and Income Maintenance in Canada and the United States*, David Card and Richard Freeman, eds. (Chicago: University of Chicago Press and National Bureau of Economic Research, 1993), 109–148.

36   John Godard, "Do Labor Laws Matter? The Density Decline and Convergence Thesis Revisited," *Industrial Relations* 42, no. 3 (2003): 458–492.

37   Mark Clothier, "Home Depot's Nardelli Ousted After Six-Year Tenure," *Bloomberg,* January 3, 2007, http://www.bloomberg.com/apps/news?pid=20601087&sid=aLphvT.qIqZI&refer=home.

38   Jon Bakija and Bradley T. Heim, "Jobs and Income Growth of Top Earners and the Causes of Changing Income Inequality: Evidence from U.S. Tax Return Data," working paper, Williams College, Office of Tax Analysis (March 17, 2009).

39   There is a connection between the previous discussion of tax policy and the current discussion of executive compensation. The sharp fall in true tax rates on very high incomes may have stimulated the rise in executive pay, since the recipients capture so much more of any rise in compensation. Carola Frydman and Raven Saks estimate that "had tax rates been at their year 2000 level for the entire sample period, the level of executive compensation would have been 35 percent higher in the 1950s and 1960s." Frydman and Saks, "Historical Trends in Executive Compensation," Sloan School of Management, MIT, working paper (2005), 31.

40   Carola Frydman and Raven E. Saks, "Executive Compensation: A New View from a Long-Term Perspective," FEDS Working Paper No. 2007–35 (July 6, 2007).

41   See figure 3AE, table 3.41 in Lawrence Mishel, Jared Bernstein, and Heidi Shierholz, *The State of Working America 2008/2009* (Cornell: Cornell University Press, 2008), 221.

42   Ibid., table 3.42.

43   Hay Group, *2006 Top Executive Compensation Study* (Philadelphia: Hay Group, 2007).

44   Kevin J. Murphy, "Politics, Economics, and Executive Compensation," *University of Cincinnati Law Review* 63 (1995): 714–746.

45   Peter A. Gourevitch and James Shinn, *Political Power and Corporate Control: The New Global Politics of Corporate Governance* (Princeton: Princeton University Press, 2005).

46   John C. Bogle, "A Crisis of Ethic Proportions," *Wall Street Journal*, April 21, 2009; John C. Bogle, *The Battle for the Soul of Capitalism: How the Financial System Undermined Social Ideals, Damaged Trust in the Markets, Robbed Investors of Trillions—And What to Do About It* (New Haven: Yale University Press, 2005).

47   Lucian Bebchuk and Jesse Fried, *Pay Without Performance: The Unfulfilled Promise of Executive Compensation* (Cambridge, MA: Harvard University Press, 2004).

48   Ibid., 100.

49   Ibid., 102, 105.

50   Ellen E. Schultz and Tom McGinty, "Executives Enjoy 'Sure Thing' Retirement Plans," *Wall Street Journal*, December 16, 2009.

51   Gourevitch and Shinn, *Political Power and Corporate Control*.

52   Arthur Levitt, *Take On the Street: How to Fight for Your Financial Future* (New York: Vintage, 2002).

53   After more than a decade of delay, and following a wave of options-related scandals, FASB finally introduced expensing in 2004. Even then there was fierce bipartisan opposition in Congress.

54   John W. Cioffi, "Building Finance Capitalism: The Regulatory Politics of Corporate Governance Reform in the United States and Germany," in Jonah Levy, ed., *The State After Statism: New State Activities in the Age of Liberalization* (Oxford: Oxford University Press, 2006).

55   Levitt, *Take On the Street*, 250; Brian J. Hall and Kevin Murphy, "The Trouble with Stock Options," *Journal of Economic Perspectives*, 17, no. 3 (2003): 51.

56   Thomas Philippon and Ariell Reshef, "Wages and Human Capital in the U.S. Financial Industry: 1909–2006," NBER Working Paper No. 14644 (January 2008).

57   Justin Lahart, "Has the Financial Industry's Heyday Come and Gone?" *Wall Street Journal*, April 28, 2008.

58   Martin Wolf, "Regulators Should Intervene in Bankers' Pay," *Financial Times*, January 16, 2008.

59   Jenny Anderson, "Atop Hedge Funds, Richest of the Rich Get Even More So," *New York Times*, May 26, 2006; Jenny Anderson and Julie Creswell, "Top Hedge Fund Managers Earn Over $240 Million," *New York Times*, April 24, 2007; Jenny Anderson, "Wall Street Winners Get Billion-Dollar Paydays," *New York Times*, April 16, 2008.

60   Christine Harper, "Wall Street Bonuses Hit Record $39 Billion for 2007," *Bloomberg*, January 17, 2008, http://www.bloomberg.com/apps/news?pid=newsarchive&sid=aHPBhz66H9eo.

61   Robert Kuttner, *The Squandering of America* (New York: Knopf, 2007).

62 David Moss, "An Ounce of Prevention: Financial Regulation, Moral Hazard, and the End of 'Too Big to Fail,'" *Harvard Magazine*, September–October 2009, 24–29.

63 Robert J. Gordon and Ian Dew-Becker, "Controversies About the Rise of American Inequality: A Survey," NBER Working Paper No. 13982 (May 2008), 25.

64 Philippon and Reshef, "Wages and Human Capital in the U.S. Financial Industry: 1909–2006."

65 Kuttner, *Squandering of America*, 77.

66 Philippon and Reshef, "Wages and Human Capital," 30.

67 Lucian A. Bebchuk, Alma Cohen, and Holger Spamann, "The Wages of Failure: Executive Compensation at Bear Sterns and Lehman 2000–2008," Harvard Law and Economics Discussion Paper No. 657 (December 2009).

68 Andy Serwer and Allan Sloan, "How Financial Madness Overtook Wall Street," *Time*, September 18, 2008.

69 Louis Uchitelle, "The Richest of the Rich, Proud of a New Golden Age," *New York Times*, July 15, 2007.

70 Daniel Gross, *Bull Run: Wall Street, the Democrats, and the New Politics of Personal Finance* (New York: Public Affairs, 2000), 14.

Chapter 3. A Brief History of Democratic Capitalism

1 The two quotes are from Michael Thompson, *The Politics of Inequality: A Political History of the Idea of Economic Inequality* (New York: Columbia University Press, 2007), 25, 45; see also Sean Wilentz, "America's Lost Egalitarian Tradition," *Daedalus*, 131, no. 1 (Winter 2002): 66–80.

2 Thompson, *The Politics of Inequality*, 27, 45, 47–48.

3 James Madison, "Federalist #10: The Utility of the Union as a Safeguard Against Domestic Faction and Insurrection," in *The Federalist Papers*, http://www.constitution.org/fed/federa10.htm, originally published in *Daily Advertiser*, November 22, 1787.

4 James Madison, "Federalist #39: Conformity of the Plan to Republican Principles," in *The Federalist Papers*, http://www.constitution.org/fed/federa39.htm, originally published in *Independent Journal*, January 16, 1788.

5 Akhil Reed Amar, *America's Constitution: A Biography* (New York: Random House, 2005), 17.

6 John Adams, "Defence of the Constitutions of Government of the United States," in *The Founders' Constitution*, vol. 1, Philip B. Kurland and Ralph Lerner, eds. (Chicago: University of Chicago Press, 1986).

7 Alexis de Tocqueville, *Democracy in America*, trans. and ed. by Harvey C. Mansfield and Delba Winthrop (Chicago: University of Chicago Press), 201.

8 Ibid.

9 The canonical model is Allen H. Meltzer and Scott F. Richards, "A Rational Theory of the Size of Government," *Journal of Political Economy* 89, no. 5 (1981): 914–927.

For a nice review, see Jo Thori Lind, "Why Is There So Little Redistribution?" *Nordic Journal of Political Economy* 31 (2005): 111–125.

10   Quoted in Steve Fraser, *Wall Street: A Cultural History* (London: Faber and Faber, 2005), 158.

11   Michael Waldman, ed., *My Fellow Americans: The Most Important Speeches of America's Presidents, from George Washington to George W. Bush* (Naperville, IL: Sourcebooks, 2003), 72–73.

12   Melvin I. Urofsky, *Louis D. Brandeis: A Life* (New York: Pantheon Books, 2009), 326.

13   Quoted in Ibid., 320.

14   Cass Sunstein, *The Second Bill of Rights: FDR's Unfinished Revolution and Why We Need It More Than Ever* (New York: Basic Books, 2004), 20–25.

15   Adam Smith, *An Inquiry Into the Nature and Causes of the Wealth of Nations* (Edinburgh: Thomas Nelson and Peter Brown, 1827), 277, 279.

16   Walter Lippmann, *Drift and Mastery: An Attempt to Diagnose the Current Unrest* (New York: Mitchell Kennerley, 1914), 36–37.

17   Ibid., 100.

18   Frances E. Lee and Bruce I. Oppenheimer, *Sizing Up the Senate: The Unequal Consequences of Equal Representation* (Chicago: University of Chicago Press, 1999); John D. Griffin, "Senate Apportionment as a Source of Political Inequality," *Legislative Studies Quarterly* 31, no. 3 (2006).

19   Robert Dahl, *How Democratic Is the American Constitution?* (New Haven: Yale University Press, 2001).

20   Lee and Oppenheimer, *Sizing Up the Senate*, 10–11.

21   David Samuels and Richard Snyder, "The Value of a Vote: Malapportionment in Comparative Perspective," *British Journal of Political Science* 31 (2002): 651–71.

22   Michael Schudson, *The Good Citizen: A History of American Civic Life* (New York: Martin Kessler Books, 1998), 182.

23   David Brian Robertson, "The Bias of American Federalism: Political Structure and the Development of America's Exceptional Welfare State in the Progressive Era," *Journal of Policy History* 1 (1989): 261–291.

24   Waldman, *My Fellow Americans*, 106.

25   Quoted in Kevin Phillips, *The Politics of Rich and Poor* (New York: Random House, 1990), 106.

26   William E. Leuchtenburg, *Franklin D. Roosevelt and the New Deal* (New York: Harper & Row, 1963), 21.

27   Rick Santelli, CNBC News, February 19, 2009 at 1 p.m. ET, http://www.youtube.com/watch?v=bEZB4taSEoA&feature=player_embedded#.

28   Frances Perkins, "Basic Idea Behind Social Security Program," *New York Times*, January 27, 1935.

29   Bruce A. Ackerman, *We the People*, vol. 1 (Cambridge, MA: Belknap Press, 1991).

30   Leuchtenburg, *Franklin D. Roosevelt and the New Deal*, 333.

Chapter 4. The Unseen Revolution of the 1970s

1   Allen J. Matusow, *The Unraveling of America: A History of Liberalism in the 1960s* (New York: Harper & Row, 1984); Rick Perlstein, *Nixonland: The Rise of a President and the Fracturing of America* (New York: Scribner, 2008). See also Allen J. Matusow, *Nixon's Economy: Booms, Busts, Dollars, and Votes* (Lawrence, KS: University Press of Kansas, 1998).

2   Kevin P. Phillips, *The Emerging Republican Majority* (New Rochelle, NY: Arlington House, 1969).

3   Phillips, *The Emerging Republican Majority,* 37, 464.

4   Robert D. McFadden, "Edmund Hillary, First on Everest, Dies at 88," *New York Times,* January 10, 2008.

5   Ted Koppel, interview by Larry King, *Larry King Live,* CNN, October 4, 2000.

6   Michael Calderone, "Health Care Talk Sinks Obama Press Conference Ratings," *Politico,* July 27, 2009, http://www.politico.com/news/stories/0709/25385.html.

7   Jeffrey H. Birnbaum and Alan S. Murray, *Showdown at Gucci Gulch: Lawmakers, Lobbyists, and the Unlikely Triumph of Tax Reform* (New York: Random House, 1987).

8   John Steinbeck, *The Grapes of Wrath* (New York: Penguin Classics, 2006), 38.

9   Jacob S. Hacker and Paul Pierson, *Off Center: The Republican Revolution and the Erosion of American Democracy* (New Haven: Yale University Press, 2005), 164.

10   Pew Research Center for the People & the Press, "Senate Legislative Process a Mystery to Many," Pew Research Center survey report, January 8, 2010, http://people-press.org/report/586/.

11   Hacker and Pierson, *Off Center,* 164.

12   For an extended discussion of such scrounging, see Paul Pierson, "The Prospects for Democratic Control in an Age of Big Government," in *Politics at the Turn of the Century,* Arthur M. Melzer, Jerry Weinberger, and M. Richard Zinman, eds. (Lanham, MD: Rowman & Littlefield, 2001), 140–61.

13   Authors' calculations from National Election Studies: http://www.electionstudies.org.

14   Larry M. Bartels, *Unequal Democracy: The Political Economy of the New Gilded Age* (New York: Russell Sage Foundation, 2008); Martin Gilens, "Inequality and Democratic Responsiveness," *Public Opinion Quarterly* 69, no. 5 (2005): 778–96.

15   Gilens, "Inequality and Democratic Responsiveness," 794.

Chapter 5. The Politics of Organized Combat

1   *National Journal,* 1974, 14.

2   David Vogel, *Fluctuating Fortunes: The Political Power of Business in America* (New York: Basic Books, 1989), 59; R. Shep Melnick, "From Tax-and-Spend to Mandate-and-Sue: Liberalism After the Great Society," in *The Great Society and*

the High Tide of Liberalism, Sidney Milkis and Jerome Mileur, eds. (Amherst, MA: University of Massachusetts Press, 2005).

3   Lewis Powell, "Confidential Memorandum: Attack on the Free Enterprise System," August 23, 1971, quoted in Kim Phelps-Fein, *Invisible Hands: The Making of the Conservative Movement from the New Deal to Reagan* (New York: Norton, 2009), 158, 160.

4   Thomas Byrne Edsall, *The New Politics of Inequality* (New York: Norton, 1984), 114.

5   Vogel, *Fluctuating Fortunes*, ch. 8.

6   Calculated from http://www.bea.gov/national/xls/gdplev.xls.

7   Ibid., 198.

8   Vogel, *Fluctuating Fortunes*, 198; John Judis, *The Paradox of American Democracy: Elites, Special Interests, and the Betrayal of Public Trust* (Pantheon: New York, 2000), 121.

9   Quoted in Sidney Blumenthal, *The Rise of the Counter-Establishment: From Conservative Ideology to Political Power* (New York: Times Books, 1986), 80.

10   Quoted in Leonard Silk and David Vogel, *Ethics and Profits: The Crisis of Confidence in American Business* (New York: Simon & Schuster, 1976), 65.

11   Blumenthal, *Rise of the Counter-Establishment*, 78.

12   Taylor E. Dark, *The Unions and the Democrats: An Enduring Alliance* (Ithaca, NY: Cornell University Press, 1999), 149.

13   Vogel, *Fluctuating Fortunes*, 209–10.

14   Ibid., 208.

15   Andrew Rich, "War of Ideas: Why Mainstream and Liberal Foundations and the Think Tanks They Support Are Losing in the War of Ideas in American Politics," *Stanford Social Innovation Review* (Spring 2005): 24. This and the previous paragraph draw heavily on Rich's research. See also Andrew Rich, *Think Tanks, Public Policy, and the Politics of Expertise* (New York: Cambridge University Press, 2004).

16   Judis, *Paradox of American Democracy*, 135.

17   Blumenthal, *Rise of the Counter-Establishment*, 80.

18   "Carter Dealt Major Defeat on Consumer Bills," *Congressional Quarterly Weekly Report*, February 11, 1978.

19   Edsall, *New Politics of Inequality*, 152.

20   "House Rejects Labor-Backed Picketing Bill," *CQ Almanac 1977* (Washington: Congressional Quarterly, 1978).

21   Ibid.

22   Ibid.

23   Richard B. Freeman and James L. Medoff, *What Do Unions Do?* (New York: Basic Books, 1985), 203.

24   "Filibuster Kills Labor Law 'Reform' Bill," *CQ Almanac 1978* (Washington: Congressional Quarterly, 1979).

25   Freeman and Medoff, *What Do Unions Do?*, 203.

26   "Filibuster Kills Labor Law 'Reform' Bill," *CQ Almanac 1978.*

27   Edsall, *New Politics of Inequality*, 125.

28   Quoted in Howard Zinn and Anthony Arnove, *Voices of a People's History of the United States*, 2nd ed. (New York: Seven Stories Press, 2009), 530–33.

29   Frank Levy and Peter Temin, "Inequality and Institutions in Twentieth Century America," NBER Working Paper No. 13106 (May 2007).

30   Thomas Ferguson and Joel Rogers, *Right Turn: The Decline of the Democrats and the Future of American Politics* (New York: Hill and Wang, 1986), 109.

31   Blumenthal, *Rise of the Counter-Establishment*, 81.

32   David O. Sears and Jack Citrin, *Tax Revolt: Something for Nothing in California* (Cambridge, MA: Harvard University Press, 1982), 233.

33   Mark Blyth, *Great Transformations: Economic Ideas and Institutional Change in the Twentieth Century* (New York: Cambridge University Press, 2002), 175–76.

34   Quoted in William A. Greider, "The Education of David Stockman," *Atlantic Monthly*, December 1981.

Chapter 6. The Middle Goes Missing

1   Suzanne Mettler, *Soldiers to Citizens: The GI Bill and the Making of the Greatest Generation* (New York: Oxford University Press, 2005); Theda Skocpol, *Diminished Democracy: From Membership to Management in American Civic Life* (Norman, OK: University of Oklahoma Press, 2003).

2   Mettler, *Soldiers to Citizens*, 19.

3   Taylor E. Dark, *The Unions and the Democrats: An Enduring Alliance* (Ithaca, NY: Cornell University Press, 1999), 57.

4   Peter L. Francia, *The Future of Organized Labor in American Politics* (New York: Columbia University Press, 2006), 1.

5   Ibid., 1.

6   Jacob S. Hacker, *The Divided Welfare State: The Battle over Public and Private Social Benefits in the United States* (New York: Cambridge University Press, 2002).

7   "Statement of George Meany, President, American Federation of Labor, Social Security Amendments of 1954," Committee on Finance, U.S. Senate, June 1954.

8   Sanford M. Jacoby, *Modern Manors: Welfare Capitalism Since the New Deal* (Princeton, NJ: Princeton University Press, 1997).

9   Derek C. Bok and John T. Dunlop, *Labor and the American Community* (New York: Simon & Schuster, 1970), 393.

10   Harry M. Scoble, "Organized Labor in Electoral Politics: Some Questions for the Discipline," *Political Research Quarterly* 16, no. 3 (1963): 666.

11   Bok and Dunlop, *Labor and the American Community.*

12   Ibid., 423.

13   Richard B. Freeman, "What Do Unions Do . . . to Voting?," NBER Working Paper No. 9992 (September 2003); Benjamin Radcliff, "Organized Labor and Electoral Participation in American National Elections," *Journal of Labor Research* 22, no. 2 (2001): 405–414. See also Patrick Flavin and Benjamin Radcliff, "Labor Union Membership and Voter Turnout Across Nations," paper presented at the annual meeting of the Midwest Political Science Association, Chicago, IL (April 2–5, 2009).

14   Martin Gilens, "Interest Groups and Inequality in Democratic Responsiveness in the U.S.," Social Science Research Network working paper (August 31, 2009).

15   Skocpol, *Diminished Democracy*, 153–56.

16   Ibid., 124.

17   Robert Putnam, "Bowling Alone: America's Declining Social Capital," *Journal of Democracy* 6, no. 1 (1995), and *Bowling Alone: The Collapse and Revival of American Community* (New York: Simon & Schuster, 2000).

18   Gabriel A. Almond and Sidney Verba, *The Civic Culture: Political Attitudes and Democracy in Five Nations* (California: Sage Publications, 1989).

19   Alex Kaplun, " 'Energy Citizens' Take Aim at Climate Legislation," *New York Times*, August 12, 2009.

20   Margaret Weir and Marshall Ganz, "Reconnecting People and Politics," in *The New Majority: Toward a Popular Progressive Politics*, Stanley B. Greenberg and Theda Skocpol, eds. (New Haven: Yale University Press, 1997), 160.

21   Jeffrey M. Berry, *The New Liberalism: The Rising Power of Citizen Groups* (Washington, D.C.: Brookings, 1999).

22   EMILY's List, Homepage, http://emilyslist.org/about/.

23   Berry, *The New Liberalism*, 57.

24   Frank R. Baumgartner et al., *Lobbying and Policy Change: Who Wins, Who Loses, and Why* (Chicago: University of Chicago Press, 2009), 258.

25   Elmer E. Schattschneider, *The Semisovereign People: A Realist's View of Democracy in America* (New York: Holt, Rinehart and Winston, 1960), 35.

26   Skocpol, *Diminished Democracy*, 171.

27   Quoted in Andrew Gelman, *Red State, Blue State, Rich State, Poor State: Why Americans Vote the Way They Do* (Princeton, NJ: Princeton University Press, 2008), 3.

28   Nolan McCarty, Keith T. Poole, and Howard Rosenthal, *Polarized America: The Dance of Ideology and Unequal Riches* (Cambridge, MA: MIT Press, 2006), 96.

29   Gelman, *Red State, Blue State*, 102–04.

30   Mark A. Smith, *The Right Talk: How Conservatives Transformed the Great Society into the Economic Society* (Princeton, NJ: Princeton University Press, 2007); Larry M. Bartels, *Unequal Democracy: The Political Economy of the New Gilded Age* (New York: Russell Sage Foundation, 2008).

31   Smith, *The Right Talk*, 65.

32   For reviews, see Bartels, *Unequal Democracy*; Gelman, *Red State, Blue State*.

33   McCarty, Poole, and Rosenthal, *Polarized America:* 99.

34   James L. Guth et al, "Religious Influences in the 2004 Presidential Election," *Presidential Studies Quarterly* 36, no. 2 (2006).

35   Ross Douthat and Reihan Salam, *Grand New Party: How Republicans Can Win the Working Class and Save the American Dream* (New York: Doubleday, 2008); Jacob Felson and Heather Kindell, "The Elusive Link Between Conservative Protestantism and Conservative Economics," *Social Science Research* 36, no. 2 (2007): 673–687.

36   American Political Science Association Task Force on Inequality and American Democracy, "American Democracy in an Age of Rising Inequality," *Perspectives on Politics* 2 (2004): 651.

37   Joe Soss and Lawrence R. Jacobs, "The Place of Inequality: Non-participation in the American Polity," *Political Science Quarterly* 124, no. 1 (2009): 95–125.

38   Andrea Louise Campbell, "Parties, Electoral Participation, and Shifting Voting Blocs," in *The Transformation of American Politics: Activist Government and the Rise of Conservatism*, Paul Pierson and Theda Skocpol, eds. (Princeton, NJ: Princeton University Press, 2007), 85–87.

39   Martin Gilens, "Preference Gaps and Inequality in Representation," *PS: Political Science & Politics* 42 (2009): 335–341; David W. Brady and Daniel P. Kessler, "Who Supports Health Reform?" *PS: Political Science & Politics* 43 (2010): 1–6.

40   Bartels, *Unequal Democracy*, 295.

41   Ibid., 287.

42   Benjamin I. Page and Lawrence R. Jacobs, *Class War?: What Americans Really Think About Economic Inequality* (Chicago: University of Chicago, 2009), 24, 96.

43   For reviews and exemplars of this research, see in particular Benjamin Page and Robert Shapiro, *The Rational Public: Fifty Years of Trends in Americans' Policy Preferences* (Chicago: Chicago University Press, 1992); Morris P. Fiorina, with Samuel J. Abrams and Jeremy C. Pose, *What Culture War? The Myth of a Polarized America* (New York: Pearson, Longman, 2004); Page and Jacobs, *Class War?*; James A. Stimson, *Public Opinion in America: Moods, Cycles, and Swings*, 2nd ed. (Boulder: Westview, 1999); and Paul DiMaggio, John Evans, Bethany Bryson, "Have Americans' Social Attitudes Become More Polarized?" *The American Journal of Sociology,* 102, No. 3 (1996): 690–755.

44   This finding is from the American National Election Studies, available online at http://www.electionstudies.org/nesguide/toptable/tab3_1.htm.

45   We review these findings in more depth in our 2005 book, *Off Center: The Republican Revolution and the Erosion of American Democracy* (New Haven: Yale University Press, 2005).

46   Jodie T. Allen and Michael Dimock, "A Nation of 'Haves' and 'Have-Nots,' " Pew Research Center for the People & the Press, September 13, 2007, http://pew research.org/pubs/593/haves-have-nots; Lydia Saad, "More Americans Say U.S. a

Nation of Haves and Have-Nots," *Gallup News*, July 11, 2008, http://www.gallup.com/poll/108769/more-americans-say-us-nation-haves-havenots.aspx.

47   Page and Jacobs, *Class War?*, 121.

48   Lane Kenworthy and Leslie McCall, "Inequality, Public Opinion and Redistribution," *Socio-Economic Review* (2007): 1–34.

49   Andrew Eggers, "Not So Deluded After All," personal Web site, May 12, 2005, http://www.people.fas.harvard.edu/~aeggers/notsooptimistic.pdf.

50   The question reads: "Looking ahead, how likely is it that you will ever be rich: Very likely, fairly likely, not too likely or not likely at all?" Conducted by Gallup Organization, January 20–22, 2003, and based on 1,006 telephone interviews. Sample: national adult. [USGALLUP.03JNY20.R04]; Methodology: Conducted by Gallup Organization, May 17–20, 1990, and based on 1,255 telephone interviews. Sample: national adult. [USGALLUP.070190.R07].

51   Lars Osberg and Timothy Smeeding, " 'Fair' Inequality? Attitudes Toward Pay Differentials: The United States in Comparative Perspective," *American Sociological Review* 71 (2006): 450–473.

52   Page and Jacobs, *Class War?*, 43.

53   Osberg and Smeeding, " 'Fair' Inequality?"

54   The 2008 question was asked in two ways: One told respondents how much households in the top 5 percent earned relative to those in the bottom 5 percent; the other informed respondents about household earnings in the top and bottom 20 percent. There was little difference in response between the two. The best source of consistent questions on public views of inequality is the General Social Survey. It has asked the "government should reduce income differences" question since 1978.

55   Leonard Downie Jr. and Robert G. Kaiser, *The News About the News: American Journalism in Peril* (New York: Knopf, 2002), 8.

56   Ibid., 138

57   Markus Prior, *Post-Broadcast Democracy: How Media Choice Increases Inequality in Political Involvement and Polarizes Elections* (New York: Cambridge University Press, 2007).

58   Hacker and Pierson, *Off Center*, 177.

59   Matthew Hindman, *The Myth of Digital Democracy* (Princeton, NJ: Princeton University Press, 2009).

60   McCarty, Poole, and Rosenthal, *Polarized America*, 1.

61   Fiorina, *What Culture War?*; Matthew Levundusky, *The Partisan Sort: How Liberals Became Democrats and Conservatives Became Republicans* (Chicago: University of Chicago Press, 2009); Sean M. Theriault, *Party Polarization in Congress* (New York: Cambridge University Press, 2008).

62   These statements are based on DW-Nominate scores, a measure of the ideological

position of members of Congress based on their roll call votes. For more on these scores, see http://www.voteview.com/.

63 Hacker and Pierson, *Off Center*, 7; McCarty, Poole, and Rosenthal, *Polarized America*, 11.

64 On self-identification, see Morris P. Fiorina and Samuel J. Abrahams, "Political Polarization in the American Public," *Annual Review of Political Science* 11 (2008): 563–588. Most striking is the increasing liberalism seen in James Stimson's "public mood" series, which uses multiple survey questions asked with the same wording over time to track the liberalism or conservatism of the American public. Stimson's data show that in 2004, the public mood was more liberal than at any point since 1961. Updated from Stimson, *Public Opinion in America*, http://www.unc.edu/~istimson/time.html.

Chapter 7. A Tale of Two Parties

1 Gary C. Jacobson, "Party Organization and Distribution of Campaign Resources: Republicans and Democrats in 1982," *Political Science Quarterly*, vol. 100, no. 4 (Winter, 1985–1986): 613.

2 Quoted in Jacobson, "Party Organization and Distribution of Campaign Resources," 616.

3 Ibid., 613.

4 Ibid., 618.

5 Ibid., 621.

6 Robert Kuttner, *The Life of the Party* (New York: Viking, 1987), 86.

7 Larry Bartels, *Unequal Democracy: The Political Economy of the New Gilded Age* (Princeton: Princeton University Press, 2008), 122.

8 Here we are drawing on several recent works that are forcing political scientists to reconsider the way they think of political parties. Marty Cohen, David Karol, Hans Noel, and John Zaller, *The Party Decides: Presidential Nominations Before and After Reform* (Chicago: University of Chicago Press, 2008); David Karol, *Party Position Change in American Politics* (Cambridge, U.K.: Cambridge University Press, 2009).

9 Paul Krugman, *The Conscience of a Liberal* (New York: Norton, 2007), 23. Krugman cites Historical Statistics 1975 for his spending figures.

10 Calculated from Campaign Finance Institute, www.cfinst.org/pdf/VitalStats_t2.pdf.

11 Calculated from Campaign Finance Institute, www.cfinst.org/pdf/vital/VitalStats_t9.pdf; www.cfinst.org/pdf/vital/VitalStats_t10.pdf; and www.cfinst.org/pdf/vital/VitalStats_t11.pdf.

12 Philip A. Klinkner, *The Losing Parties: Out-Party National Committees, 1956–1993* (New Haven: Yale University Press, 1994), 133.

13 Ibid., 139.

14 Federal Election Commission data in Paul S. Herrnson, "National Party Organizations at the Dawn of the Twenty-First Century," in L. Sandy Maisel, *The Parties Respond: Changes in American Parties and Campaigns* 4th ed. (Boulder: Westview Press, 2002), table 3.1, 55.

15 Gary C. Jacobson, "The Republican Advantage in Campaign Finance," in John E. Chubb and Paul E. Peerson, eds., *The New Direction in American Politics* (Washington, D.C.: The Brookings Institution Press, 1985), 154.

16 Kuttner, *Life of the Party*, 83.

17 Herrnson, "National Party Organizations," 55; Campaign Finance Institute, table 3–10.

18 Klinkner, *The Losing Parties*, 64–77.

19 Herrnson, "National Party Organizations," table 3.1, 55.

20 Klinkner, *The Losing Parties*, 143.

21 Ibid., 157.

22 Ibid., 159.

23 Ibid., 164.

24 Herrnson, "National Party Organizations," 55.

25 David Vogel, *Fluctuating Fortunes: The Political Power of Business in America* (New York: Basic Books, 1989), 245.

26 Kuttner, *Life of the Party*, 62, 63.

27 Ibid., 71.

28 Klinkner, *The Losing Parties*, 181–82.

29 Karol, *Party Position Change*, 67.

30 The next three paragraphs draw on Kenneth S. Baer's sympathetic history of the DLC, *Reinventing Democrats: The Politics of Liberalism from Reagan to Clinton* (Lawrence: University Press of Kansas, 2000).

31 Baer, *Reinventing Democrats*, 73–74.

32 DLC, "New Orleans Declaration: A Democratic Agenda for the 1990s," statement endorsed by the Fourth Annual DLC Conference, March 1, 1990.

33 Jonathan Chait, *The Big Con: The True Story of How Washington Got Hoodwinked and Hijacked by Crackpot Economics* (Boston: Houghton Mifflin, 2007), 223.

34 David A. Stockman, *The Triumph of Politics: The Inside Story of the Reagan Revolution* (Avon: New York, 1986), 241. On Breaux's successful brand of "non-partisan chic" see Chait, *The Big Con*, 225–28.

35 Kuttner, *Life of the Party*, 53.

36 For a detailed discussion see Mark Smith, *The Right Talk: How Conservatives Transformed the Great Society into the Economic Society* (Princeton: Princeton University Press, 2007), chapter 7.

37 Quoted in Paul Barrett, "What Brought Down Wall Street?" MSNBC.com, September 19, 2008, http://www.msnbc.msn.com/id/26793500.

38 Barbara Rudolph, Gisela Bolte, Richard Hornik, and Thomas McCarroll, "The Sav-

ings and Loan Crisis: Finally, the Bill Has Come Due," *Time*, February 20, 1989, http://www.time.com/time/printout/0,8816,957083,00.html.

39 See Thomas Ferguson and Joel Rogers, *Right Turn: The Decline of the Democrats and the Future of American Politics* (New York: Hill and Wang, 1986), 130–37.

40 Eisenhower, Dwight D. Personal and confidential to Edgar Newton Eisenhower, November 8, 1954. In *The Papers of Dwight David Eisenhower*, L. Galambos and D. van Ee, eds., doc. 1147.

41 Jeffrey Eisenach, executive director of GOPAC, quoted in Daniel J. Balz and Ronald Brownstein, *Storming the Gates: Protest Politics and the Republican Revival* (Boston: Little, Brown, 1996), 145.

42 Thomas Byrne Edsall, *The New Politics of Inequality* (New York: Norton, 1984).

43 Balz and Brownstein, *Storming the Gates*.

Chapter 8. Building a Bridge to the Nineteenth Century

1 Calculated from http://elsa.berkeley.edu/~salz/TabFig2007.xls. These figures include capital gains.

2 Patrice Hill, "McCain Adviser Talks of 'Mental Recession,'" *Washington Times*, July 9, 2008; "Obama on Gramm: 'America Already Has One Dr. Phil,'" Associated Press, July 10, 2008.

3 Arthur Levitt, *Take On the Street: How to Fight for Your Financial Future* (New York: Pantheon, 2002), 205.

4 Eric Lipton and Stephen Labaton, "A Deregulator Looks Back, Unswayed," *New York Times*, November 17, 2008.

5 Ibid.

6 David Corn, "Foreclosure Phil," *Mother Jones*, May 28, 2008.

7 "Transportation—DeLay Stands in Path of Proposal to Expand TEA-21 Spending," *Congress Daily PM*, March 17, 2003.

8 Kevin Drum, "The New Model Republican Party," www.washingtonmonthly.com/archives/individual/2003_10/002380php.

9 Lyman A. Kellstedt, John C. Green, James L. Guth, and Corwin E. Smidt, "Religious Voting Blocs in the 1992 Election: The Year of the Evangelical?" *Sociology of Religion* 55, no. 3 (1994): 311.

10 Thomas Byrne Edsall with Mary D. Edsall, *Chain Reaction: The Impact of Race, Rights, and Taxes on American Politics* (New York: Norton, 1992), 131–34.

11 Kimberly H. Conger and John C. Green, "Spreading Out and Digging In: Christian Conservatives and State Republican Parties," *Campaigns and Elections*, February 2002, http://www.find.articles.com/p/articles/mi_m2519/is_I_23;shai_82757259.

12 Thomas Frank, *What's the Matter with Kansas? How Conservatives Won the Heart of America* (New York: Metropolitan Books, 2004), 109.

13   Bob Woodward, *The Agenda: Inside the Clinton White House* (New York: Simon & Schuster, 1994), 161.

14   Quoted in Dan Balz and Ronald Brownstein, *Storming the Gates: Protest Politics and Republican Revival* (Boston: Little, Brown, 1996), 175.

15   Ibid., 182, 183.

16   David Maraniss and Michael Weisskopf, "Speaker and His Directors Make the Cash Flow Right," *Washington Post*, November 27, 1995, http://www.washington post.com/wp-srv/politics/special/campfin/stories/cf112795.htm.

17   Calculated from http://www.opensecrets.org.

18   Data from the Senate Office of Public Records. Calculations by Center for Responsive Politics, www.opensecrets.org/lobby/index.php.

19   This discussion draws from Jacob S. Hacker and Paul Pierson, "Tax Politics and the Struggle Over Activist Government," in Paul Pierson and Theda Skocpol, eds., *The Transformation of American Politics: Activist Government and the Rise of Conservatism* (Princeton: Princeton University Press, 2007), 256–80.

20   Eliza Newlin Carey, "Moore's Club for Growth Causing a Stir in the GOP," *National Journal*, October 26, 2002, 3128.

21   William G. Gale, Peter R. Orszag, and Isaac Shapiro, "Distributional Effects of the 2001 and 2003 Tax Cuts and their Financing," Washington, DC: Brookings Institution and Tax Policy Center, available at http://www.brook.edu/views/papers/gale/20040603.htm.

22   Carey, "Moore's Club for Growth Causing a Stir in the GOP," 3128; Matt Bai, "Fight Club," *New York Times Magazine*, August 10, 2003, 24.

23   Sean M. Theriault, *Party Polarization in Congress* (New York: Cambridge, 2008), 197.

24   Quoted in Balz and Brownstein, *Storming the Gates*, 15.

25   David R. Mayhew, "Clinton, the 103rd Congress, and Unified Party Control: What Are the Lessons?" in *Parties and Policies: How the American Government Works* (New Haven: Yale University Press, 2008), 114.

26   Calculated from data available at the Tax Policy Center, a joint project of the Urban Institute and the Brookings Institution: http://www.taxpolicycenter.org/numbers/Content/Excel/T02–0024.x ls. Includes provisions affecting marginal tax rates, the 10 percent bracket, the child tax credit, the child and dependent care credit, the limitation on itemized deductions, the personal exemption phaseout, the AMT, as well as the standard deduction, 15 percent bracket, and EITC provisions for married couples. Excludes retirement and education provisions.

27   Jacob S. Hacker and Paul Pierson, "Abandoning the Middle: The Bush Tax Cuts and the Limits of Democratic Control," *Perspectives on Politics* 3 (2005): 39; Memo from Michele Davis to Treasury Secretary Paul O'Neill, February 2, 2001. From Ron Suskind, "The Bush Files," http://thepriceofloyalty.ronsuskind.com/thebush files/archives/000058.html.

28 Citizens for Tax Justice, "Year-by-Year Analysis of the Bush Tax Cuts Shows Growing Tilt to the Very Rich," 2002, http://www.ctj.org/html/gwb0602.htm.

29 Joint Economic Committee, U.S. House, "The Alternative Minimum Tax for Individuals: A Growing Burden," Washington, D.C., May 2001, http://www.house.gov/jec/tax/amt.htm.

30 Aviva Aron-Dine and Robert Greenstein, "The AMT's Growth Was Not 'Unintended': How the Administration and Congressional Leaders Anticipated the AMT Problem and Knowingly Made It Worse," Washington, D.C., Center on Budget and Policy Priorities, November 30, 2007, available at http://www.cbpp.org/files/11–30–07tax.pdf.

31 Ibid., 2.

32 Ron Suskind, *The Price of Loyalty: George W. Bush, the White House, and the Education of Paul O'Neill* (New York: Simon & Schuster, 2004).

33 Michael Graetz and Ian Shapiro, *Death by a Thousand Cuts* (New Haven: Yale University Press, 2006).

34 Peter A. Gourevitch and James Shinn, *Political Power and Corporate Control: The New Global Politics of Corporate Governance* (Princeton: Princeton University Press, 2005).

35 Robert Kuttner, *The Squandering of America: How the Failure of Our Politics Undermines Our Prosperity* (New York: Knopf, 2007), 78.

36 Jesse Westbrook and David Scheer, "Cox's SEC Hindered Probes, Slowed Cases, Shrank Fines, GAO Says," *Bloomberg*, May 6, 2009.

37 Christine Dugas, "Workers Sue over 401k Losses," *USA Today*, August 20, 2001; Albert B. Crershow, "A 401(k) Post Mortem: After Enron, Emphasis on Company Stock Draws Scrutiny," *Washington Post*, December 16, 2001, H1.

38 John W. Cioffi, "Building Finance Capitalism: The Regulatory Politics of Corporate Governance Reform in the United States and Germany," in Jonah Levy, ed., *The State after Statism: New State Activities in the Age of Liberalization* (Oxford: Oxford University Press, 2006), 185–229.

39 Ibid.

40 Ibid.

41 CBS News, "Bush and Gore Do New York," October 18, 2000, available at http://www.cbsnews.com/stories/2000/10/18/politics/main242210.shtml.

Chapter 9. Democrats Climb Aboard

1 Terry McAuliffe, *What a Party!* (New York: St. Martin's, 2007), 212–18.

2 Patrick Healy, "The Schumer Book (No, He's Not Running for President)," *New York Times*, January 30, 2007, http://thecaucus.blogs.nytimes.com/2007/01/30/the-schumer-book-no-hes-not-running-for-president/.

3 Eric Lipton and Raymond Hernandez, "A Champion of Wall Street Reaps the Ben-

efits," *New York Times*, December 14, 2008, A1. The next two paragraphs draw on this article.

4   On this "invisible primary," see Marty Cohen, David Karol, Hans Noel, and John Zaller, *The Party Decides: Presidential Nominations Before and After Reform* (Chicago: University of Chicago Press, 2008).

5   Lipton and Hernandez, "Champion of Wall Street."

6   Fredreka Schouten, Ken Dilanian, and Matt Kelley, "Lobbyists in 'Feeding Frenzy,' " *USA Today*, September 25, 2008.

7   Center for Responsive Politics, "Finance Sector Gave 51 Percent More to House Bailout Bankers," *Capitol Eye Blog*, weblog entry posted on September 29, 2008, http://www.opensecrets.org/news/2008/09/finance-sector-gave-50-percent .html; Center for Responsive Politics, "Finance/Insurance/Real Estate—Long-Term Contribution Trends," http://www.opensecrets.org/industries/indus.php? ind=F.

8   Schouten, Dilanian, and Kelley, "Lobbyists in 'Feeding Frenzy.' "

9   Louise Story, "Top Hedge Fund Managers Do Well in a Down Year," *New York Times*, March 24, 2009.

10   Lipton and Hernandez, "Champion of Wall Street."

11   Patrick McGeehan, "Wall Street Must Recover Before City Can Overcome Recession, Economists Say," *New York Times*, April 14, 2010.

12   FEC figures from Paul S. Herrnson, "National Party Organizations at the Dawn of the Twenty-First Century," in L. Sandy Maisel, *The Parties Respond: Changes in American Parties and Campaigns* (Boulder: Westview Press, 2002), 55, 58.

13   John Judis, "Abandoned Surgery: Business and the Failure of Health Reform," *American Prospect*, March 21, 1995.

14   Paul Pierson, "The Deficit and the Politics of Domestic Reform," in Margaret Weir, ed., *The Social Divide* (Washington, D.C.: Brookings Institution Press, 1998).

15   Bob Woodward, *The Agenda: Inside the Clinton White House* (New York: Simon & Schuster, 2005), 161.

16   Irving Kristol, "The Battle for Reagan's Soul," *Wall Street Journal*, May 16, 1980, A22.

17   Malcolm Gladwell, "Game Theory," *New Yorker*, May 29, 2006.

18   Michael Lewis, *Moneyball: The Art of Winning an Unfair Game* (New York: Norton, 2003).

19   Larry Bartels, *Unequal Democracy: The Political Economy of the New Gilded Age* (Princeton: Princeton University Press, 2008); Mark Smith, *The Right Talk: How Conservatives Transformed the Great Society into the Economic Society* (Princeton: Princeton University Press, 2007).

20   George Packer, "The Hardest Vote," *New Yorker*, October 13, 2008.

21   John D. Griffin, "Senate Apportionment as a Source of Political Inequality," paper presented at the American Political Science Association Meeting, September 2004.

22   Matthew Shugart, "Reform the Senate, But Don't Take Away the Filibuster," *Daily Herald* (Provo, Utah), May 5, 2005, 3.

23   Ari Berman, "K Street's Favorite Democrat," *Nation*, March 19, 2007.

24   Quoted in Ibid.

25   Jacob S. Hacker and Paul Pierson, *Off Center: The Republican Revolution and the Erosion of American Democracy* (New Haven: Yale University Press, 2005).

26   David R. Mayhew, *Parties and Policies: How the American Government Works* (New Haven: Yale University Press, 2008), 273–87.

27   Barbara Sinclair, "The '60-Vote Senate': Strategies, Process and Outcomes," in Bruce I. Oppenheimer, ed., *U.S. Senate Exceptionalism* (Columbus: Ohio State University Press, 2002), 241–61.

28   Sarah A. Binder, *Minority Rights, Majority Rule: Partisanship and the Development of Congress* (Cambridge: Cambridge University Press), 1997; Gregory J. Wawro and Eric Schickler, *Filibuster: Obstruction and Lawmaking in the U.S. Senate* (Princeton: Princeton University Press, 2006).

29   Ezra Klein, "The Rise of the Filibuster: An Interview with Barbara Sinclair," *Washington Post*, December 26, 2009.

30   Mark Schmitt, "When Did the Senate Get So Bad?" American Prospect, November 24, 2009.

31   Klein, "The Rise of the Filibuster."

32   Michael C. Jensen, Kevin J. Murphy, Eric G. Wruck, "Remuneration: Where We've Been, How We Got to Here, What Are the Problems, and How to Fix Them," Harvard NOM Working Paper No. 04–28 (July 12, 2004).

33   Arthur Levitt, *Take on the Street: What Wall Street and Corporate America Don't Want You to Know* (New York, Pantheon, 2002), 118. Fed researchers suggest that between 1995 and 2000, expensing stock options would have lowered earnings growth in the S&P 500 from 12 percent to 9.4 percent.

34   Levitt, *Take On the Street*, 112–18.

35   Richard Posner, *A Failure of Capitalism: The Crisis of '08 and the Descent into Depression* (Cambridge: Harvard University Press, 2009), 294.

36   Louis Uchitelle, "The Richest of the Rich, Proud of a New Gilded Age," *New York Times*, July 15, 2007.

37   Eric Dash and Louise Story, "Rubin Leaving Citigroup; Smith Barney for Sale," *New York Times*, January 9, 2009.

38   Naftali Bendavid, *The Thumpin': How Rahm Emanuel and the Democrats Learned to be Ruthless and Ended the Republican Revolution* (New York: Doubleday, 2007), 156–57.

39   John Carney, "Rahm Emanuel: Wall Street's Man in the White House," *Business Insider*, November 7, 2008, http://www.businessinsider.com/2008/11/rahm-emanuel -wall-street-s-man-in-the-white-house.

40   Bendavid, *The Thumpin'*, 157.

Chapter 10. Battle Royale

1   Emmanuel Saez, "Striking It Richer: The Evolution of Top Incomes in the United States (Update with 2007 Estimates)," August 5, 2009, http://elsa.berkeley.edu/ ~saez/saez-UStopincomes-2007.pdf.

2   Carmen DeNavas-Walt, Bernadette D. Proctor, and Jessica C. Smith, *Income, Poverty, and Health Insurance Coverage in the United States: 2008* (Washington, D.C.: U.S. Census Bureau, September 2009), http://www.census.gov/prod/2009pubs/ p60-236.pdf.

3   Lynnley Browning, "Ex-UBS Banker Pleads Guilty in Tax Evasion," *New York Times*, June 20, 2008.

4   Andrew Ross Sorkin, *Too Big to Fail: The Inside Story of How Wall Street and Washington Fought to Save the Financial System—and Themselves* (New York: Viking, 2009), 489.

5   Barbara Sinclair, "Barack Obama and the 111th Congress: Politics as Usual?" *Extensions* (Spring 2009).

6   Barack Obama, "Renewing the American Economy," March 27, 2008. http://www .nytimes.com/2008/03/27/us/politics/27text-obama.html?pagewanted=print.

7   Charles Homans, "The Party of Obama," *Washington Monthly*, January 2010. www .washingtonmonthly.com/features/2010/1001.homans.html.

8   Lisa Taddeo, "The Man Who Made Obama," *Esquire*, November 3, 2009. www .esquire.com/features/david-plouffe-0309.

9   Doris Kearns Goodwin, *Team of Rivals* (New York: Simon & Schuster, 2005).

10   Matt Bai, "Taking the Hill," *New York Times Magazine*, June 2, 2009.

11   Ibid.

12   Ezra Klein, "The 'Congressionalist' White House," *The Washington Post*, June 8, 2009. http://voices.washingtonpost.com/ezra-klein/2009/06/the_congressional ist_white_hou.html.

13   Rebecca Johnson, "On the Money," *Vogue*, March 2010.

14   Dan Balz and Ronald Brownstein, *Storming the Gates: Protest Politics and the Republican Revival* (Boston: Little Brown, 1996), 118–26; Julian E. Zelizer, *On Capitol Hill: The Struggle to Reform Congress and Its Consequences 1949–2000* (New York: Cambridge University Press, 2004).

15   Alexander Bolton, "Collins, Snowe Stymie Dems' Tactics," *The Hill*, April 21, 2010.

16   Jacob Hacker and Paul Pierson, *Off Center* (New Haven: Yale Press, 2005), 110.

17   Project calculated from DW nominate scores, a measure of the ideological place-ment of members of Congress developed by Keith Poole and Howard Rosenthal, available at www.voteview.com/dwnomin.htm.

18   Arguably, the real puzzle is why the GOP did not become more moderate as it grew. As the Democrats expanded their ranks in 2006 and 2008, their scores in the House moderated somewhat. Through good times and bad, however, the GOP maintained its steady rightward march.

19   Sean Theriault, "Party Polarization in the 111th Congress," www.apsanet.org/~lss/Newsletter/jan2009/Theriault.pdf.

20   Ibid; extension of remarks, published in the *Legislative Studies Newsletter*, Ameri-can Political Science Association, January 2009.

21   Andrew Ross Sorkin, *Too Big to Fail* (New York: Penguin, 2009), 499, 504; Eve Fair-banks, "From the GOP's New Guard, The Audacity of Nope," *Washington Post*, October 5, 2008.

22   Theriault sees little rise in conservatism in the GOP Senate caucus after 2008, but he wrote assuming that Coleman would win and before Specter left the caucus. The Poole-Rosenthal scores reported January 4, 2010 show a considerable right-ward shift.

23   William E. Brock, "A Recipe for Incivility," *Washington Post*, June 27, 2004, B7.

24   For a detailed discussion of asymmetric polarization, see Hacker and Pierson, *Off Center*.

25   Jim DeMint, "The American Option: A Jobs Plan That Works," *Heritage Lecture #1108*, January, 2009.

26   Ben Furnas, "Senate Conservatives Propose $3.1 Trillion 'Stimulus Plan,' Three Times More Costly Than Obama's Plan," Center for American Progress, February 2, 2009, http://wonkroom.thinkprogress.org/2009/02/02/senate-conservatives-plan.

27   However, according to the *National Journal*, ten senators were more conservative than him on economic issues in 2007, http://nj.nationaljournal.com/voteratings/sen/cons.htm?o1=con_economic&o2=desc#vr.

28   Bruce Bartlett, "Supply-Side Economics, RIP," October 13, 2009, www.capitalgains andgames.com/blog/bruce-bartlett/1168/supply-side-economics-rip.

29   Bruce Bartlett, "Why I Am Anti-Republican," August 30, 2009, www.frumforum .com/why-i-am-anti-republican.

30   Pete Nickeas, "Enzi Sees Healthcare Impasse: Senator Takes Credit for Blocking Democrats' Reform Legislation," *Star-Tribune* (Casper, Wyoming), February 16, 2010.

31   The House bill received support from one Republican, Joseph Cao, who had won a fluke victory in 2008 as a result of the scandal involving William Jefferson and found himself marooned in an overwhelmingly Democratic district.

32   The letter, originally posted and discussed in a blog by Ezra Klein, "How a Letter

from 1964 Shows What's Wrong with the Senate Today," *Washington Post Blog*, November 25, 2009, http://voices.washingtonpost.com/ezra-klein/2009/11/how_a_letter_from_1964_shows_w.html.

33   Lindsay Renick Mayer, Michael Beckel, and David Levinthal, "Crossing Wall Street," Center for Responsive Politics, November 16, 2009.

34   Gregory Koger and Jennifer Nicoll Victor, "Polarized Agents: Campaign Contributions by Lobbyists," *PS: Political Science and Politics*, July 2009, 485–88.

35   This and the following paragraph draw from Jeffrey Birnbaum, "Big Bank Brings In a Face from the Clinton Administration," *Washington Post*, May 27, 2008, A11.

36   The next paragraphs draw heavily on the important efforts of the Sunlight Foundation to chart networks connecting lobbying operations to particular members of Congress. See for example www.sunlightfoundation.com/projects/2009/health care_lobbyist_complex and www.sunlightfoundation.com/projects/2009/11/09/the-max-baucus-energy-climate-lobbyist-complex/.

37   Center for Responsive Politics, "Federal Lobbying Climbs in 2009 As Lawmakers Execute Aggressive Congressional Agenda," *Capital Eye Blog*, February 12, 2010.

38   Center for Responsive Politics, "New Lobbying Reports Show Big Business Keeps Spending to Influence Politics," *Capital Eye Blog*, January 21, 2010.

39   Public Citizen report cited in Eliza Newlin Carney, "Big Banks Are Back in the Game," *National Journal*'s Under the Influence blog, December 14, 2009.

40   Eliza Newlin Carney, "Big Banks Are Back In The Game," National Journal.com, December 14, 2009, www.nationaljournal.com/njonline/rg_20091214_8881.php.

41   Brody Mullins and Neil King Jr., "GOP Chases Wall Street Donors: Data Show Fund-Raisers Begin Capitalizing Over Banker Regret On Backing Obama," *Wall Street Journal* Online, February 4, 2010, http://online.wsj.com/article/SB100014 24052748703575004575043612216461790.html?mod=WSJ_hps_MIDDLEThird News; Center for Responsive Politics, "Efforts by Health Business Industries Help Push Influence Peddling to New Heights," February 12, 2010.

42   Peter H. Stone, "Health Insurers Funded Chamber Attack Ads," *National Journal*, January 12, 2010, http://undertheinfluence.nationaljournal.com/2010/01/health-insurers-funded-chamber.php

43   Jim VandeHei, "Political Cover: Major Business Lobby Wins Back Its Clout by Dispensing Favors," *Wall Street Journal*, September 11, 2001, A1; Stephen Power, "No Deal: Chamber Battles Obama," *Wall Street Journal*, November 2, 2009.

44   Associated Press, "Chamber of Commerce Opposes Obama's Plans," August 9, 2009, http://abcnews.go.com/Business/wireStory?id=8286157.

45   Kimberly A. Strassel, "The Weekend Interview: Business Fights Back," *Wall Street Journal*, October 23, 2009. Spending figures from Center for Responsive Politics, "New Lobbying Reports."

46   Strassel, "Weekend Interview."

47   Noam Schreiber, "Could Wall Street Actually Lose Congress?" November 23, 2009, www.tnr.com/blog/the-stash/could-wall-street-actually-lose-congress.

48   Media Matters for America, "Report: Despite Warnings from Many Economists That Stimulus May Be Too Small, Network News Rarely Raised the Issue," March 6, 2009, http://mediamatters.org/reports/200903060025.

49   Elizabeth Drew, "The Thirty Days of Barack Obama," *New York Review of Books*, March 26, 2009; Ryan Lizza "The Gatekeeper," *New Yorker*, March 2, 2009.

50   Frank Luntz, "The Language of Financial Reform," The Word Doctors, Arlington, VA, January 2010; Eric Dash and Nelson D. Schwartz, "As Reform Takes Shape, Some Relief on Wall Street," *New York Times*, May 24, 2010, B1.

51   Carl Hulse and Adam Nagourney, "Senate GOP Leader Finds Weapon in Unity," *New York Times*, March 16, 2010.

52   Michael Tomasky, "Something New on the Mall," *New York Review of Books*, October 22, 2009. On the conflicting estimates of the crowd size, see www.politifact .com/truth-o-meter/article/2009/sep/14/tea-party-photo-shows-large-crowd -different-event/.

53   CNN Opinion Research Poll of 1,023 adult Americans, including 954 registered voters, February 12–15, 2010, http://i2.cdn.turner.com/cnn/2010/images/02/17/ rel4b.pdf.

54   Pew Research Center survey of 1,003 adult Americans, January 14–17, 2010, http://people-press.org/reports/questionnaires/586.pdf.

55   CNN Opinion Research Poll of 1,160 adult Americans, December 16–20, 2009, http://i2.cdn.turner.com/cnn/2009/images/12/21/rel19a.pdf.

56   Kaiser Health Tracking Poll of 2,002 American adults, January 7–12, 2010, ww.kff .org/kaiserpolls/upload/8042-C.pdf; Nate Silver, "Health Care Polls: Opinion Gap or Information Gap?" FiveThirtyEight.com, January 23, 2010, www.fivethirtyeight .com/2010/01/health-care-polls-opinion-gap-or.html.

Conclusion: Beating Winner-Take-All

1   The golden ticket analogy has been offered by Gregory Mankiw, "The Wealth Trajectory: Rewards for the Few," *New York Times*, April 20, 2008.

2   Ronald D. Orol, "If Senate OKs Bank Bill, Expect a Year of Debate," Marketwatch .com, March 17, 2010.

3   "Gohmert Calls for Amendment Convention by States," March 23, 2010, http:// gohmert.house.gov/index.cfm?sectionid=125&parentid=44&sectiontree=4,44,125 &itemid=805.

4   ABC News, "Boehner: 'Hell No' on Bill," March 22, 2010, http://abcnews.go.com/ Health/video/john-boehner-blasts-health-care-bill-10165837.

5   Carl Hulse and Adam Nagourney, "Senate GOP Leader Finds Weapon in Unity," *New York Times*, March 16, 2010.

6   Glenn Beck has gone so far as to liken proposals for filibuster reform to repeal-
    ing the Bill of Rights. Former vice president Dan Quayle complained that com-
    pleting health-care reform legislation through the reconciliation process is to
    "effectively . . . take away the filibuster in the United States Senate . . . so therefore
    you have . . . 51 votes in the Senate. That is not what our Founding Fathers had
    in mind. That is not the constitutional process." Dan Quayle appearance on Fox
    News, http://tpmlivewire.talkingpointsmemo.com/2010/02/quayle-51-votes-not
    -what-our-founding-fathers-had-in-mind.php.

7   Alexander Hamilton, Federalist #22, in Alexander Hamilton, James Madison, and
    John Jay, *The Federalist Papers* (Oxford University Press, 2008), Lawrence Gold-
    man, ed.

8   James Madison, Federalist #58, ibid.

9   Indeed, we have offered many of them in our past writings. Jacob S. Hacker and
    Paul Pierson, *Off Center: The Republican Revolution and the Erosion of American
    Democracy* (New Haven, CT: Yale University Press, 2005); Jacob S. Hacker, *The
    Great Risk Shift: The New Economic Insecurity and the Decline of the American
    Dream*, rev. and exp. (New York: Oxford University Press, 2008).

10 James Fallows, "How America Can Rise Again," *Atlantic Monthly*, January/
    February 2010, 49.

11 Eric Patashnik, *Reforms at Risk: What Happens After Major Policy Changes Are
    Enacted* (Princeton, N.J.: Princeton University Press, 2008).

12 Paul Ryan, "A Road Map for America's Future Version 2.0," U.S. House of Rep-
    resentatives, Washington, D.C., January 2010, http://www.roadmap.republicans
    .budget.house.gov/UploadedFiles/Roadmap2Final2.pdf.

13 Ari Melber, "Year One of Organizing for America," President Special Report (Janu-
    ary 2010), www.techpresident.com/ofayear1.

14 Michael Waldman, *My Fellow Americans: The Most Important Speeches of Ameri-
    can Presidents, From George Washington to George W. Bush* (Naperville, IL:
    Sourcebooks, 2003), 106; Michael Sandel, "Obama and Civic Idealism," *Democracy*
    16 (Spring 2010): 10.

Index

Page numbers in *italics* refer to figures and tables.

Wagner, Robert, 306
Wagner Act (1935), 129, 140
Walker, Charls, 120, 124–26, 133–34, 135
Wall Street, 1, 2, 6, 51, 66–68, 70, 104, 194, 195, 197, 209, 221–30, 232, 247–50, 256, 261, 274, 282, 290–91; *see also* financial services industry
Wall Street Journal, 47, 59, 77, 275
Wal-Mart, 32, 64, 104, 240, 318*n*
Walton family, 218, 240
War on Poverty, 200
Washington, George, 269–70
Watergate scandal, 98, 117
Waxman, Henry, 260
Wealth of Nations, The (Smith), 82
Weber, Vin, 190
Weill, Sanford, 71, 249–50
welfare, 52, 97, 107, 181, 182, 193
What a Party! (McAuliffe), 223–24
What's the Matter with Kansas? (Frank), 204
White, Maureen, 225
White, William Allen, 79
Williams, Edward Bennett, 125
Williams, Harrison, 131
Wilson, Woodrow, 86, 89
winner-take-all politics:
    conservatism and, 5, 7, 41–42, 43, 54, 77, 115, 189, 204
    Democratic vs. Republican support for, 8, 182, 185–86, 194–95, 221–22, 224–25, 228–30, 235, 236–37, 255, 257, 261, 268, 278, 289–306

as economic norm, 2–3, 41–42, 74, 77–79, 87, 100, 134, 253–55
government's role in, 33, 41, 42–47, 70–72, 100, 134, 193, 199
historical development of, 7–8, 17, 41–72, 100
inequality and, 3–4, 11, 15–18, 29, 32, 37–40, 41, 45, 74–77, 91, 149–51, 225–26, 256, 302–3, 306, 328*n*
liberalism and, 5, 7, 43, 54, 115, 256–57
political influence in, 5–8, 159–60, 241, 256–57, 283, 286–88, 305–6
reform of, 7–8, 17, 41–72, 100, 256–57, 289–306
social impact of, 13, 14, 28–29, 41–42, 52–53, 74–84, 87, 89, 90–91, 100, 139–40, 152–53, 296–97
taxation and, 44, 99, 105–7, 132–34, 179–80, 187–88, 208, 212–14, 218, 229
Winner-Take-All Society, The (Frank and Cook), 45
Wolf, Martin, 67
women's rights, 22, 27, 80, 126, 145–46, 179, 258, 263, 306
workplace conditions, 26–30, 74, 79, 80, 86, 97, 116–17, 119
WorldCom, 65–66, 220–21, 295
World War II, 137–38, 140
Wright, Jim, 191
Wyoming, 84, 268

Zandi, Mark, 280
Zimmer, Dick, 226

About the Authors

Jacob S. Hacker is the Stanley B. Resor Professor of Political Science at Yale University. He is the coauthor, with Paul Pierson, of *Off Center: The Republican Revolution and the Erosion of American Democracy*. His other books include *The Great Risk Shift: The New Economic Insecurity and the Decline of the American Dream*. He lives in New Haven, Connecticut.

Paul Pierson is the John Gross Professor of Political Science at the University of California at Berkeley. He is the coauthor of *Off Center* and the author of *Politics in Time* and *Dismantling the Welfare State?* He lives in Berkeley, California.